Dwarf Conifers

A COMPLETE GUIDE

Part of the Pygmy Pinetum at Devizes, Wilts

DWARF CONIFERS

A Complete Guide

by

H. J. WELCH

with a foreword by

J. S. L. GILMOUR, M.A., F.L.S., V.M.H.
Director of the University Botanic Garden at Cambridge

FABER AND FABER
24 Russell Square
London

First published in mcmlxvi
by Faber and Faber Limited
24 Russell Square, London WC1
Printed in Great Britain
by Jarrold & Sons Ltd, Norwich

© *1966 by H. J. Welch*

Contents

Illustrations

ILLUSTRATIONS

Foreword

by J. S. L. Gilmour

Dwarf conifers, as garden plants, exhibit two outstanding features—the fascination that they exercise on their devotees, and the unrivalled complexity of their nomenclature! That the latter appears in no way to diminish the former says much for their horticultural value and attractiveness—not to mention the patience and persistence of their devotees! They are, indeed, ideally suited to small gardens, and I have no doubt that Mr Welch's book will stimulate many more owners of gardens, both large and small, to join this happy band.

Mr Welch is particularly well qualified to deal with his subject. Not only does he grow a very extensive collection in his "Pygmy Pinetum" at the Wansdyke Nursery near Devizes, he has played a leading part in the recent attempt by a Committee of the Royal Horticultural Society to bring some order into the near-chaos of dwarf conifer nomenclature. Many of the results of the work of this Committee are embodied in this book, which should thus help to spread more widely the suggestions for nomenclatural simplification and standardization made by the Committee.

It is worth recording that Dr B. K. Boom of Wageningen was also a valued member of the Royal Horticultural Society's Committee and that the recently published *Manual of Cultivated Conifers* by the late Mr P. den Ouden and Dr Boom (The Hague, 1965) employs broadly the same nomenclature as Mr Welch's volume—thus avoiding a "clash" and helping further, it is hoped, to stabilize dwarf conifer names. Following the work of the Committee, the Royal Horticultural Society has been appointed International Registration Authority for Garden Conifers and one of their main tasks will be to produce a list of names of cultivars already in cultivation. The publication of Mr Welch's book will, it is hoped, stimulate growers and others to comment on the names he uses, thus providing valuable information towards compiling the Society's list.

Plant nomenclature is a difficult subject and Mr Welch has not been rash enough to assume that his readers will appreciate the significance of the names he uses without some help; this he has provided in an excellent chapter on the general principles of botanical nomenclature—a chapter that will certainly be of value to a wider audience than specialist dwarf conifer growers.

Mr Welch, of course, deals with many aspects of dwarf conifers besides their names. His chapters on garden use, cultivation, and pests and diseases form a valuable background to his main theme of identification and naming. The wealth of illustrations, and especially the "Identification Plates", add greatly to the usefulness and visual appeal of a book which will, I am confident, come to be recognized as a landmark in the study and appreciation of these remarkable little plants.

1 : General Introduction

Most books on gardening and similar recreational activities seem to begin with this sort of remark: "When it was first suggested that I should write a book on lilies (or alpine gardens or wood carving or as the case may be) I said: 'What! Another one, there must be dozens on the subject already!' But on further consideration I felt there might perhaps be a need . . . etc. etc." But when I was approached about writing a book on dwarf conifers I had no such first reaction because there is an almost complete dearth of books on the subject.

This is surprising in view of the growing interest being taken in them by the gardening public in these days of small gardens, and not only is there a dearth of books, there seems to be a corresponding lack of writers knowledgeable in this corner of horticulture. I had had occasion to make a close study of the dwarf conifers, so when the suggestion came that I might write a book on the subject I readily agreed to make the attempt.

To avoid any misunderstanding, perhaps I should explain straight away that throughout this book the term "dwarf conifer" relates to plants that are naturally dwarf, whether they be species, variety or cultivar, and I have nothing to say about Bonzai trees, i.e. artificially dwarfed plants (they may or may not be conifers) which owe their size to root pruning and other cultural practices. This art has been developed by the Japanese, and for those interested there is now available a book in English written by a Japanese expert—*BONSAI–Japanese Trees* by Kan Yashiroda, available from the publishers of this book.

While writing the present book, I have regarded myself primarily as a grower and lover of these fascinating little plants writing for others who grow them or would like to. I have had in mind that what everyone is crying out for is some means of identifying their treasures (and their purchases) and some guide in the selection of suitable plants for use in particular situations. I have therefore limited myself to those forms which are either readily available in the trade or at least are obtainable by a little searching amongst the nurseries specialising in dwarf conifers.

The vexed question of nomenclature is now receiving long overdue attention by the botanists and the Royal Horticultural Society has recently agreed to act as International Registration Authority for Garden Conifers. As the number of these runs into thousands and as there are many synonyms in the botanical literature of the world it will be some time yet before all the queries can be investigated and a Register issued, but one of the first things which the Advisory Committee appointed by the Society has done has been to establish certain principles based upon the *Rules of Nomenclature for Cultivated Plants*, but supplementing them as necessary to arrive at a satisfactory scheme of nomenclature for garden

11

conifers. This was done because of this and other books on conifers known to be in preparation.

Most urgent of these was a book since published entitled *The Manual of Cultivated Conifers* by the late P. den Ouden with the collaboration of Dr B. K. Boom of Wageningen, Holland, the latter of whom is also a member of the Advisory Committee. Having myself had a part in what has been going on in this connection and also having, through the kindness of Dr Boom, seen the manuscript of that book prior to publication, I can safely say that while the nomenclature in the present book is not official it is not likely to be altered in many places when the Register comes to be issued.

And when that time comes it will not be a major tragedy if a few of my names have to be changed. If in the meantime we have all been helped to identify our plants by means of this book and its illustrations according to the names I have used, my principal object in writing it will have been realized. Most of the present almost hopeless confusion will have been dissipated if in this matter we follow the injunction of St Paul in another connection, and "all speak the same thing".

The use of dwarf conifers had quite a vogue in the middle years of the last century, in the days when horticultural keeping up with the Jones's meant the possession of a better arboretum than Lord So-and-so's in the next county. The few such plantings of those spacious days as still survive remain as a proof (or otherwise) of their claim to be dwarf forms, but with the decline in the number and spending power of those large establishments the demand for the dwarf forms virtually disappeared, and many recorded varieties appear to have been lost to cultivation by the end of the century.

With the rise in the vogue for alpine gardening and of rock garden construction based on the aim of simulating nature as closely as possible, a new and altogether happier use for these conifer microforms was found and the demand increased. Apart, however, from occasional references in gardening journals and in general textbooks on conifers there was no literature on the dwarf forms and so when the late Murray Hornibrook published the first edition of his work *Dwarf and Slow-growing Conifers* in 1923 he was breaking quite new ground.

In that book he described and listed about 250 varieties. The appearance of the first edition gave rise to a lot of interest and doubtless many garden owners and others would have brought additional forms to Hornibrook's notice, for by the time his second edition appeared in 1938 he was able to extend it to cover about 530 forms. In a recent survey of the subject I have estimated that about one quarter of these are lost to cultivation. On the other hand, many new forms have been introduced. I now have lists of most of the principal collections throughout the world. It is difficult to be precise, because of duplication of names, but I estimate that if they were all combined into one grand "global" list this would come out at round about the thousand mark.

Several outstanding collections have been made, both in the British Isles and in North America, and it is fortunate that the collectors seem in most cases to have held

1 Masterly use of one rock and a single dwarf conifer in an area of greensward.

the result of their lifelong labour of love as a public trust, for several of these collections have eventually been made over or bequeathed to some national or state arboretum. None of these collections has to my knowledge covered much over 500 forms and the largest of several at present in course of formation in this country is still I believe not beyond this total, if undescribed forms on trial be disregarded. My own Pygmy Pinetum at Devizes is still well down the field with a total of about 400 forms.

There is therefore plenty of scope here for would-be breakers of world records, and at this point may I make a suggestion for consideration by the members of Park Authorities of all kinds and their advisers, i.e. that an attraction of local or even regional interest could be made in less space and at less cost of public money by a good collection of dwarf conifers than perhaps in any other way.

The widest range offered by any nursery today is I believe about 150 varieties. A careful search might bring to light in other nurseries a further fifty or so. After that, the hunt would be on. But the average gardener has no interest in astronomical figures. Hardly a garden exists that would not benefit from the presence of some dwarf conifers, and when he first becomes dwarf conifer conscious the garden owner is mainly concerned with how many he should introduce (and, of course, which ones) so as to secure the greatest improvement in his garden without altering its character.

The builder of the tiniest trough garden knows he must have his one or two pygmy trees to give his miniature world scale and an air of permanence and maturity, and the garden or rockery is small indeed that cannot make good use of a half-dozen suitably chosen specimens. A large garden could accommodate 100 or more dwarf conifers without their becoming at all obtrusive. Most gardens will lie between these two extremes, and the planting plan for the average suburban garden might very well find good use for anything from a dozen dwarf conifers upwards.

The best way to purchase dwarf conifers is to go to a nursery which specialises in them. Most local nurseries with a general trade will from time to time buy in a mixed parcel (often from the Continent) and these will be planted out in some odd corner to await the advent of the occasional customer asking for dwarf conifers. Even if when he arrives he is fortunate enough to find the labels still legible he is unlikely to find on that type of nursery anyone able or willing to answer his invariable question "How big will it grow?" I must admit sooner or later, and this seems a good moment to do it, that there are very few truly dwarf conifers. The great majority of those so classed are more strictly described as slow-growing. A plant is not like an animal. If you want a dog of a certain size you can go to a reliable pet shop and be sure that the pup you are buying will grow to the size you want, give or take an inch or so, and then stop. But a tree, although its rate of growth very greatly reduces as it approaches its maturity, will continue very slowly to increase in size for many years to come. The right answer, out of an honest and true heart, to the enquiry "How big will it grow?" is therefore a difficult matter even to the specialist with wide experience of the particular plant in question, so that your general practitioner nurseryman is not to be

Good use of upright-growing forms to give a strong foreground interest—▲ 2 In the Royal Botanic Garden, Edinburgh. ▼ 3 At Creevy Rocks, Saintfield, Co. Down. N.I.

15

Dwarf conifers can be equally well used—

▲ 4 In the "grand manner".

◄ 5 In a small garden corner.

16

blamed if he evades the question. He is, however, at fault if he misleads the customer by pretending to know when he does not and is greatly to be blamed if he sells as a "dwarf" a variety which he knows to be no such thing.

Most, perhaps all, of the nurseries who specialize in dwarf conifers advertise in the journals of the Alpine Garden Society and/or the Scottish Rock Garden Club, and many of these are regular exhibitors at the shows sponsored by these bodies and at the larger flower shows both in London and at many provincial centres, and these can in general be relied upon. I add one word of caution, this being that when I say "specializing in dwarf conifers" I do mean exactly what I say. There are excellent firms who specialize in alpines and stock a few dwarf conifers merely because they go together well in the order book, and there is just the risk of finding that such firms, however reliable they may be within their own speciality, will not be as knowledgeable or (alas that it has to be said of a few cases) as careful as they might be when it comes to labelling their dwarf conifers. It is not without significance that a nurseryman whose name is a household word with all who grow alpines and whom I personally would not at all include in the warning I have just given sees fit to state in his catalogue "We make no guarantee as to the correctness of the names we use" when he comes to the dwarf conifers. It would be most gratifying to me if this book were to bring forward the day when such extreme caution was no longer deemed necessary.

Of course many gardeners will choose trees the appearance of which at a show or in a nursery appeals to them, caring little or nothing whether they are labelled correctly or at all, but for the keen plantsman who must have his plants correctly named I would say, go to the nurseries who make a speciality of dwarf conifers. There are not many of these, but their number is on the increase. There even is one nowadays which grows nothing but dwarf conifers.

So far as possible get plants that are "on their own roots". This means simply that they have been propagated from cuttings (less commonly by layering) and not by grafting. There is actually no inherent objection to grafted plants. *Pinus*, *Cedrus*, *Pseudotsuga*, *Larix*, some of the *Picea* and a few varieties of some other genera are impossible to propagate economically from cuttings so these must be increased by grafting and the resulting plants are healthy and long-lived. But conifers respond to rootstock vigour just as much as do fruit trees. As is well known, an apple variety worked on the dwarfing stock EM IX remains small and suitable for use as a cordon or dwarf bush whereas the same variety worked on a vigorous stock such as EM XVI will soon become a large tree. Similarly, a dwarf conifer grafted on to a strong-growing seedling of the arboreal species will make much stronger growth than we want and may even lose character entirely. Unfortunately, producers of nursery stock (the continental growers who supply a large part of this country's needs among them) whose normal aim is, of course, to produce a strong, vigorous and healthy-looking plant, tend to overlook the different requirements when it comes to dwarf forms and this has brought all grafted plants of dwarf conifers under a cloud of suspicion. It is always possible to detect a grafted plant—the healed-over but still discernible remains

6 Informal use of dwarf conifers on the rockery in the National Botanic Garden, Glasnevin, Dublin. (Photo by kind permission of the Keeper.)

of the graft will be found on the trunk an inch or so above the soil, but it is impossible to tell with certainty what rootstock has been used. Some estimate of the vigour of the plant can be formed by a careful inspection of the amount of annual growth it has been making in the nursery, but the safest course is to avoid grafted plants whenever possible. This is specially the case if you are buying the real pygmy forms for a trough garden or window-box.

There is another important advantage in buying dwarf conifers from a specialist nursery in this country who raises his own stock which is seldom mentioned and that is that the importation of conifers in several genera is prohibited under the *Importation of Forest Trees* (*Prohibition*) *Orders*. Nurseries dependent upon obtaining supplies from continental sources will consequently be unable to supply *Abies*, *Larix*, *Picea*, *Pinus*, *Pseudotsuga*, *Sequoia*, *Tsuga* and *Thuja*, and many of our choicest dwarf forms are found in these genera.

I should have liked to finish this chapter for the benefit of my scientifically-minded readers with a learned account of how dwarf forms originate but it would appear that little is known of the mechanism giving rise to nature's freaks and oddities amongst which (let us admit it) our cherished dwarf forms have to be classed. At the practical level of the average gardener's mind however, sufficient is known to enable us to group the dwarf forms to our own satisfaction, the advantage of so doing being the knowledge it brings us of the probable behaviour of our plants, especially with regard to their likelihood of reversion.

GENERAL INTRODUCTION

A gardener's classification is as follows:

Seedling Mutations

From time to time seedlings will appear showing some distinct variation from the rest. This may be a peculiarity in vigour (in this way arise giant and dwarf forms) in colour (presenting us with golden and glaucous forms) in habit (fastigiate, weeping and globose forms) or foliage (threadlike, congested and monstrous forms). Where these variations are frequent the species is spoken of as a "variable" one, but occasionally even in species not prone to show variation a seedling with a pronounced departure from the normal will occur. It is probable that dwarf seedling forms arise more frequently than we suppose but the chances of survival in the wild or in a forestry nursery where the culling of the runts is normal practice are very small indeed. Occasionally one such plant has been rescued from destruction by someone with an eye to its value as a garden plant, and by subsequent vegetative propagation it has found its way into our gardens as a named dwarf form. These seedling forms as a class are stable and show no tendency to revert to the typical arboreal form, although there is a tendency for the peculiarity to become less pronounced with age, i.e. golden forms become greener, congestion of foliage gets less noticeable, dwarf forms develop more vigour and so forth.

Examples of seedling mutations are *Chamaecyparis lawsoniana* and *C. obtusa* (most cultivars), *Chamaecyparis pisifera* 'Nana', *Picea abies* 'Clanbrassiliana' (probably) and most if not all the cultivars of *Thuja occidentalis*. Unfortunately for us, a trick Nature has done once she can do again, so at any time a seedling may turn up showing the same peculiarity or combination of peculiarities as an already established cultivar in anything from a broadly similar to an indistinguishably identical manner. At either end of the range the situation is clear enough. Where there are marked differences from all existing cultivars and the new seedling is felt after prolonged trial to have some distinctive garden value it can be propagated and given a new cultivar name, as has been done in the case of all the various globose forms of *Thuja occidentalis* that have been named. At the other end of the range a seedling so like an existing cultivar as to be indistinguishable from it even in old age may sometimes get propagated in its place and no harm will have been done. In any intermediate situation on the other hand, in cases where small differences from existing cultivars are discernible (or are found to develop as the new seedling ages) the possibility of confusion arises in two ways. The plant may stray into cultivation under an existing cultivar name and so give it a reputation for being variable (this is the probable explanation in the *Chamaecyparis lawsoniana* forms 'Forsteckensis' and 'Tamariscifolia' where in both cases I believe there are several clones in cultivation) or it may be enthusiastically "named" by its excited and impatient owner, only to turn out in the end to be for all practical purposes a synonym of an existing cultivar. In every case the exercise of caution and restraint on the part of the raiser is necessary and no attempt should ever be made to introduce a new cultivar until the mother plant has been allowed to grow freely for some years so as to have outgrown any merely juvenile tendencies, and even then the opinion of some authority should be sought on whether the new form is worth introducing, before any action is taken which may merely add one more name to our lists but no more beauty to our gardens.

In this connection it might be well to point out that unless and until a new form is propagated and distributed it is not a cultivar within the definition given in Article 11 of the Cultivar Code, and if it is necessary to distinguish it during its period of trial I would suggest that it be grown under a number, or a name containing a number, to avoid any confusion. "A/40" or "Bill's No. 1" will define a plant as well as any name and its temporary nature will be self-evident, for such number-names are frowned on heavily in Recommendation 21A of the Code.

We are told that "Nature preserves her species by making her freaks sterile" so, as we should expect, most of the seedling mutations we have in our gardens do not set seed. But once in a while Nature relaxes her vigilance and lets one get by and in that event it is usually found that the resulting seedlings or most of them have reverted to the typical, arboreal habit of the species, but occasionally a seedling will arise in which the peculiarity of its mother is accentuated. In Chapter 5 I retell the story of how the pygmy forms of *Chamaecyparis obtusa* arose from seeds developing on the usually sterile dwarf form *Chamaecyparis obtusa* 'Nana Gracilis'. In recent years *Chamaecyparis lawsoniana* 'Fletcheri' has been seeding freely and a few pygmy seedlings have been reported. I hope we are not in for another collection of named forms almost impossible to tell apart after a few years, and that raisers of these interesting plants will exercise patience and restraint.

The true weeping forms are of the seedling mutation class and so this peculiarity is stable. These forms will need to be grafted on to a stem as is done with standard roses or be trained up to a cane in their nursery days unless they are to remain for ever a sprawling victim of their own congenital inability to lift their branches off the ground. Left to grow like this they are usually more curious than beautiful, but where a bold rock-face is to be clothed they can be very effective. Plants in this group are *Picea abies* 'Inversa' and 'Reflexa' and *Cedrus libani* 'Sargentii'.

JUVENILE FIXATIONS

This might be considered a sub-form of the previous class.

All seedling conifers commence life with a type of foliage quite unlike the adult form which the plant develops later. Occasionally a seedling can continue to carry only juvenile foliage all its life. These fixed juvenile forms may grow into trees (see Chapter 5 for remarks on the special case represented by the Junipers) and may even set seed on juvenile foliage, but in the majority of cases they also show much reduced vigour, so are amongst us as dwarf forms. Several of them are excellent garden plants.

The juvenile foliage of all conifers is very similar in general appearance and the longer and more freely held leaves were once thought by someone to give a plant

7 A fine specimen of *Picea glauca* 'Albertiana Conica' dominating the scree at the Royal Botanic Garden, Edinburgh.

something of the appearance of heather. As a result, most of these forms have been given the cultivar name 'Ericoides' so it is not surprising that there is much uncertainty in gardens as to the correct labelling of these forms. At one time two botanists named Siebold and Zuccarini supposed that they were all species of a distinct genus which they named *Retinospora*, but the occasional development of adult foliage dispels this notion and these juvenile forms have been distributed, not without difficulty, amongst the species to which they each belong. The name *Retinospora* survives on many old labels and, incredibly enough, in a few nurseries (where often it is not even spelt correctly) although it has been officially abandoned by botanists for more than a quarter of a century. "This nuisance must now cease" fits the case and will be the case if and when the public refuse to purchase any plant labelled *Retinospora* or *Retinispora*.

In some species there are also forms with foliage intermediate between the juvenile and the adult form. A familiar case is *Chamaecyparis pisifera* in which the juvenile forms are given the name 'Squarrosa' and the intermediate forms the name 'Plumosa'. As might be expected in the circumstances these forms are often variable and sometimes unstable. A few (e.g. *Chamaecyparis pisifera* 'Squarrosa Minima') may suddenly throw up strong adult growth which soon "takes over" if not removed. Others may show plumose growth on squarrose forms and vice versa, and even the stablest of the juvenile forms may occasionally throw a small spray of the typical, adult foliage. This, by revealing to us the specific loyalty of our plant, is very interesting, but any tendency of the plant to extend this habit should be cut away immediately.

21

GENERAL INTRODUCTION

BUD MUTATIONS

This is the usual origin of variegated forms. These have arisen as "sporting" branches showing this peculiarity on a normal green plant. It can be argued that any departure from the normal must represent in some degree a loss of perfect health and this may be the reason why these variegated forms are often lacking in vigour, although apparently quite healthy in other respects. As this loss of vigour makes them slow-growing it is an advantage from the gardener's point of view.

Another fruitful source of dwarf forms has been the "Witch's broom" growths which are occasionally seen on *Picea, Larix* and few other genera. The origin of these is uncertain. The gardener in his practical but unscientific way thinks of some sort of virus having entered the plant through some accidental wound to cause the abnormal development of a mass of congested and often stunted foliage looking from a distance like an enormous bird's-nest, but he has found that cuttings or grafts taken from the broom will develop into dwarf plants with a quaint charm that is all their own and in this way he has produced some of our most-sought-after forms. *Picea abies* 'Pygmaea' is a good example.

A characteristic of all bud mutations is a tendency to revert to the normal colour, type of foliage or habit, as the case may be. Our gardener friend here amplifies his theory and explains that the virus-infected plant is always trying to throw out the invader and that what we call reversion is actually the plant succeeding in "throwing off the virus". Whether or not this turns out to be the scientifically correct explanation it does cover the facts and stresses the point that we should keep a watch on these forms and at once cut out any undesirable growths that appear. Especially is this important in the case of the dwarf *Picea abies* forms.

ALPINE FORMS

Several species of conifer whose range include an area of high mountains, although normally of tree-like habit have developed stunted, shrubby or even prostrate forms, many of which make excellent garden plants. As these are established in the wild and have a natural habitat they are given varietal rank by the botanists so they will have names of latin form such as *Abies balsamea* var. *hudsonia*, even although they have been brought into garden cultivation. Because they are botanical varieties we find them more or less variable and in a few cases an outstanding clone has been given a cultivar name.

Because of their origin these alpine or mountain forms (the word alpine is commonly used with a wider meaning than its true sense of "from the Alps") are indestructibly hardy and within the life-span of a single plant seldom revert to the lowland habit of the species and so they are a very useful group. Many are appropriate subjects for Bonzai specimens or, with less rigorous attention, for trough gardens.

8 Formal groups of contrasting habit-forms on a level site at the Arboretum Blijdenstein, Hilversum, Holland. Note the isolation by distance from all large trees or other plant masses.

CULTIVARIANTS

This is a word I have coined to describe a class of plant which is not at present recognised by the Cultivar Code although the plants in question are "distinguished by characters . . . significant for the purposes of . . . horticulture" which are sufficiently stable when reproduced asexually for the plants to fill a distinct place in our planting schemes and consequently to be called for by the gardening public.

In this class there are two distinct groups, although they both arise from the deliberate selection of propagating material. The first group was drawn attention to by the late Murray Hornibrook in his classic work on the dwarf conifers where in his remarks on *Chamaecyparis lawsoniana* 'Fletcheri' he points out the possibility of securing diminutive and often bun-shaped plants from this and certain other upright varieties by the selection of cutting wood from weak-growing shoots low down on the plant.

Our hypothetical gardener friend will come up here with one of his pseudo-scientific theories in explanation. This time he will talk in terms of a mysterious substance (he will probably call it a hormone) which collects at the growing tips of plants and controls their growth. An upright or pyramidal habit, according to him, is caused by the plant sharply differentiating between the central leader and all other growing tips in its distribution of this substance; a globose habit on the other hand results from its even distribution. The cutting away of the leading shoot or shoots compels the plants to step up the supply to the remaining shoots, causing them to "break" in the expected manner. A plant that can mobilize its remaining stocks of the hormone to initiate new growth buds when the whole plant has been cut hard back survives, one that cannot do this dies under such hard treatment, and so on.

23

9 An example of true "leader" growth being put out by a young Norway Spruce after being decapitated.

According to this theory, weak-growing shoots low down on the plant will be so far down the plant's scale of priorities for a ration of this growth substance that they will be so poorly endowed with it (even to the point of its being entirely absent) that when used for cuttings they will produce plants with little or even no ability ever to throw up leader growth. There are some obviously thin places in this theory but it does delightfully cover the known facts. These are that the slow-growing dense-foliaged forms often put on the market as "var. *nana*" frequently romp away quite suddenly after years maybe of very slow growth, as though the plant had suddenly learned how to use its meagre stock of the growth hormone (or perhaps had found out how to make some for itself) yet that it is undeniably possible to obtain in this way pygmy forms which remain so indefinitely and retain their character when propagated. In the Pygmy Pinetum there is a plant which I call *Chamaecyparis lawsoniana* 'Ellwood's Pygmy', obviously a very old plant, which measures 45 cm high by 60 cm across. Rooted cuttings are indistinguishable from the normal 'Ellwoodii' but if (as has happened on occasion) I get the two varieties muddled they are unmistakably distinct after one year's growth.

The other group of "cultivariant" consists of the low-growing forms of *Abies* or *Picea* frequently found labelled or listed as "var. *prostrata*" which could probably be produced by appropriate selection of grafting wood from any species in these genera. If a tree of either *Abies* or *Picea* be examined it will be found to carry two types of shoot, leader growth on which the foliage is radial, and side growth on which it is not. The nurseryman knows that the best trees are always produced by the use of

24

leader growth as grafts, but unfortunately there is never enough of this and so he has to use side growth as well, in spite of the additional trouble he knows he will have to take with the resulting plants by careful staking and other professional know-how to induce it to form the symmetrical, upright plant which most of his customers demand. But left to itself a graft from side wood will maintain this horizontal habit however large the plant grows. A large prostrate specimen so produced of any of the good forms of the beautiful blue spruce *Picea pungens*, or of any other of the more spectacular *Abies* or *Picea*, tumbling down over the rocks for a dozen or more feet from where it was planted can be a magnificent sight and it is amusing to recollect that most of such plants started life as a graft intended for sale in the normal upright form which was accidentally left (nurserymen are busy folk) until it had become too late to take its training in hand.

Because of this inability for side growth to change its habit, plants of these genera are very liable to lose their symmetry if the leader becomes damaged or destroyed. To meet this situation Nature has endowed them with the ability to throw up new leader growth from what I believe botanists call a plastic bud. This can on occasion have curious results. Sometimes several such buds will develop, producing a small clump of leader shoots from which one will eventually assume the mastery and become the tree's new leader. Rarely, one fails to appear on or near the trunk (or it may have been neatly removed by a passing cow) but one will develop at the end of a horizontal branch after the stimulation from later damage. The resulting tree, looking like half a swastika, is usually too unsightly to be left and so this effect is rarely seen, but the fact that it does happen gives us a clue to the reputed instability of these pseudo-prostrate forms. The fact probably is that they are completely and indefinitely stable, subject to the aptitude the plant has for initiating leader growth from a plastic bud following damage. I know of several of these prostrate blue spruces (there is one at Kew, another at Edinburgh) where this has happened and whenever it does occur the tree always loses its grace and becomes something of a monstrosity, so it behoves us (ourselves, our offspring and our cattle) not to walk about on such plants and to prune them as little as possible. If pruning is necessary it would probably be worth while to watch closely for the appearance of the unwanted leader growth the following spring and literally to nip it in the bud.

A word of warning is needed as to the figures for annual rates of growth given by writers on dwarf forms. Where these have been measured on plants growing in pots or on recently transplanted specimens they will bear no reference whatever to the growth of a healthy, well-established plant in the open ground.

2 : The Uses of Dwarf Conifers

The late Murray Hornibrook, who in his early days no doubt had a paragraph all to himself in Burkes' *Landed Gentry of Ireland*, obtained most of his information from the large estates around him in some of which extensive plantings of dwarf conifers had been made.

Now, alas, many of these fine gardens are no more. They are either uninhabited, like Kilmacurragh, or are occupied by new owners with different interests, like Curragh Grange and Rostrevor, and very few indeed of the collections mentioned in his book *Dwarf and Slow-growing Conifers* still survive. And in England, where the social changes of our day have proceeded with perhaps less turbulence than in Hornibrook's native land many of the stately homes now manage to run the garden with two men and a rotavator where at one time they needed twenty men and several boys.

During the same period enormous numbers of smaller houses have been built in every town and village and with them that worthy character the owner/occupier (who, with the local Council's Parks Department is the mainstay of the nursery trade these days) has been increasing in his millions.

And it is in these small gardens of today that the dwarf conifer has come into its own. Instead of a visit from Capability Brown, finishing up with his famous stock remark, "Your estate has great capabilities, my lord", your new landed proprietor, when he had ejected the brick ends, cement bags and other debris left by the builder has to set to work to get his landscape effects in a fraction (often a small fraction) of an acre. The centre of gravity of gardening has shifted from the great estate to the suburban plot, and the obvious plant to reproduce on the new scale the effect of serenity and restful maturity produced on the grand scale by plantations of majestic conifers is, of course, the dwarf conifer.

Not only so, but many of the new generation of home landscapers are finding that neither the small rock garden nor the garden pool, so popular today, really looks complete without one or two dwarf conifers on or near it.

The dwarf conifer is being "discovered", and what is so interesting to me is to see it steadily making its way into public favour in spite of the handicap that the lack of a literature represents to any group of plants. There is probably no type of planting which, around the year and over the years, will give greater pleasure for the cost and trouble involved than a group of dwarf conifers such as in Ills. 13 and 18, yet the literature is extremely poor, being virtually limited (so far as the complete range of dwarf conifers is concerned) to Hornibrook's book, last issued in 1938 and long since out of print. I hope this present book, whilst it does not attempt to be a textbook, will go part of the way to meet the immediate need and will help overcome the

10 A group of young specimens in the Pygmy Pinetum at Devizes. Dwarf conifers may be "moved on" when they outgrow a particular situation.

"ignorance resistance" to the extension of the dwarf conifer vogue that undoubtedly exists.

As though the lack of adequate and authoritative literature were not handicap enough there are, alas, very few collections that I know of in the public gardens and arboreta of the British Isles where dwarf conifers are displayed to best advantage or correctly labelled. One of the finest displays I know is at the National Botanic Garden at Glasnevin in Dublin. Here can be seen many of the original plants donated by Hornibrook in about 1921 and whilst this original planting is now much past its best, in other parts of the garden dwarf conifers have been used skilfully and effectively and the whole collection is well and (so far as our present uncertain knowledge permits) accurately labelled. There is a smaller and younger collection in the University Botanic Garden at St Andrews in Scotland where also the labelling can be relied upon, but this is more than I can honestly say about any other collection that I have seen. On the rock garden at Kew, dwarf conifers have been planted very effectively but the accuracy of the labelling comes short of what we expect from the country's senior horticultural establishment. At the Royal Horticultural Society's garden at Wisley there are some fine specimens in the rock garden and a large collection is planted in three groups near the Heather Garden, although the best use is not at present being made of the plants available in these groups. They originally came to the Society as very small plants and I have no doubt that they will be rearranged in due course now that they are bigger. There are good collections at the

27

11 Dwarf conifers quite at home at one of "England's stately homes".

12 Dwarf conifers equally happy in a suburban front garden.

Royal Botanic Garden at Edinburgh and at the University Botanic Garden at Cambridge and in many public parks but nowhere, it seems, can absolute reliance be placed on the labelling.

Along with this lack of an authoritative and faultless lead in the labelling in these famous gardens there will be found (and probably both can be traced to the paucity of the literature on dwarf conifers) a reluctance on the part of botanists great and small to commit themselves to any firm opinion on problems of identification and nomenclature.

What I should like to see is an "official" or "national" collection of dwarf conifers under the control of some adequate public authority in some place readily accessible to the public, where each plant would be labelled with unimpeachable care so as to be in practice the end of all controversy on all questions of indentification and nomenclature.

Pending some such development I am doing the best I can as an individual here in Devizes to fill the gap. My "Pygmy Pinetum" (as I euphemistically call it) is being planted on an open hillside which lends itself to the construction of a rockery (I use the word deliberately, with apologies to the alpine gardeners who dislike its association with the inartistic rockwork of long ago) on a rather bold scale, in which the large blocks of stone available can be used to simulate rocky outcrops. My collection embraces over 400 varieties and as well as taking great pains to get my labelling correct I have tried to exploit the various potential uses of their differing form, colour, texture and habit. All is still in the formative stage but I should be pleased to see anyone interested in seeing what is being done here if they care to write to me c/o the publishers.

In my planting I have observed few rules, believing that in this as in every form of art to look right is to be right. But certain conclusions have formed in my mind as the result of some of my experiments and experience here, particularly as to the most effective use to be made of certain varieties, and these I refer to in Chapter V under the names of the plants concerned.

There is, however, one basic and inescapable rule, I believe, for the use of dwarf conifers (along with miniature plants of any kind, no doubt) and that is, ALWAYS PLANT THEM IN THE OPEN, AWAY FROM OTHER LARGE PLANT MASSES. The dwarf conifers are serious, dignified little plants and they resent being made to look ridiculous. Our object must be to use dwarf conifers to set the scale of the miniature garden picture and not let them become out of scale by the over-towering presence of larger plants.

The key word in the use of dwarf conifers is "scale" and from this arises another useful principle, which is to plant dwarf conifers wherever possible together in groups. This is more of a recommendation than a rule as there are clear exceptions, but in a general way it can be said that dwarf conifers usually look best together. Planted in this way they are in scale with each other. If dwarf conifers are used in the traditional way, on a rockery, they thereby automatically achieve this grouping more or less, but

13 A delightful formal group of dwarf conifers in the National Botanic Garden, Glasnevin, Dublin. (Photo by kind permission of the Keeper.)

there are many other ways of using them and if your space (or pocket) indicates the purchase of any particular number of trees—be it only half a dozen—I would say without hesitation that you would probably get more landscape value and pleasure from your new treasures by grouping them together as a "feature" than by dotting them about here and there all over the garden where they can only be viewed one at a time.

Such a feature could well be made on a lawn. On a large lawn it could look well a little to one side of the main area so as not to appear lost, yet have mown grass all round it. The bed should be raised up very slightly towards the middle, near which one conifer larger than the rest and of a sturdy upright habit will look well dominating the lower varieties around it. In a large planting, other dominant specimens will need to be used to form fresh centres of interest at other spots and it is not at all a bad plan in planting to start with these dominant plants, adding the lower planting around them.

On a smaller scale the same principles can be followed in grouping your dwarf conifers to form a definite garden picture. If a good composition is achieved it is at all times pleasing to the eye and since many of the dwarf conifers change colour two or even three times a year the tone values of the group is constantly altering. Some of our plants put on their richest colouring during the winter and what could be expected to give more pleasure than a group such as the above planted where it can be seen from a principal living-room window from whence its winter beauty could be enjoyed in comfort whatever the weather happened to be outside.

In every case the background is important and needs careful consideration. In the

30

14 Dwarf conifers planted in association with evergreen azaleas and other low-growing shrubs at the Royal Botanic Garden at Edinburgh.

large plantings referred to (a very good example is the Nisbet collection at the Royal Horticultural Society Gardens at Wisley) the group will be large enough to hold one's attention from whatever direction one approaches it and isolation itself may be all the background that is necessary, but in smaller plantings it will generally be the case that our garden picture will mainly or always be viewed from one direction and here the background must be chosen (as a picture-frame is chosen) to set off the picture and isolate it from its surroundings. A background of tall trees—at a respectful distance—is excellent and where space is limited an evergreen hedge may be the answer; or the group may be placed so that a fence or even a building will serve the purpose.

The use of dwarf conifers in rockeries and alpine gardens is, of course, well established and many would say that this is the best use for them. As well as suggesting an "alpine" atmosphere their evergreen sturdiness of itself sets off the usually low-growing flora around them and any who have attempted alpine gardening without the use of dwarf conifers will be surprised at the improvement brought about by the introduction of a few well-chosen specimens.

For this class of work the selection of the right form of tree is especially important. It should always be remembered that one is seeking to reproduce a scene from nature in one of her wilder moods, so anything savouring of smugness is to be avoided and plants should be selected for each situation of a form which would be expected in just that situation in the wild. For this reason the globose forms and others of a neat and formal outline are in a general way the least useful. Wholly prostrate forms of the *Juniperus horizontalis* type should be used sparingly, for they almost all spread

31

15 Upright-growing forms used effectively to give height and interest on an undulating, informal site at Edinburgh.

eventually over a large area that could be more usefully used for other alpines, but in this class both *Juniperus conferta* and *Juniperus procumbens* 'Nana' are useful plants because of their willingness to grow downhill. They are consequently valuable for covering banks or old tree roots, and the former will even hang down and cover vertical rock faces like an aubrieta.

The dwarf *Picea* are a very useful group. They range from low-growing forms which never reach much over 30–40 cm high but spread slowly outwards (examples are *Picea abies* 'Nidiformis', 'Repens' and 'Tabuliformis') through less prostrate cushion and bun forms ('Pumila', 'Pumila Nigra' and 'Gregoryana' and its various forms) to globose plants ('Clanbrassiliana') and pyramidal forms ('Remontii'). In this latter class comes the popular *Picea glauca* 'Albertiana Conica', none the less useful for its change of name. This plant grows into a neat green cone which with a little attention may, if you wish, be made to look as though it had been turned on a lathe. A single specimen of this variety always catches the eye, and a group (for preference of varying heights) can be most effective, but always—because of its formal symmetry—it should be planted somewhere on the low ground and well out in the open.

Low-growing varieties of irregular outline of the *Juniperus sabina* 'Tamariscifolia' type are very useful and this variety itself can be utilised in most alpine gardens. It will in time become a large plant but it stands being kept to size by heavy pruning better than most of us do.

Many of the real pygmies will be quite at home in suitable nooks and crannies amongst the rocks and there are several of the slow-growing and bushlike forms of Juniper which if taken young and carefully left unpruned will grow into lank, gawky, one-sided plants which will look most attractive at the foot of a rock-cliff where it will appear as though the plant had so grown in an attempt to reach up and outwards to the light. There is quite a colour range of these, giving us scope for selection of plants either toning or contrasting with the colour of the rock-cliff behind. *Juniperus × media* 'Blaauw' is an uncommon and most attractive blue-grey, 'Kaizuka' is a rich grass green. 'Plumosa' (green) and 'Plumosa Aurea' (a rich golden yellow for most of the year) and the two variegated forms, if left to themselves, form lower-growing and more compact plants and may need some training to give us the ruggedness of outline we want just here, but the rich colour of 'Plumosa Aurea' is worth the effort. In the same group 'Shimpaku' is a miniature gem, but unfortunately it is still in short supply in this country.

It is, however, on the higher parts of the rockery, at the tops of the rocky outcrops, where the greatest care in the choice of suitable varieties is so important. At a first glance these more prominent positions would seem just fine for showing off the beauty and symmetry of some dwarf tree of upright or pyramidal habit and so the tendency is to plant such a tree where in nature it would have been either blown out of the ground in a gale many years ago or at best have been so knocked about by the wind over the years as to have lost all pretension to symmetry of outline. We may not be able to analyse our failure but the eye is instinctively disturbed by such incongruity, whereas a dwarf pine in the same spot (planted with its stem well out of the upright and with its lower branches and all the foliage below the branchlets removed so as to expose the bare bones of the poor wind-swept veteran) will look just inevitably right and so be aesthetically satisfying. There are several dwarf pines that will serve us, although but few of them are in easy supply. *Pinus sylvestris* 'Beuvronensis' and 'Watereri' (frequently listed as 'Pumila') and *Pinus densiflora* 'Umbraculifera' are obtainable and either of these will be excellent. For the larger spot the Mountain Pine, *Pinus mugo* will be suitable, a very good example of its use being the Rock Garden at Kew (*Ill.* 215). Certain very close-growing selections have been named on the Continent but as this pine varies considerably from seed it is usually possible to pick out desirable plants in the nursery rows.

For any situation more than three or four feet above the level of the path from which it is to be seen I personally feel that the spreading forms should be limited to those with definitely pendulous branch-tips, as those with stiff, up-turned growing points give to my eye an unpleasant "shock-headed" effect. Plants of the form I prefer are *Juniperus virginiana* 'Kosteri', *Chamaecyparis lawsoniana* 'Elegantissima' and, of course, the dwarf weeping Cedar of Lebanon, *Cedrus libani* 'Sargentii'.

Juniperus recurva var. *coxii* is quite entitled to a paragraph to itself because of its unique charm as a young plant, especially when planted near water. A specimen in the Wansdyke Nursery about 1 m high is without question my best salesman. It has had the lower branches removed and the upper main branches trained out horizontally so that the hanging foliage is well spread out, sufficient of this having been removed to expose the trunk and main framework, and few indeed are the visitors who do not fall for its charms, although warned that (inasmuch that the tree is called the Coffin Juniper because of the demand for its timber in Burma for this purpose) they must expect it to get too big in time (*Ill.* 152).

A few dwarf conifers are essential in the heather garden. Here, contrary to the general rule, they should be isolated plants relatively few and far between, only enough of them being used to emphasize the open, wind-swept terrain. The prostrate forms are quite out of place but the choice may fall on any of those varieties which grow with a rugged, untidy outline such as the varieties of juniper already mentioned in this chapter, and here out in the open safer use can be made of the upright to conical forms. The dark blue-green mass of *Chamaecyparis lawsoniana* 'Ellwoodii' or the slender grace of *Juniperus communis* 'Suecica' or 'Cracovia' can make a delightful contrast with the low masses of the surrounding heather and I know of no better combination than the winter-flowering *Erica carnea* and the loosely conical shape of *Thuja occidentalis* 'Ellwangeriana Aurea', with its twisted golden foliage. This is at its best when the *Erica* are in flower and it seems to revel in the hardest winter weather that comes. A good example of the skilful use of dwarf conifers in this type of garden can be seen in the Valley Garden in Windsor Great Park.

In the United States, where large numbers of houses are of the prefabricated type erected on low walls of concrete the development of what is there called "foundation planting" has been necessary. This consists of evergreens planted close to the house to hide the concrete foundations, and for this conifers are widely used. In this country where it is more usual to carry the facing brickwork down to ground level such planting is unnecessary but it is still quite usual for a path to follow the outline of the house and two, three, four or more feet away. The border so formed is always a problem. Its nearness to the house makes it architecturally important but it is always dry and frequently very draughty—both being conditions in which few plants are happy. Hence the sound advice given in books on garden layout to make it as wide as possible.

Provided that there is sufficient width (4 ft being perhaps a fair minimum) several of the dwarf conifers can be used in such a border with good effect. Care should be taken to avoid over-planting. This tendency is inevitable where the need to cover unsightly foundations as soon as possible can easily lead to the use of varieties much too vigorous for such a restricted spot, but in this country we have no such excuse.

As a group the junipers are probably the best able to deal with the dry conditions, and the semi-prostrate forms of *Juniperus × media* and *Juniperus sabina* are particularly useful. Where there is ample room for it to develop a plant of *Juniperus × media* 'Pfitzeriana' planted right at the main corner of the house can be very impressive, but in most gardens today it would be well to choose the compact form 'Pfitzeriana Compacta' or *Juniperus sabina* 'Tamariscifolia'. Low-growing, conical and upright forms can be used to give a point of emphasis where needed, but these

16 Varieties of dwarf conifer with an irregular and "rugged" outline always look well amongst heather and other ground-cover plants.

should not (for both practical and architectural reasons) be planted in front of windows. In this sort of situation, where the wall of the house forms the background, regard must always be had to its colour and tone in order to secure a good contrast, and in the choice of planting the amount of sunshine the plants will get should be borne in mind.

The entrance door to the house needs special attention. In a very simple small fore-court garden a pair of Irish Yews (the golden form where the house walls are grey stone or dark red brickwork and the dark green form where the walls are of any light colour) may be all that is necessary to give simple emphasis to the doorway. Where there is greater room more elaborate planting can be attempted and where there is plenty of space a grouping of conifers to flank the entrance can be made quite a feature, especially if the ground rises towards the house, necessitating a low flight of steps. These large groups should be planned not only for the effect architecturally as one approaches the building but so as to give a "picture" from the doorway itself, from whence it will most frequently be viewed both by our visitors and ourselves. In all but the simplest schemes it is usually better to secure balance than to attempt symmetry.

In all these suggestions I do not want to give the impression that dwarf conifers should be used alone. Although, as I have said, they are usually most effective used in groups they readily and happily associate with other plants, provided these are not too exuberant. The evergreen azaleas and the smaller daphnes, for example, even when not in flower, make a good combination with dwarf conifers by virtue of their contrasting foliage texture, and doubtless the same can be said of most of the slow-growing broad-leafed shrubs. Carpeting plants can be allowed to grow right to the trunks of the trees and thereby save much weeding, providing that care be taken to avoid the more rampant and invasive species and varieties. Many dwarf bulbs look beautiful when in flower (if planted in fairly bold groups rather than individually dotted about under the dwarf conifers) but the garden varieties usually look out of scale.

I am frequently asked whether any of the dwarf conifers are suitable as indoor plants and my invariable reply is to suggest that two or preferably three little trees should be established in pots so that they can be brought indoors in turn. By this system of horticultural shift work they should all continue in excellent health and a small tree or two can give a lot of pleasure to an invalid or to one whose own green-finger days are over, and they would need far less constant attention than do Bonzai specimens. The trees should be changed around every month or two. During their indoor "shift" they should have the coolest and lightest position available and they should be plunged to the rims in the garden during their off-duty shifts.

In any garden a few selected dwarf conifers established in pots can be very useful in many ways. They can be used as ornaments in their own right in a cold greenhouse or on the terrace and they may be plunged here and there in the alpine garden or border wherever and whenever a note of evergreen is needed to emphasize the floral picture of the moment. It should be borne in mind that all conifers in pots will need care in the matter of regular watering and they will enjoy frequent heavy syringings on summer evenings (all conifers like this) especially in the dusty atmosphere of large cities.

Amongst the miscellaneous uses to which dwarf conifers can be effectively put is the planting of graves. Provided that care be taken to select varieties that can be relied upon to remain dwarf and that full advantage is taken of the range of available colours and habits of growth, a simple group of dwarf conifers can be quite as effective as any attempt to grow flowers in such a restricted area, and of course will be far less trouble to maintain. It is a particularly useful solution to the problem set by those graves that are cared about but which are impossible to visit frequently.

3 : Cultivation Requirements

As a broad generalization covering the present chapter I can state that dwarf conifers are hardy and tough; do well in any ordinary soil and are of easy cultivation.

As regards their being hardy and tough: Whilst this is a fair enough general statement, they do in fact range on the hardiness scale from almost indestructibility downwards to a few which need to be given a sheltered spot, and even in these cases winter hardiness appears to be more a dislike of strong wind than inability to withstand low temperatures.

In more detail again: *Abies, Cedrus, Juniperus, Picea, Pinus, Thuja* and *Thujopsis* seem to stand up to any winter weather, this being especially true as one would expect of the mountain forms such as *Abies balsamea* var. *hudsonia* and the low-growing forms of the tree junipers. The dwarf forms of *Chamaecyparis, Cupressus, Podocarpus* and the other genera with which we are concerned follow their full-size relatives with respect to hardiness. That means to say that they will stand a great deal of exposure but may suffer in an extreme winter. Usually the golden and white-tipped forms are more susceptible to winter damage than the green forms and in all genera (except perhaps *Juniperus*) the fixed juvenile forms seem to be the least reliable. These forms should therefore be given as much shelter as possible from cold winds or (what is worse) draughts. A few of the *Podocarpus* are reliably hardy only in the south-west of England.

Turning now to the matter of soil: My statement about the dwarf conifers doing well in any ordinary soil can be amplified by stating that any garden soil we are likely to meet comes within that description. On soil overlying chalk or with a very high lime content choice should be limited to the *Juniperus* and *Taxus* and, fortunately for those who have to garden under those conditions, these genera include a very wide range of colour, habit and texture forms, but other than this no worry need be felt about planting dwarf conifers in any soil in which gardening at all is possible. If conifers do well in your district you can be assured of success. If they are conspicuously absent from the local landscape it is much more likely to be an unsuitable climate than any peculiarity of the soil. In such conditions you may have to provide an immediate environment for your dwarfs that is more to their liking if they are to succeed.

An idea sometimes met with is that the dwarf conifers need peat. This may have arisen from the general practice with trade exhibitors at flower shows of using a thin covering of this material to complete their exhibits, but it has no substance; it may in fact lead to losses because of the difficulty of really firm planting in peaty mixtures. I know of one case where a collection of dwarf conifers given to a well-known garden was planted in stations prepared by heavy additions of peat and

17 Dwarf conifers give height and a sense of maturity in the alpine border at Beech Park, Clonsilla, Co. Dublin.

losses occurred which might have been avoided had the trees been planted out straight into the soil and been trodden really firmly.

Many people have noticed that the golden forms of *Chamaecyparis lawsoniana* and other colour forms acquire a much richer colouring in some situations than in others and I remember a "bought-in" consignment of *Thuja occidentalis* 'Rheingold' which compared so poorly with my own stock of this variety that at first I thought I had been supplied with the wrong plants. But gradually the new stock developed the rich colour I had been used to in the Pygmy Pinetum and now the plants are indistinguishable. My own opinion, for what it is worth, is that these colour variations are due to the effect of the soil rather than to climatic conditions. I have noticed a richer colour on sandy and gravelly soils than on clay or peat soils. It does not seem to depend upon the acidity (pH value) of the soil and it may be due to the influence of iron or some other trace element. I have never come across any account of research having been done on this point and should be interested to hear through the publishers from anyone who can enlighten me on the subject, with a view to the inclusion of a paragraph on the matter in any subsequent edition. For if richness of colouring can be shown to depend upon the presence of some particular element in the soil it should be very simple and cheap to ensure its inclusion in soil in which these colour forms are to be potted or grown.

Another notion that one meets is the idea that because dwarf conifers are choice and sought-after plants they need to be planted in exceptionally good soil. In a general

38

way the truth is just the opposite to this, for both slowness of growth and ultimate dwarfness are functions of the rate of growth, and given a rich diet even the slowest of growers must be excused for responding with unusual and unwelcome vigour. Conversely, the strongest grower will be slow-growing if kept on near-starvation diet. Considerable control can therefore be exercised over the future growth of any dwarf conifer as of any plant. So if you have only been able to obtain a very small specimen of some choice rarity, one that would be quite ineffective in the place you have in mind for it, the thing to do is to plant it temporarily in a rich spot, encouraging it with a handful of bonemeal mixed thoroughly into the soil at the time of planting. If on the other hand you have large specimens that you do not want to increase greatly in size, plant them in the poorest soil you can find or (more effective still) use a container of some sort to restrict the root spread. This can be anything from a large flower pot to a derelict dust-bin with a few holes knocked in its bottom for drainage.

The check to growth resulting from being lifted and replanted is itself a useful deterrent to any plant and a specimen that is "just right" in a particular situation can be kept from increasing in size almost indefinitely by being lifted and replanted occasionally, the opportunity being taken to do a little discreet root pruning each time.

Arising out of this last suggestion I might point out what a great deal of fun can be had with dwarf conifers by getting right away from the idea that we are planting them in permanent homes. With large-growing trees of all kinds (and even down to such things as roses) this from the nature of the case has to be our outlook and the utmost we can do is to interplant our permanent trees with something quick-growing that can later be grubbed when it has served its purpose, but with the dwarf forms there is no need whatever to regard anything we do as finality. Each tree as it increases in size can be used in the situation for which it is ideally suited at the time and be moved into a larger home when it needs one and is large enough to fill it adequately.

Once this idea has taken root in any real gardener's mind he will enjoy many happy hours during each summer, planning the autumn's moves. Special meetings of the Garden Planning Committee will be called to discuss this proposal and that amendment during the summer evenings when backs are beginning to ache too much for any more bending tonight, and as soon as there has been some real soaking rain to soften the ground the re-arrangements decided upon can be carried out in plenty of time for the little trees to settle down and make fresh roots in their new homes while the soil is still warm; in time too for the matter to be put right before the winter really sets in if, in spite of all the planning, it is felt that a mistake has been made. This paragraph will probably make me very unpopular in the nursery trade because re-arranging one's trees can be nearly as much fun (fortunately not *quite* as much) as buying new specimens, but there is always the possibility of the gardener forgetting that a tree—especially a large one—is very liable to suffer from dryness at the roots during the first summer after a move of this kind and finding that he has to visit the nursery in search of a replacement for the tree he has unfortunately "lost" through his forgetfulness.

Dwarf conifers can either be purchased in pots or from the open ground according to the tradition in the nursery to which you go, some inclining towards growing all their stock in pots and others preferring to grow them in the more natural conditions of open ground cultivation. Still other firms keep their young stock in pots and grow the larger sizes under field conditions. Plastic containers are being used increasingly in place of the traditional clay pots, but the effect is similar.

As a general rule plants from the open ground are stronger and more in character than their counterparts in pots, which may have long been suffering conditions of semi-starvation and an efficiency considerably below one hundred per cent on the part of the boy responsible for the watering. On the other hand you can buy (and plant) dwarf conifers from pots at any part of the year, whereas nurseries carrying the whole of their stock in the open ground will probably be willing to take an order for autumn delivery but will refuse to serve you during the summer. There may be some truth in the point sometimes made that plants already established in pots are the best if they are to be grown on in the same way. Over against that is the somewhat greater probability that open-ground plants establish in the garden better than pot-grown stuff, but there is probably insufficient in either theory to worry unduly about.

However your plants come to you, see that the roots are spread out as carefully as you would when planting any other tree. If your plant has been growing in a pot the chances are that it will have its roots in a dense tangle with one or more long roots going round and round the bottom of the pot. These long roots are of no more use to the plant than the clock springs they resemble and they should be cut hard back. Carefully unravel the tangled mass of smaller roots with as little damage to them as possible. Even if you have to wash most of the soil off in a bucket of water it is better to free the root system so that it can be spread out as the planting proceeds, with all the main roots radiating from the plants in their natural manner (this especially goes for what you have left behind of the clock-spring roots) than to plant the pot ball as it is. If plants from the open ground are delivered with the roots in a ball tied round with hessian or some similar material this must be removed. The root system in this case must be broken into sufficiently to enable sizeable roots to be spread out as the soil is back-filled. The aim always is to have the main roots spreading downwards and outwards, separated by soil, in the same way that the branches spread upwards and outwards, separated by air. In the case of very large specimens with a heavy ball it may be better to lower this into a hole dug to the exact depth before cutting the hessian away. In this case a small piece must be left in the ground where it will rot and do no harm, but the roots all round can be teased out of the ball and spread in the soil as previously described.

The essential thing in the case of either a pot ball or a hessian ball is to break up at least the surface of the ball and to ensure that some main roots radiate from it into the surrounding soil. Omission of this precaution is probably the greatest single cause of failure to establish balled plants, for if the ball (consisting almost certainly of soil with very different physical properties to the surrounding earth) is just dumped into a hole in the ground it is quite possible for capillary connection never to be established between it and its surroundings. In this case the plant, having drawn every trace of moisture out of the ball when growth commences in the spring can perish from drought when the rest of the garden may still be too wet to do anything with. If, in addition, the ball is approximately spherical a wonderful ball-and-socket effect is produced and the poor plant rocks to and fro in every wind with no possibility of ever anchoring itself, for any new roots which do succeed in crossing from the ball into the socket are sheered off during the next breezy spell before they ever attain any mechanical strength.

Dwarf conifers can be successfully transplanted at any time from early autumn to late spring, but due to the danger of desiccation before a plant can re-establish itself, planting should not be done when cold weather is due. This means that the months of December, January and sometimes February are best avoided, especially in the case of very small plants. If the vulnerability of spring-planted trees to dryness at the roots during the following summer is remembered, spring is probably the best time as the roots are then active and soon get hold in their new quarters, but human frailty being what it is the autumn is probably the safest time. If sufficient trouble is taken, however, it is quite practicable to move conifers at any time of the year. During the hot summer of 1960 I moved a number of quite large specimens. The ground at the time was as dry as a brick and they were each lifted with a great block of soil of the consistency of concrete and brought home in the back of the car. They were stood for several days in a mist-propagation house, during which time the "ball" was, frequently watered. When it was nice and soft all through and the foliage was fresh and green from the effect of the mist the trees were planted out in a shaded corner to which no sunlight penetrated and I did not lose a single plant. They are now some of the best specimens in the Pygmy Pinetum.

For amateurs without mist houses the same effect could have been secured by very frequent spraying or syringing and where natural shade is not available artificial shade can be provided by the erection of a rough timber tripod over the plant with two of its sides covered with hessian, canvas or any available opaque material. This wigwam should have one side left open towards the north and it should be large enough relative to the size of its occupant to allow air to circulate freely around the plant and yet shelter it from the sun throughout the whole day.

No attempt should be made to plant trees purchased in pots during summer in the way described above until the autumn. If you are impatient to see them in place they should be stood in a bucket of water for several hours and then be dropped into position (with or without the pot) and watered regularly until they can be dealt with thoroughly later on.

In America plastic sprays are widely used to seal the surface of the leaves and so help the plant to recover after being transplanted, by reducing transpiration. A spray

18 Dwarf conifers associate well with garden pools. Some of the weeping forms are effective if planted so as to overhang the water.

of this kind is now available in this country. I have no experience of its use but I have no doubt it could be used with advantage whenever late spring or summer transplanting is unavoidable.

No one should attempt to grow plants of any kind indoors or under glass who is not prepared to shoulder conscientiously the full responsibility usually carried by Nature herself in the matter of water supply. All I therefore need to do here is to remind such that a dwarf conifer is probably more prone to suffer from its owner's lapses of memory than other plants because it is often left for years in a more or less pot-bound state and because conifers do not advertise their sufferings like most other plants do by wilting in time for the application of a quick refresher. When conifers show distress they are usually in a very bad way indeed and are probably beyond the point of recovery. Treatment in such circumstances is to stand the pot in a bucket of water for several hours until the whole ball is soaked through, and then to put the plant where it will be in complete shade, syringing the leaves as frequently as possible until it recovers its usual bright, healthy appearance. It may ease its own burden of recovery by shedding some of its foliage (the gaunt, unfurnished appearance of many pot-grown plants is due to a succession of such crises in their lives) but it will soon show which way things are going, and the abandoned foliage can be rubbed off as soon as it is completely shrivelled and dry.

I have already remarked that newly planted conifers in the open need regular attention during their first summer, especially if May, June or July are dry months, and they should never be allowed to become dry at the roots. Their second year they are, of course, less vulnerable and after that most conifers can safely be left to themselves unless drought conditions develop. Note should be taken of the clause "in the open" which qualifies the last but one sentence, for conifers planted in hollow stone walls, near buildings and in crazy paving and other inherently dry places will always need watering during the summer.

Almost all conifers thrive best in areas of high rainfall and in consequence of that they all enjoy being sprayed or syringed with water whenever the weather is warm and dry. This is especially so in the grimy atmosphere of cities where the foliage gets not only dry but coated with dust, and always the syringing seems most effective when done during the evening, so that the leaves remain wet during the night.

Pruning is no mysterious art to be understood only by the initiated few; it is just the simple knowledge of how plants react to damage (in this case our pruning) applied with common sense and a clear idea of what we are trying to do in each case.

Pruning serves two purposes. In the early, formative years of the tree it usually accompanies staking of the central stem to form a trunk, and other practices which would come under the wider term, Training. This type of pruning may consist of either the removal of rival leaders and lower or overcrowded branches where, as in the case of *Juniperus recurva* var. *coxii*, the beauty of the tree lies in an open habit, or on the other hand the shortening of growing tips to encourage buds to break lower down in order to produce denser growth, where this is what is required. In either case no amateur is likely to overdo matters and frequently he needs reminding of the importance of "trunk training" and formative pruning. I well might paraphrase the words of the wise king of old and say "Train up a tree in the way it should go and when it is old it will not depart from it".

Some judicious shortening of the growth after transplanting will always help a plant to re-establish itself after its move, by reducing the burden on the root-system until it has had time to make new root hairs and in many cases, such as the prostrate forms of juniper, hard cutting back of the leading growths each spring for several years is necessary to encourage the plant to form a dense mat. This is exactly the same as the hard cutting back advocated in the gardening textbooks for newly planted hedges and is done for the same reason.

The second object of pruning is to keep the tree within bounds. This can be done—less successfully with some species than others—to a limited extent only, for the reason that hard pruning encourages strong growth. So if you try to restrict a tree to a size *greatly* below its natural inclination you are starting up a vicious circle and would be well advised to move the tree to where it will have more room to develop and plant a dwarfer form in its place.

When I am asked about the pruning of dwarf conifers and the best tool to use I always advise the use of nail scissors. I do this not only because a pair of nail scissors is in fact a very convenient tool but because by recommending its use I hope I am impressing the enquirer with the desirability of "little and often" over against the leaving of pruning until stronger and larger tools are needed. A nurseryman uses a knife and for the heavier cuts this is the best tool *provided it is kept sharp*. "Nail scissor" pruning can be done at any time of the year (what an invitation to the gardener to while away the hours pottering about and fiddling with his trees!) but any heavy cutting is best done in late spring when life is active and new growth will soon cover the scars of battle.

Although this book does not deal with the art of Bonzai (which I personally regard as in the same moral category as keeping pit ponies and the old custom, also from China, of binding little girls' feet to keep them small) yet there are some things we can learn from the Bonzai technique and profit by if used with restraint, as possibly is the case with every vice. I have already suggested the use that can be made of root pruning in keeping our trees from putting on size and the necessity of staking certain varieties in their early years, and if in any particular case a curved trunk would be more pleasing to the eye than a straight one or a branch be required to grow in a particular shape or direction, no objection could be raised to our getting the effect we want by a curved stake or the temporary use of wire loosely twined corkscrew-fashion around the trunk or branch we wish to train until it takes the shape we have chosen. It is important to remember that the season's growth hardens or lignifies during the late summer and autumn, so any training devices should be in position by early August at the latest and will be found to have served their purpose by the winter, whereas once growth has hardened into wood it has become inert and will never change its shape. Force will be needed to bend it where we want it to go and we shall have to hold it there by force in a state of internal stress until the following season's growth has hardened around it during the following autumn. Even then when we release the ties the mechanical strength of the old wood that has merely been held in a state of stress all the time will assert itself against the strength of the new wood and the plant will "give" a bit and take up a shape intermediate between its original and the one we want. Of course, if we have allowed two years' growth before taking the training in hand, not only shall we need to use greater force and stronger ties—we shall need to leave them in place for two autumns at least. Hence the importance of training young growth during that first summer.

Certain forms, particularly those with juvenile foliage, are prone to the browning of their leaves by scorching sun or keen wind. In the case of plants suffering in this way in more or less normal weather the answer is to move them to a more sheltered spot, but even the more robust forms may be affected during an exceptional winter or even a prolonged spell of cold wind.

In every case the nursing of a badly burnt plant back into health and symmetry is a difficult task and requires much patient care, sometimes extending over several years, but it is in some obscure way a rewarding one. If only the foliage tips are burnt all that is necessary is to wait until it is completely shrivelled and brown and then at some time when the foliage is quite dry to vigorously beat, brush, shake or otherwise coax all the dead leaves to fall off. The wind will do it for you in time but the sooner the dead bits are gone the sooner the tree will recover its good looks. If large areas of foliage die it will indicate that some part of the branch system is also dead. Whether or not such a plant will ever recover a pleasing shape will depend firstly upon the distribution and extent of the die-back and secondly upon the ability of the species in question to break from old wood. In any event the dead patches must be cut away, for they are most unsightly. Dead tissue never comes to life again and the presence of dense areas of dead foliage will prevent the tree from ever regaining its shapeliness. Cutting these away will let light in, encouraging buds to break from the old wood, and a healthy plant will soon colonize the blank spaces. But here a word of caution is necessary: Do not be too eager to cut anything out until you are sure it is dead, for the plant may take some time making up its mind just how much of its branch system it is going to abandon and premature knife action may result in the loss of wood, "with life in it" where it perhaps can ill be spared from the tree. The safest course is to go over the plant several times at intervals during the spring, each time cutting out only what is indisputedly dead, beginning with the browned foliage and only cutting into old wood when little pinheads of new growth indicate the points at which the plant intends to start re-furnishing itself.

A very common misapprehension is that conifers, because they are evergreen, do not drop their leaves, but the only difference between an evergreen and deciduous plants is that the latter discard their leaves after a few months, leaving the branches bare during the winter and until the new growth commences in the spring, whereas evergreens hold on to theirs much longer—at least until the next year's leaves develop. The different species vary in their ideas of how long to keep their old leaves but they all let them ripen and fall off in the end. This can have two effects worth mentioning here. One is that certain conifers can look very bedraggled for a few weeks during the summer just when the old leaves are ripening and preparing to drop. This can easily be taken for a sign of ill health (or even impending death) but a close look at the foliage will soon disclose what is taking place and the tree will soon recover its good looks.

The other result of the dropping of the dead leaves is the tendency with many of the more bushlike and densely branched conifers for the dead leaves to collect and build themselves into a dense solid mass in the interior of the plant, especially amongst the lower branches. This is a common cause of the fastigiate forms of *Chamaecyparis lawsoniana* and *Thuja orientalis* becoming bare at the base, for the dense peatlike mass excludes light and completely inhibits growth buds. Gardeners should realize that this is a form of neglect, and they will often find a considerable improvement in the general appearance of a tree result from a thorough spring cleaning of its interior. It is not at all unusual to be able to get a wheelbarrow full of trass out of a single large plant. A convenient tool for this work can be easily made out of a piece of stout wire bent into a hook, but the best way I have found is to use the garden hose with a narrow bore nozzle or with one's finger held against the open end so as to produce a

19 Dwarf conifers effectively used amongst heather and other low-growing flowering shrubs at Creevy Rocks, Saintfield, Co. Down. N.J

high velocity jet, and to work this to and fro right in among the branches. There will probably be considerable doubt as to which has got wetter, you or the tree, but if you have persevered, at close enough range, all the dead rubbish will have been cleared away and you may very possibly be rewarded next spring by the appearance of new foliage much lower down the tree than you had ever again expected to see it.

Older plants of the dense and bushy forms, especially the juvenile forms of *Thuja orientalis* such as 'Rosedalis' consist of a dense surface covering of foliage but the interior will be found to contain much dead wood—the remains of branches that have failed to meet the competition for light and air. If as much of this dead wood as possible be cut away occasionally it will contribute to the health and longevity of the tree. Some of these forms tend to become untidy and irregular in outline as they age and the more open the interior of the plant can be kept the more encouragement there will be for buds to start into growth from the old wood and these will thicken the growth, colonize any bare patches and keep the tree vigorous and shapely in its old age.

Damage from heavy snow can be avoided (or at worst greatly minimized) if the trouble be taken to shake the plant free of the snow as soon as possible after it has fallen and before the subsequent effect of wind, rain, frost or a combination of them increases the burden of snow being carried by the plant to the point of damaging the main branches. Branches of fastigiate forms may need tying up (few gardeners would respond to advice to tie them up before the winter, I am afraid) but surprisingly

46

20 Another view of the same garden.

little damage will have been done if action is taken immediately following the falling of the snow.

It is hardly to be expected that anyone will have anything fresh to say on the subject of weeding and least of all would you expect to find such a thing in a book on dwarf conifers. But weeding is such a problem that it is only right to pass on anything one has found out to reduce this work. I remember several years ago there was an exhibit put on by one of the Horticultural Institutes at the Chelsea Flower Show. I forget the details but the general import was a schedule of the commoner weeds and the proved longevity of their seeds, and to this day I remember the awful impact on my mind of seeing that some of the weeds now germinating in my garden could have been there in the ground since Queen Victoria's day. With this in mind there is everything to be said for disturbing the ground as little as possible once your permanent planting is done, for it is only the turning over of the soil and the consequent bringing to the surface of these seeds that causes them to germinate. The principle is that the weeding should be done with as little disturbance of the soil as possible. For this the best tool that I know of is a fern trowel, which is a very narrow trowel with a semicircular end. This needs to be sharpened on a grindstone to a very sharp edge, and the technique of its use is to grasp the weed with one hand and pull whilst using the sharpened trowel in the other hand (as though it were a chisel) to cut off the roots just below ground level. This is no use, of course, for deep-rooted subjects such as docks and dandelions that can regenerate from pieces of root, nor for couch grass, but for most of the annual weeds including the grasses it is most effective, and

47

the root is destroyed with virtually no disturbance of the soil. For the long tap-rooted subjects the tool to use is a small handfork, preferably one that has been stamped out of a sheet of steel so that the blades are as thin as possible. This is pushed into the ground at an angle of about 45° close to the plant so that the tines pass across the tap root, which will now lie between them. If now the weed be grasped with the other hand and pulled hard whilst the fork is waggled from side to side it will either come up in its entirety or will be cut off by the thin tines of the fork at such a low level as to render its regeneration unlikely. If the weeding be consistently done in this way, and the weeds be never allowed to seed, the seed population of the top layer of soil will be reduced by quite a surprising amount, with a consequent reduction in the burden of weeding.

Another way to discourage the germination of weeds is the use of ground cover planting, as already mentioned in Chapter 2, and yet another alternative is to cover the surface of the soil with small stone chippings.

I understand that the William T. Gotelli collection, thought to have been the finest private collection of dwarf conifers ever to have been made, was kept in this manner before it was passed over to the United States Arboretum at Washington. I have only seen photographs of the collection when it was in Mr Gotelli's garden but from these it would appear that many of the rarer and more botanically interesting specimens were planted in sunk containers in a large flat area, with space all round each plant to facilitate inspection by visitors, and that the whole of this area was covered with stone chippings. Apart from the fact that their being grown in containers kept his plants dwarf, I understand that Mr Gotelli liked them grown in this way so that whenever he felt inclined he could have them all lifted and the complete layout altered with the minimum of trouble, the disturbance being quickly covered by means of a few barrow loads of new chippings. Part of Mr Nisbet's collection at Gosport was similarly treated and it is an idea that might be well copied in smaller collections and for the same reasons.

The propagation of dwarf conifers on a commercial scale is carried out nowadays with quite elaborate equipment, in propagating houses provided with controlled bottom heat and mist apparatus, but there is nothing to prevent the home gardener striking a few cuttings of his treasures with the simplest of apparatus. A cold frame on the north side of a hedge or low building where it is fully open to the light but receives no direct sunlight is ideal, but much can be done on a small scale with a few bell-jars or even a bottomless wooden box covered with a sheet of glass. The light (in the case of the cold frame) or the sheet of glass (in the case of the box) should be a close fit and unless the frame is a very substantial affair of brick or concrete it would be all the better for being sunk into the ground until the glass is at or a little above ground level. This sinking will greatly further our aim of sheltering the cuttings from fluctuating and extreme temperatures, which is the reason for the use of the cold frame at all. The wooden box can be similarly sunk, or two boxes can be used, one much larger than the inner one where the cuttings are to go and with the space

▲ 21 Dwarf conifers in a formal layout at Castlewellan, Saintfield, Co. Down, N.I., home of a fine collection of conifers. ▼ 22 Another view of the same garden.

between them filled up with soil. Sinking must not, of course, be done where there is the slightest danger of flooding.

Three to four inches of rooting medium should be provided. This could consist of 50 per cent sharp, coarse sand or grit, 25 per cent finely sieved soil and 25 per cent peat. The exact mixture is not important, provided it is what the gardener calls "open". This means that it cannot readily become sodden. So, provided the sand predominates and is coarse enough, the soil adds a little nutriment to feed the new roots we hope for and the peat buffers fluctuations in the moisture level, but the proportions are not critical.

In the taking and preparation of the cuttings standard gardening practice should be followed. There is nothing special about cuttings of dwarf conifers except that the cuttings will vary (according to the subject) from the usual 4–5 in long down to about an inch in the case of some of the very slow-growing forms. They should be of well ripened one-year-old wood with or without a heel or small portion of second-year wood. One of the most important points with cuttings of all kinds (and dwarf conifers are no exception) is to make quite sure that the soil is well firmed around the base of the cuttings. It is useless to ram the soil at the surface if the base of a cutting is dangling in a pocket of air or loose soil. This is a very frequent source of failure.

Conifers do not seem to be very fussy regarding the time of year at which the cuttings are taken. It can be done either during the autumn or in early spring, but bearing in mind that the cuttings will have to remain in the frame for twelve months or longer and that they are more likely to suffer from excessive heat during the summer than extreme cold during the winter, autumn cuttings will have the advantage during the first and most critical six months.

I intend to be quite non-committal regarding the use of plant hormones as an aid to rooting, for although I usually use a powder dip myself I know several very experienced dwarf conifer "fans" who maintain that conifers dislike the treatment and root better without it. A dip into a powder fungicide such as Orthocide (Captan) in any case is a wise precaution against the ingress of stem-rot before the cutting has had time to close its defences by forming callus tissues over the wound.

Even with such simple apparatus as described, reasonably good results can be expected from most varieties of *Abies*, *Chamaecyparis*, *Cryptomeria*, *Juniperus*, *Picea*, *Taxus* and *Thuja*, but *Cedrus*, *Cupressus*, *Pinus*, *Pseudotsuga* and some *Abies* and *Picea* range between "Very Difficult" and "Impossible", at least on any worthwhile scale, and in consequence the dwarf forms of these genera have to be propagated commercially by grafting, a process which calls for equipment and skills rather outside the range of this book. It might not be amiss, however, to remark that propagation by grafting is necessarily much more costly than the production of plants from cuttings and this is why these genera must always be offered by nurserymen at higher prices.

Most, probably all, conifers can be increased by layering. In some cases all that

23 Dwarf conifers effectively used in the new rock garden at the Royal Horticultural Society's gardens at Wisley.

needs to be done is to lower a plant bodily into the ground (or earth it up) so that only the young growths at the tips of the branches are to be seen and leave it so for one or perhaps two growing seasons until a little exploratory digging at the side of the plant indicates that rooting has taken place freely up the buried branches. The plant can then be taken up and cut with sharp secateurs into two or more rooted pieces, each of which can be treated as a new plant. Where a whole plant cannot be sacrificed in this way the layering of a single branch in the normal textbook manner can always be relied upon to produced roots in time.

I have no experience of air-layering conifers but see no reason to suppose it would not be successful where no branch near enough to the ground is available for layering in the normal manner. But it is at best a cumbersome method—a propagator's last ditch.

51

4 : Nomenclature

All concerned with dwarf conifers would agree that their nomenclature is in a state of great confusion. Botanists, nurserymen and the general gardening public can be relied upon to respond as one man to any lugubrious mention of this fact.

But although we agree we do not all mean the same thing.

Nurserymen and their customers will mean that there is so much uncertainty as to the identity of particular plants; that there is such blameworthy carelessness by persons other than the current complainer that there can be no confidence in any sources of supply, and that there exists no apparent means of sorting out the resulting muddle and ill-feeling.

Botanists will probably concur, but they will primarily have in mind the official Codes of Nomenclature and the fact that the dwarf conifers, as a group, are about as far from fitting into these Codes as they very well could be.

I have sympathy with both points of view. It would be no exaggeration to say that it would be possible to order the same dwarf conifer from six reputable sources and receive that number of distinct varieties or to order six different varieties and receive the same plant from every source of supply. I well recall a large consignment from a nursery no longer in business which at the time specialized in dwarf conifers, in which a little more than half the plants turned out to be wrongly labelled.

This raises trouble enough, but the botanists' problem is the more difficult of the two. The gardeners' problem is one of identification. The botanists' task is classification and nomenclature.

In this book, particularly by the liberal use of photographs and what I call my "Identification Plates" I am making a stab at the first part of the problem where the greatest uncertainty exists—identification—and as I have already mentioned, the botanists are at work on questions of classification and nomenclature. Time may therefore require alterations in a few of the names I use, but there is no indication that sweeping changes are in prospect.

Most keen gardeners these days will have a general idea of the system of classification used by botanists. With their higher categories—Families, Orders, Classes and Divisions—we have little concern, as all the conifers giving us dwarf forms belong to either the family Pinaceae or the family Taxaceae, both of the Order Coniferales. We are therefore only concerned about the Genera and the Species and their subdivisions (where these occur) together with the names used by gardeners, i.e. the Cultivar names.

The nomenclature of the former group is controlled by an International Association for Plant Taxonomy who issue an *International Code of Botanical Nomenclature*, the current edition of which is dated 1961. Curiously enough, there seems nothing to control botanical classification, as distinct from nomenclature. Botanists have no real agreement amongst themselves, for example, as to an exact definition of a species. Individual botanists study particular groups of plants and from time to time one of them comes up with a monograph in which he may suggest the amalgamation of species or genera or the creation of new species (or even genera, or worse) and so far as I have been able to ascertain (not being myself a botanist) there is nothing to stop him save the sobering reflection that his fellows will laugh at him and agree to ignore his contribution if his suggestions are unfounded or too far-fetched. They have a jolly little magazine of their own called *Taxon* (which Alice would have had a poor opinion of as it contains neither pictures nor conversations) in which one can come across this sort of remark:

"The organs termed paraphyses by bryologists are apparently less different from the paraphyses in our sense than are some of the so-called paraphyses (paraphysoids, pseudophyses and hyphidia, pseudoparaphyses) of some mycologists. On the other hand, the paraphyses of pteridology are evidently not homologous with or similar to the paraphyses of the fungi, but might be comparable to the paraphyses as characterized by us. It would be desirable to have the opinion of competent specialists in the bryological and pteridological field in order to determine whether the word paraphysis can be used in mycology, as well as in bryology, and what other term, if any, should replace the term paraphysis in Pteridoptera."

I can well understand that folk who lap up this sort of thing set quite a value on their reputation with the others, so it does seem that the risk of not being drawn into the discussions on the genera *Mnium* L., *Mnium* Hedwig and *Calypogeja* Raddi at the *Splitters and Lumpers Club* or, worse still, of being cold-shouldered at the *Green Petiole* (or wherever it is that botanists foregather and where the final word is given on these matters) acts as a wholesome safeguard against lighthearted irresponsibility.

Whether or not it acts powerfully enough I cannot say. Some gardeners would hotly contest this. What, however, is clear is that once he has decided to take the plunge and suggest some change in classification your botanist is entirely controlled in his nomenclature by the Code of Nomenclature already referred to. This is a system of rules of such rigidity as to make the law of Moses or the Council's Building Byelaws read like a brochure for a holiday camp, and he is tied by its inexorable decrees even to the spelling he uses. Unfortunately the Code does not also share the immutability of the laws of the Medes and Persians because it can be amended at any International Botanical Congress. These are held every fifth year, and unfortunately they usually like to have another look at their brain child each time they meet.

Botanists for the past few hundred years and in many countries have been describing and naming allegedly new species without always being so careful in their search through what had gone before as they are at the Patent Office, and it has frequently happened that the same plant (or taxon as I should say) had been given several names

24 A corner of the rockery at the Pygmy Pinetum at Devizes, Wilts.

at different times and places. Early in the formulation of the Botanical Code it was decided that the only way to secure international agreement—and hence, eventually, stability—was to agree to use the first name that could be shown to have been given in a proper manner to the plant. This is known as the "Priority Rule" and this is the rule that is responsible for those changes in the names of garden plants which so irritate gardeners, many of whom have difficulty in grasping the thought that nomenclatural stability can lie at the end of a road of alteration. It is perhaps particularly hard to accept it with a good grace when we do reconcile ourselves to the abandonment of a well-known name and painstakingly familiarize ourselves with a new (actually an older) name and are then told that a still older one has since been discovered the use of which is now our botanical duty. The whole process may be likened to a log being washed up the beach by successive waves on a rising tide. However many times the log may be shifted, eventual stability is certain, because there must eventually come one wave, as the tide turns, which is the last with any power to float the log.

So far I have only been writing about the *International Code of Botanical Nomenclature*, often abbreviated to the *Botanical Code*. There is another, the *Cultivar Code*, which deals with matters important from the gardeners' point of view about which the botanists do not concern themselves. I shall have more to say about this Code later on but we are not yet by any means clear of the problems which the Botanical Code can provide for us when ordering the labels for our dwarf conifers.

54

NOMENCLATURE

Most people these days are familiar with the binomial system introduced by the Swedish botanist Linnaeus in or around the year 1753. By this system the name of each species of plant normally consists of two words of latin form, the first—the generic name—being the genus in which it is (at the moment of going to press) placed by the botanists and the second—the specific epithet—the species to which (repeat words in brackets) it belongs. The illustration frequently used, of the first being analogous to a man's surname and the second to his christian name is only partly true because whilst there can be many John Smiths in the world the botanical system is such that there can never be any repetition of this binomial name, even although the same specific epithet can be used in more than one genus. We can therefore have *Thuja orientalis* and *Picea orientalis*, and if you are wanting a name for a new species of juniper you have found out east you can use *Juniperus orientalis* (no one having yet used the specific epithet *orientalis* within the genus *Juniperus*, so far as I am aware).

To go back to the analogy with human names: if we allowed other parents to use the name John but could contrive it that there were to be only one family of Smiths in the whole world, all of whom we could compel to live in Biggleswade (and hence in Bedfordshire and hence in England and hence in Europe) the analogy would be much better. In those circumstances, to meet someone called John would tell us nothing more than to be told that a certain plant was called *orientalis*. To hear that someone was called Smith, however, would tell us a lot more—we should from that fact alone know or be able to look up the town, county, country and (if it mattered to us) the continent where he belonged. All we should not know would be "Which of the Smiths is he?". So that to know that our plant is a *Thuja* is sufficient to tell us that it is of the family Pinaceae and in the order Coniferales and (if we are further interested) of the class Gymnosperma and of the Division Spermatophyta. All we need to know is, "Which of the *Thuja* is it?". But to know that we have *Thuja orientalis* fixes our plant just as much as would the knowledge that we were speaking to the only John Smith in existence.

So far this sounds all very simple and easy. But the botanists have also introduced at all ranks a whole lot of intermediate classifications which can be used as and when any particularly complicated problem of grouping makes a few further sub-divisions handy. Thus between the ranks Genus and Species we may have Subgenus, Sectio, Subsectio, Series and Subseries and below the rank of Species we find Subspecies, Varietas and Forma. The use of any of these intermediate ranks does not affect the binomial rule (we still have only one John Smith, even if we have now discovered that he is one of the red-haired members of his family, or that he lives in North Biggleswade) except in the sub-ranks below that of Species. Here the analogy with human names breaks down entirely, and an additional latin-form word has to be added to the binomial (making three) to define our plant. In practice there is much short-circuiting, but whilst many plants get by most of the time with a name like *Chamaecyparis pisifera* 'Rogersii' or at a pinch as *Thuja* 'Rheingold' there are unfortunate plants which (when medals are being worn) have to bear up under full-dress names such as *Saxifraga aizoon* var. *aizoon* subvar. *brevifolia* forma *multicaulis* subforma *surculosa* Engler and Irmscher.

It might very well occur to an optimistic reader previously unacquainted with the subject that we were now coming to the end of the matter, but in those groups of plants that have been of most service to mankind the work of selection has been going on in some cases for centuries, and a real need exists for our being able to make distinctions of significance to horticulture between cultivated varieties (usually abbreviated to the word cultivar). This can and often does continue down even to the point at which we are actually distinguishing between individual plants, for all "named" varieties of apples, roses, etc., originate by the selection of a single seedling plant considered by its raiser to have sufficient distinctiveness to be worth propagating asexually. Thus, for example, all the Cox's Orange Pippin apple trees in the world have been propagated from and so are really a part of the original seedling raised by the retired brewer of the name who at that time lived at Slough. A company of plants originating by vegetative propagation from a single plant is termed a clone.

With their lowest ranks, Varietas and Forma, the botanists wash their hands of the matter and hand the problem over to another body, an International Commission appointed by the International Union of Botanical Sciences who have produced the *International Code of Nomenclature for Cultivated Plants* (usually referred to as the Cultivar Code) the current edition of which is dated 1961.

It is to my way of thinking unfortunate (even if doubtless unavoidable) that the task of controlling the nomenclature of plants had to be divided between two bodies each producing its own Code because not only have we the duty of complying with each Code, where it applies—we have the additional complication of having to decide in border-line cases as to which Code is to control the naming of the particular plant we are dealing with. The boundary line (which roughly speaking is the distinction between cultivated plants and wildlings brought into cultivation) is essentially an artificial distinction, more or less arbitrarily made, and this third problem is a special nuisance in the nomenclature of the dwarf conifers because these lie along the boundary-line between the two Codes, more perhaps than any other group of plants.

The Cultivar Code has necessarily had to be superimposed upon the Botanical Code, the requirements of which still control the botanical part of the name by which the cultivar is to be known, and it follows the same rules where this has been found possible, but it makes the one great departure, this being that in future the cultivar name must be what the Code calls a "fancy" name, i.e. one that is markedly different from a botanical name in Latin or of latinised form. Cultivar names already in use (zero hour was 1st January 1959) in latin form are to remain, but there are to be no more of them and all cultivar names are to be clearly distinguished from botanical names by the way they are printed. They may for instance (as in this book) be printed with capitals and single quotation marks. Thus our old friend *Thuja occidentalis* 'Little Gem' finds itself in the clear provided we use a capital "L" and a capital "G" and use single quotation marks. Similarly *Chamaecyparis lawsoniana* 'Forsteckensis'

25 Dwarf conifers used effectively in stone troughs in Miss Anne Ashberry's garden at Chignal-Smealey, Chelmsford, Essex.

and *Thuja orientalis* 'Elegantissima' are acceptable (or we may write *Chamaecyparis lawsoniana* cv. Forsteckensis or *Thuja orientalis* cv. Elegantissima and be equally correct) because these cultivar names were in use before 1st January 1959. No new cultivar names in latin form can, however, be accepted. They must now consist of one, two or at a pinch three words forming a "fancy" name. This will be more or less a departure in the dwarf conifer world, where latinized names have in the main been used and where in consequence "fancy" names have appeared undignified, and we shall have to get ourselves more accustomed to names of the 'Little Gem' and 'Rheingold' type. I do hope, however, that choosers of names will maintain the dignity of these serious little plants by the choice of suitable names, and not descend to frivolous and topical allusions which might be quite suitable in the case of a narcissus or a gladiolus—or a racehorse. Provided that restraint is used in this way no doubt good will come of the new rule for it is undeniable that the coining of latin-form multinomials has been overdone. The stringing together of such descriptive adjectives as *nana*, *compacta*, *pygmaea*, *compressa*, *aurea* and *lutea* as and when fresh mutations were propagated and introduced has given substantial grounds for the popular complaint that the smaller the tree the longer its name.

The Botanical Code comes in a fair-sized volume with the text printed in English, French and German, and will increase your overdraft by 35s., but all serious gardeners should invest in a copy of the Cultivar Code, the cost of which is 2s. 6d. In England this is distributed by the Royal Horticultural Society, Vincent Square, London S.W.1. and in America by Dr Donald Wyman of the Arnold Arboretum, Jamaica

Plain 30, Mass. U.S.A. It defines the word cultivar in Article 5 as follows: "The term cultivar, abbreviated cv., denotes an assemblage of cultivated individuals which is distinguished by any characters (morphological, physiological, cytological, chemical or others) significant for the purposes of agriculture, forestry or horticulture, and which, when reproduced (sexually or asexually), retains its distinguishing features." To this Article is appended a note to the effect that throughout the Code the words cultivar and variety are exact equivalents.

In my opinion the retention of the word variety at all is unfortunate. I understand it had to be on account of the use of the word in American Plant Patent law, but I hope it will be found possible to drop it in future issues of the Code. Although it is used as the exact equivalent of the word cultivar, in English (and also several other languages, where it appears as variété, variedad, varieteit or varietà) it is woefully easy to confuse with the botanical rank Varietas, a rank between Species and Forma. In its abbreviated form "Var." the two terms are indistinguishable and in spite of what the Code allows (for the reason given above) gardeners should now drop the words "variety" and "form" used in any technical sense.

Having now explained the general operation of the two Codes I turn to their particular application to the nomenclature of dwarf conifers, and it is here that I must alter the stops to make the music much more plaintive.

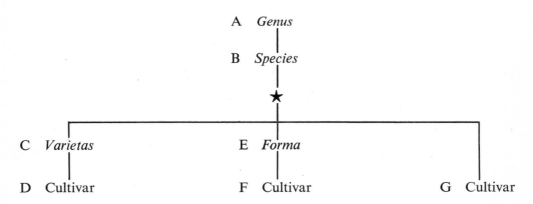

In the above diagram, names controlled by the Botanical Code are printed in italics and names controlled by the Cultivar Code in ordinary type. If I have made myself reasonably clear thus far my reader will understand that the simplest case must have a name of the form A—— B——. Conifers thus simply dealt with are *Juniperus rigida* and *Podocarpus alpinus*.

The next simplest case is probably that of the seedling turning up in the seedbeds with sufficient distinctiveness—the seedling with a difference—to be propagated as a "named variety". Many cultivars arise in this way, a representative example being *Chamaecyparis lawsoniana* 'Forsteckensis'. Here the name is of the form A—— B—— G——, and the G—— part has now to conform to the Cultivar Code. Other cultivars of the A—— B—— G—— form arise by the appearance of variegated foliage or other bud mutations, or by the appearance (in certain species) of "witch's brooms", and in other ways.

Next in the ascending scale of complexity is that of the plant which the botanists view as a Varietas or as a Forma. An additional rank Subspecies could arise, in which case it would show up where the star is on the chart, but so far as I am aware none of the conifer species has been so divided, so we have been thus far spared this complication. Another possibility is the case of a Forma of a Varietas. So that bad as things are for us they might have been worse and a sobering exercise is to re-draw the chart to show the greatest number of possible sequences under which a name can arise. (Continuing the same system my attempt at doing this brings into use all the letters of the alphabet down to Q.—No prize is offered for bettering this.)

As was mentioned earlier regarding the term Species, no precise definition of the words Varietas or Forma seems to have been agreed upon. I therefore use the word Varietas to cover an assemblage of plants differing in one or more major characteristics from the typical species and found in the wild in some particular geographical area or otherwise in relatively large numbers and (in gardeners' language) breeding true, and Forma to cover plants occurring in the wild as occasional individuals showing some peculiarity (such as threadlike foliage or an unusual habit). Such forms may or may not "breed true" and are frequently sterile.

With the definitions of the terms used in the classification being uncertain it is not surprising that doubt arises from time to time as to the proper botanical classification of a particular plant. There appears doubt for instance about the correct name for the Coffin Juniper, some botanists regarding it as merely a varietas of *Juniperus recurva* and others as meriting specific rank. In the one case its correct name would be *Juniperus recurva* var. *coxii* (a case of A—— B—— C——) and in the other it would be plain *Juniperus coxii* (a simple case of A—— B——).

Another good example is the popular little best-selling dwarf conifer grown for many years as *Picea albertiana conica*. Now the botanists tell us that the Albertan spruce is merely a varietas of *Picea glauca*, so its correct botanical designation has now to be *Picea glauca* var. *albertiana* f. *conica*.

Taken on the whole there is not much uncertainty as to genus and species with the majority of the dwarf conifers. The fixed juvenile forms give us a little difficulty, there being several of the cultivars named 'Ericoides' which are still doubtful and one or two forms with peculiar foliage the same, but in the great majority of cases the generic and specific names are in no doubt, and we are fortunately able to side-track most of our remaining difficulties by taking advantage of the remarkable, if little known, fact that a plant can have two correct names—one under the Botanical Code and one under the Cultivar Code.

In other words, if a dwarf form arises as a seedling in my nursery and is brought into cultivation it is a cultivar and must be named as such under the Cultivar Code, but if later a botanist finds the same plant "in the wild" he is entitled to rename it under

26 Part of a batch of 2,000 *Picea abies* 'Nidiformis' being grown in the nursery of F. J. Grootendorst and Sons at Boskoop, Holland.

the Botanical Code as a varietas or forma (whichever he thinks appropriate) in which case he is expected to latinize my name in order to minimize confusion.

Conversely if a botanical varietas or forma comes into general use as a garden plant we gardeners are in order if we use its botanical appellation as a cultivar name, provided we do so in accordance with the Cultivar Code, which may mean anglicizing the Latin name. So our old friend known as *Picea glauca* var. *albertiana* f. *conica* by the botanists can quite properly become *Picea glauca* 'Albertiana Conica' in gardening circles.

In this book much use of this liberty has been made. A few varietal and form names are used where the plants are rarely met with in gardens or have little garden value, but as I am writing for gardeners about garden plants, in the great majority of cases I use the names in their cultivar form. This will probably commend itself to the majority of my readers but they must remember that in many cases my cultivar names can be just as correctly used in their botanical form.

Both "names" are equally "correct".

5 : Varieties currently available

This will probably be my best-read chapter. It is more than just the usual list of personal recommendations, but it stops well short of an attempt to describe every known form of dwarf conifer. Rather is it an attempt to bring together a reasonably complete list of all the varieties that are at the time of writing known to be obtainable in British and American nurseries. Many of the varieties described are easily obtained and are stocked by most nurseries who sell conifers, but others are rare and may need searching for amongst nurseries who specialise in the dwarf forms.

The descriptions, whilst more than a mere appraisal of the garden value of each variety, stop short of complete botanical descriptions. This latter is a task I hope to undertake at some later date but in this book all I have attempted to do is to give such general descriptions as will help towards recognition and enable the garden use of each variety to be appreciated, with information in more detail where it is necessary for distinguishing between two or more closely related forms. In this the free use that has been made of photographs should help considerably.

Whilst I hope the remainder of this book will be of interest (and perhaps, of use) to any garden-minded person, in *this* chapter I have assumed that my readers have some general knowledge of conifers and their dwarf forms (or have friends who do) and have access to some good general textbook on conifers, especially as regards descriptions of the genera and species—matters outside the scope of this book.

In some cases where a cultivar is well known in the trade and not the subject of disputed identity and where Hornibrook has given a detailed description I have not repeated this.

IDENTIFICATION PLATES

This might be a good opportunity for giving a few explanatory details regarding the Identification Plates to be found on pages 62 to 100. It is not claimed that these will ensure recognition of every form of dwarf conifer illustrated, but studied together with the descriptions and with reference also to other photographs in the book they should enable anyone with some general knowledge of dwarf conifers to put the correct name to unidentified dwarf forms in many cases, and they are certainly adequate to show up the inaccuracy of many existing labels throughout the land.

All the photographs have been taken against a background ruled with 1 cm squares. This gives a scale for each picture. In many cases the spray has been simplified by pruning away growth that would have been outside the picture plane. In some cases, where this would have resulted in unduly denuding the spray, the leaves or branches that have been pruned off have been laid alongside in as near their original position as possible. In these cases the spray has therefore been somewhat flattened, as

61

[*continued on page 102*

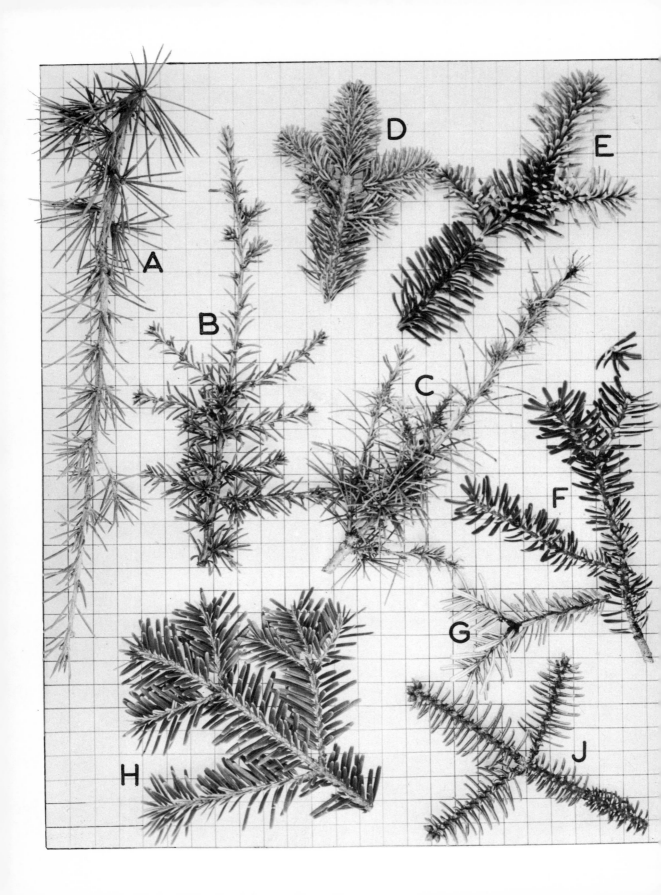

IDENTIFICATION PLATE 1

ABIES AND CEDRUS

A. *Cedrus libani* 'Sargentii'. Has a completely pendulous habit, and unless trained up as a young plant will merely sprawl on the ground. (p. 113)

B. *Cedrus brevifolia*. Becomes a small tree in time, but grown in a pot or other container will remain small for many years. Note the shortness of the leaves. (p. 110)

C. *Cedrus libani* 'Nana'. Usually seen as a large bush, with dense and congested foliage. There is variation amongst the various clones in cultivation, of which 'Comte de Dijon' is but one. (p. 111)

D. *Abies lasiocarpa* 'Compacta'. One of the best of dwarf conifers. Has grey-green foliage and a neat conical habit. Sometimes found under the obsolete name *A. arizonica* 'Compacta'. (p. 108)

E. *Abies procera* (formerly *A. nobilis*) 'Prostrate'. This, and its glaucous counterpart 'Glauca Prostrate' are amongst the finest of dwarf conifers for a prominent spot on a large rockery. There is a form, 'Robusta', of the species with leaves almost twice as long as in the photograph and a specimen of the prostrate cultivariant—its name would be 'Robusta Prostrate'— would develop into a magnificent plant where it had room. (p. 108)

F. *Abies alba* 'Compacta'. Upper side of foliage dark, dull green. (p. 105)

G. *Abies alba* 'Compacta'. The very glaucous underside of the leaves with the prominent green mid-rib. (p. 105)

H. *Abies koreana*. An alpine species which varies considerably from seed. The densely set foliage is a rich, glossy, medium green and the underside is white. (p. 108)

J. *Abies pinsapo* 'Glauca'. Not a dwarf form, but the unusual foliage habit—the leaves spreading radially almost at right angles to the shoot—and the light-grey colour make it an interesting small specimen.

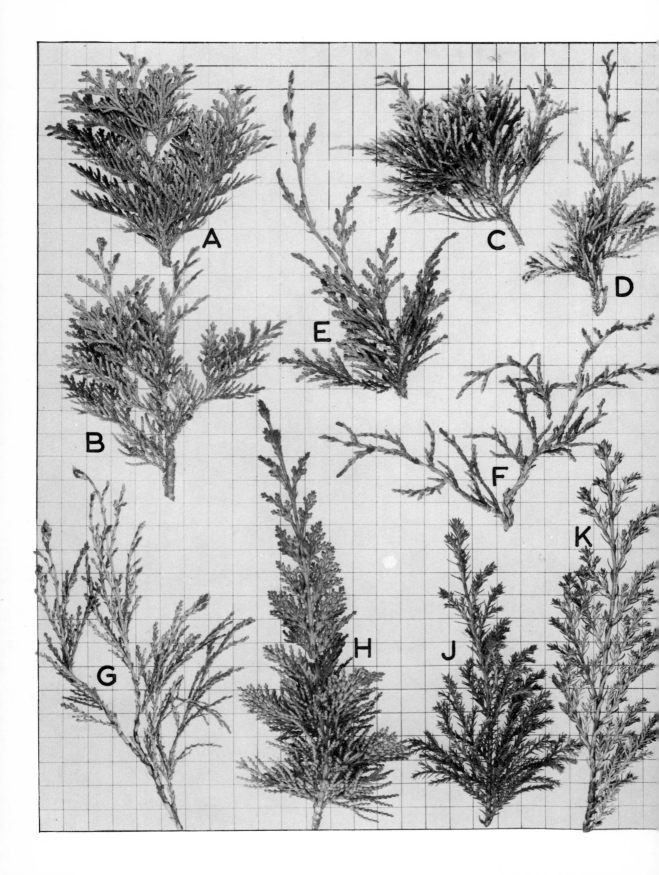

IDENTIFICATION PLATE 2

CHAMAECYPARIS LAWSONIANA 1

A. *Chamaecyparis lawsoniana* 'Minima'. Usually seen as a globose bush with no central trunk but with numerous main branches springing from at or near ground level. Note the neat, rounded outline of the spray. This gives a very trim and dense appearance to the whole plant. Colour: yellow-green, but the blue-green 'Minima Glauca' is more commonly seen. (p. 123)

B. – – 'Nana'. Usually more squatly-conical than 'Minima' and with a well-defined and thick central trunk. Note the more "ragged" or uneven spray outline, resulting in a looser and more untidy look to the plant. (p. 123)

C. – – 'Forsteckensis'. The tight, "mossy" type of growth which is characteristic of this globose little plant when well grown. (p. 121)

D. – – The looser sprays by which the plant increases in size. By pruning away the latter, the plant can be kept very dense indeed. (p. 121)

E. – – 'Tharandtensis Caesia'. The difference between this form and 'Forsteckensis' (above) reflects the greater vigour of the former, and the colour is a distinctly blue-grey, quite different to the dull, dark green of the latter. (p. 128)

F. – – 'Lycopodioides'. Will become a large upright bush or small, rounded tree in time, but the twisted shoots all over the plant are unmistakable. (p. 123)

G. – – 'Duncanii'. Of the thread-leaf forms, 'Duncanii' is the coarsest, and it forms a large, spreading plant (p. 119). 'Filiformis Compacta' (p. 119) has finer and more flexible foliage and is never larger than a small bush. 'Erecta Filiformis' and 'Masonii' are strong-growing forms, of erect branch habit.

H. – – 'Wisselii'. Usually seen as a tall, columnar tree, but is effective grown as a large bush. Colour: very dark green. (p. 129)

J. – – 'Ellwoodii'. A popular variety, usually seen as an upright-oval to columnar bush up to 2 m, but will slowly grow much larger in time. Colour: dark blue-green. (p. 119)

K. – – 'Fletcheri'. Another popular variety, but by no means a dwarf form as it grows much more rapidly than 'Ellwoodii'. Colour: light grey-green. (p. 120)

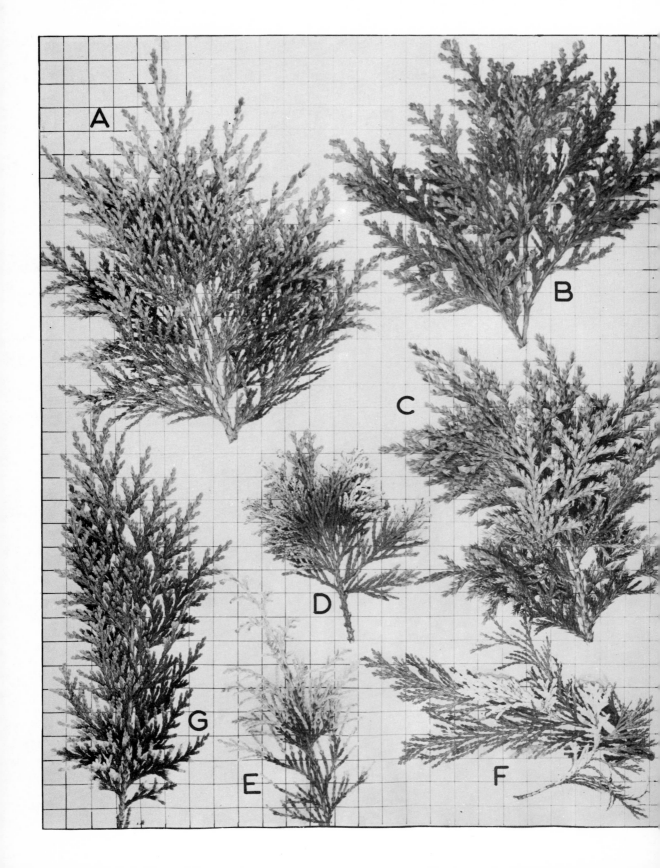

A. *Chamaecyparis lawsoniana* 'Tamariscifolia'. Note the free-standing leaf tips and the triangular shape of the leaf-spray. This form is slightly glaucous on the underside. (p. 127)

B. – – 'Nidiformis' (syn. *C.* × *nidifera*). Note the dense, overlapping foliage (both at front and back of spray) and the rounded leaf-spray; usually curled. Slightly glaucous above, very glaucous beneath. (p. 126)

C. – – 'Dow's Gem'. Note the coarse, open foliage, which lies in boldly curved sprays, imparting a good deal of "character" to the bush. (p. 119)

These three forms, and 'Knowefieldensis' below, are low-growing and wide-spreading plants, usually seen as wide as or wider than high.

D. – – 'Pygmaea Argentea'. Neat, dense foliage and habit similar to 'Minima', but all growing tips facing the light a creamy-white. Elsewhere the colour is grey-green. (p. 127)

E. – – 'Nana Albospica'. Forms a small upright ovoid bush with branches ascending and all growing tips nodding. All young growth creamy-white and when the plant is growing strongly this colour dominates the whole bush. (p. 124)

F. – – 'Albovariegata'. There are several forms in cultivation. In the most desirable, the white variegation is sufficient to give a striking appearance to the whole plant, the all-white sprays on this form being 2–2·5 cm across. (p. 115)

G. – – 'Knowefieldensis'. Note the long, parallel-sided sprays with the central stem always predominant. The resulting clearly-defined, long, narrow, triangular outline is repeated in larger sprays on the plant. Colour: rich, mid-green; only very slightly glaucous below. (p. 122)

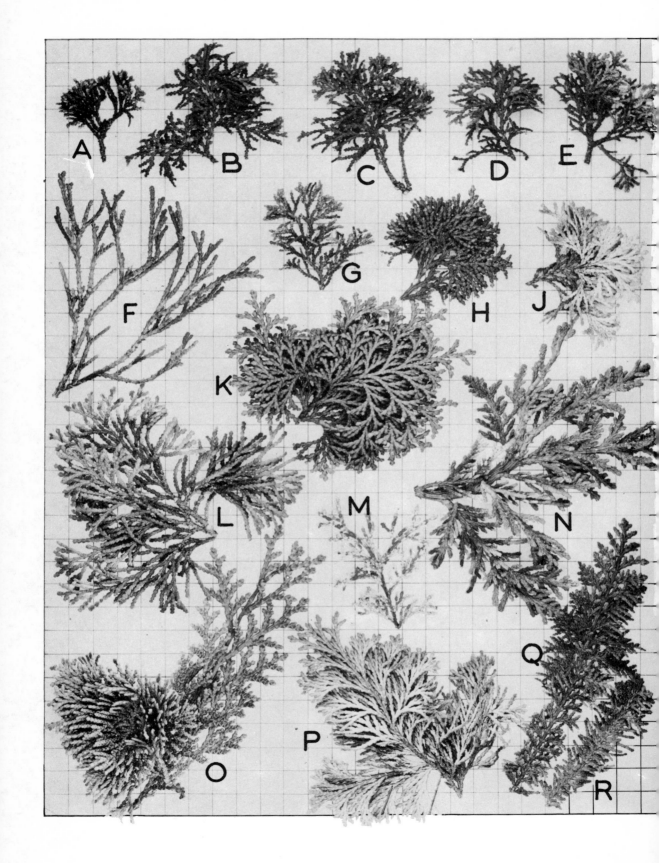

IDENTIFICATION PLATE 4

Chamaecyparis obtusa

A. *Chamaecyparis obtusa* 'Caespitosa'. A tiny, bun-shaped plant with dark-green, up-curved sprays and tiny, tightly appressed leaves. (p. 131)

B. – – 'Chilworth'. Usually seen as an upright and quite "miniature-tree-like" plant. Leaf sprays noticeably down-cupped. (p. 131)

C. – – 'Intermedia'. Foliage dense and of a dark green. (p. 134)

D. – – 'Juniperoides'. Forms a small bun-shaped or globose plant with foliage in open lace-like sprays with closely appressed leaves, more suggestive to me of the typical foliage of *C. thyoides* than that of any juniper. (p. 134)

E. – – 'Juniperoides Compacta'. As its name indicates, a smaller and altogether denser version of 'Juniperoides'. Colour: yellow-green. (p. 134)

F. – – 'Coralliformis'. Can become a large bush in time. Tends to become loose and straggly unless trimmed back occasionally. (p. 131)

G. – – 'Minima'. A tiny, bun-shaped form similar to 'Caespitosa' (above) but with light-green foliage consisting of a dense mass of tetragonal branchlets, not the flat sprays of the latter variety. (p. 131)

H. – – 'Nana'. The true 'Nana' has very dark-green, dense, rounded saddleback-shaped leaf-sprays all held more or less horizontally. (p. 136)

J. – – 'Nana Lutea'. A new form, much smaller in all its parts than 'Nana Aurea', and of a much brighter colour, well maintained throughout the year. Leaf-spray similar in shape and size to 'Nana'. (p. 138)

K. – – 'Kosteri'. Note the slightly twisted foliage—one branchlet over and the other under its neighbours—which is characteristic of this form. Sometimes a little bronzed, similar to 'Pygmaea'. (p. 134)

L. – – 'Pygmaea'. Forms a flat-topped, spreading plant, green in summer and slightly bronzed in winter. 'Pygmaea Aurescens' differs mainly in colouring. (p. 139)

M. – – 'Mariesii'. Usually seen as a small, rather straggly plant. The foliage is plentifully speckled with a creamy-white variegation. (p. 136)

N. – – 'Lycopodioides'. Will become a large bush in time. Usually has an irregular branch habit and with foliage on the strongest-growing branches very coarse—even, at times, monstrous. (p. 135)

O. – – 'Nana Gracilis'. Usually seen as a picturesque, squat or more or less conical bush densely clothed with its rich mid-green foliage in large, dense, flat sprays (see on left) held at all angles, but leader growth is occasionally much looser (see on right). (p. 138)

P. – – 'Nana Aurea'. Usually an upright plant, differing from 'Nana Gracilis' (not from 'Nana') mainly in colour. (p. 138)

Q. – – 'Filicoides'. Often seen as a rather gaunt and open small tree and pays for regular shortening of strong growth when a young plant. On a vigorous plant, the leaf-sprays (which are quite flat) can be two or three times as big as shown. (p. 133)

R. – – 'Pygmy Fernspray'. A diminutive form of 'Filicoides', smaller in all its parts. (p. 133)

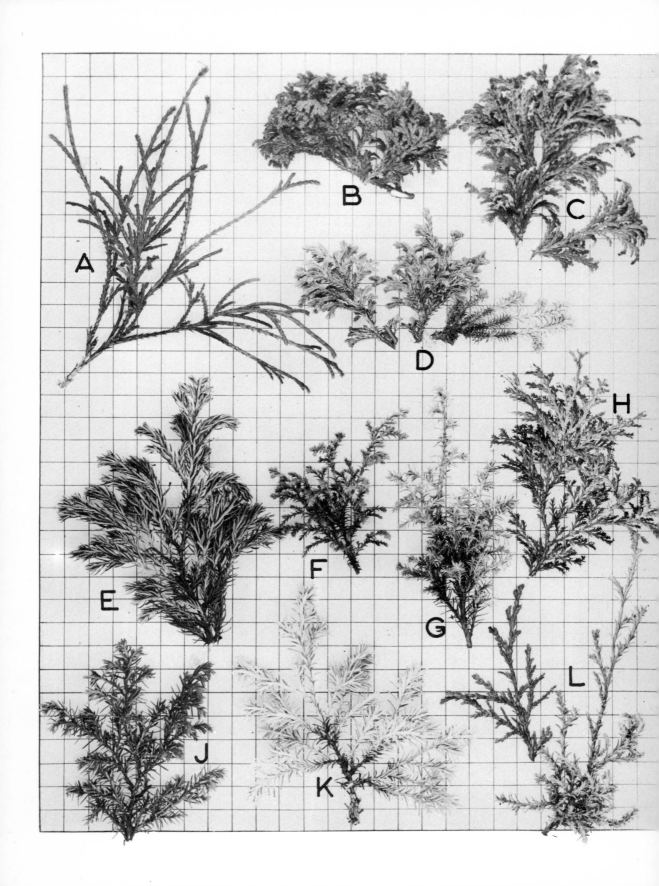

IDENTIFICATION PLATE 5

CHAMAECYPARIS PISIFERA

A. *Chamaecyparis pisifera* 'Filifera Nana'. The dwarf thread-leaf form makes only a low, mop-like bush. There are several colour variants. (p. 147)

B. – – 'Nana'. Never more than a low hemispherical little bushlet with dark green foliage, very glaucous beneath. (p. 145)

C. – – 'Compacta'. Much larger leaf-sprays and coarser growth than 'Nana' and more common in its variegated form 'Compacta Variegata'. (p. 145)

D. – – 'Plumosa Compressa'. Forms a low bun-shaped mound with dense but very variable foliage (the three small sprays were taken from a single plant). It varies in colour also, from yellow-green to a greyish-green. (p. 148)

E. – – 'Boulevard' (syn. 'Squarrosa cyano-viridis'). A very popular newcomer, with foliage a lovely silvery-blue-grey. The dull greys and brown sometimes seen seem to be due to unsuitable soil conditions. (p. 144)

F. – – 'Plumosa Flavescens'. Usually a low, spreading to globose plant, with young foliage a striking sulphur-yellow. The colour passes to a nondescript green by winter. (p. 150)

G. – – 'Plumosa Rogersii'. Forms a more or less conical plant and retains its golden colour well into the winter. The long, much recurved leaves are similar in other garden forms which differ from 'Plumosa Rogersii' in vigour or habit. (p. 150)

H. – – 'Plumosa Albopicta'. The variegation persists throughout the year but is difficult to photograph as it consists of white flecks here and there all over the bush. It is most noticeable in spring. (p. 148)

J. – – 'Squarrosa Dumosa'. Forms a globose bush with soft dull green foliage, grey in winter. All the 'Squarrosa' forms have very similar foliage and differ mainly in colour and size of leaf. (p. 151)

K. – – 'Squarrosa Lutea' is the golden-yellow and has the largest leaf of any 'Squarrosa' form. (p. 153)

L. – – 'Squarrosa Intermedia' has the smallest leaf. The congested foliage at the base is more characteristic of the doubtfully separable 'Squarrosa Minima' and to the left is a small piece of the dreaded reversion. Apart from its adult foliage, it is green in colour—quite distinct from the glaucous grey-green of the squarrosa foliage. (p. 151)

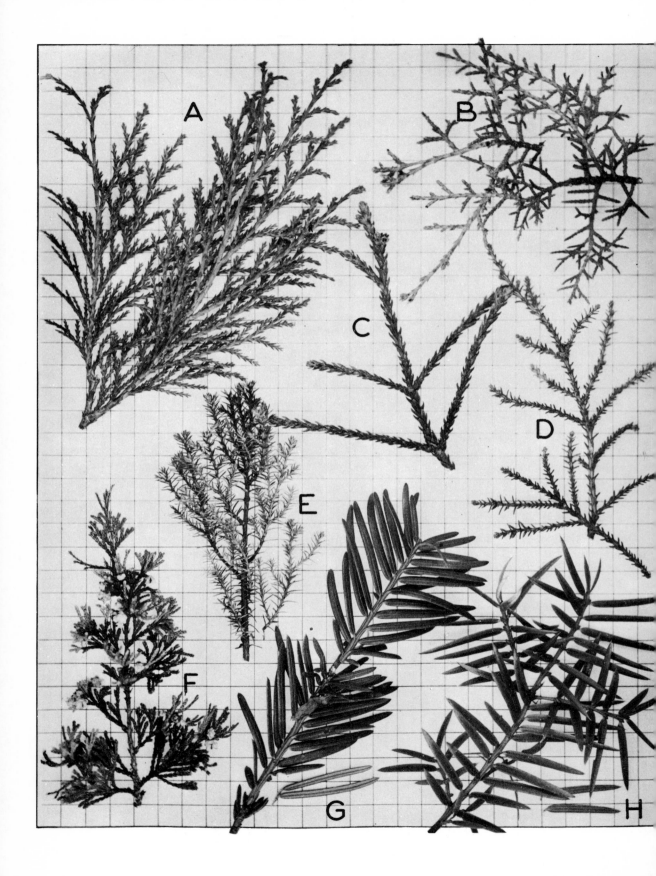

IDENTIFICATION PLATE 6

ATHROTAXIS, CEPHALOTAXUS, CHAMAECYPARIS, CUPRESSUS, FITZROYA AND TORREYA

A. *Chamaecyparis nootkatensis* 'Compacta'. Is usually seen as a large, upright bush or small tree. The tips of the leaves are free-standing and neither side of the spray is glaucous. (p. 129)

B. *Cupressus arizonica* 'Compacta'. The true form is very dense and congested, with no leader and a confused, interlocking branch system, but loose forms are often supplied under this name. (p. 164)

C. *Athrotaxis laxifolia*. Forms a small, rather open tree. The foliage is intermediate between the loose, free-standing leaves of *A. selaginoides* and the tightly appressed foliage of *A. cupressoides*. (p. 109)

D. *Fitzroya cupressoides*. Usually seen as a small tree with pendulous branches. Note that the cupressus-like leaves are in whorls of three. (p. 167)

E. *Chamaecyparis thyoides* 'Ericoides'. Usually a regular, conical bush with ascending branches and juvenile foliage, dark green in summer and plum-purple (variable) in winter. (p. 154)

F. – – 'Andelyensis'. A very slow-growing form which forms a narrowly columnar plant usually carrying a small amount of juvenile foliage near the ground. The photograph shows a shoot with young cones. These are frequently produced in considerable quantity. (p. 153)

G. *Cephalotaxus harringtonia* 'Prostrate'. Note the difference between this species and H (below) in the leaf-shape and the stomatic bands on the underside of the leaves. (p. 114)

H. *Torreya nucifera* 'Prostrata'. See note under G (above). Both of these plants form large, wide-spreading plants useful for ground cover under tall trees. (p. 317)

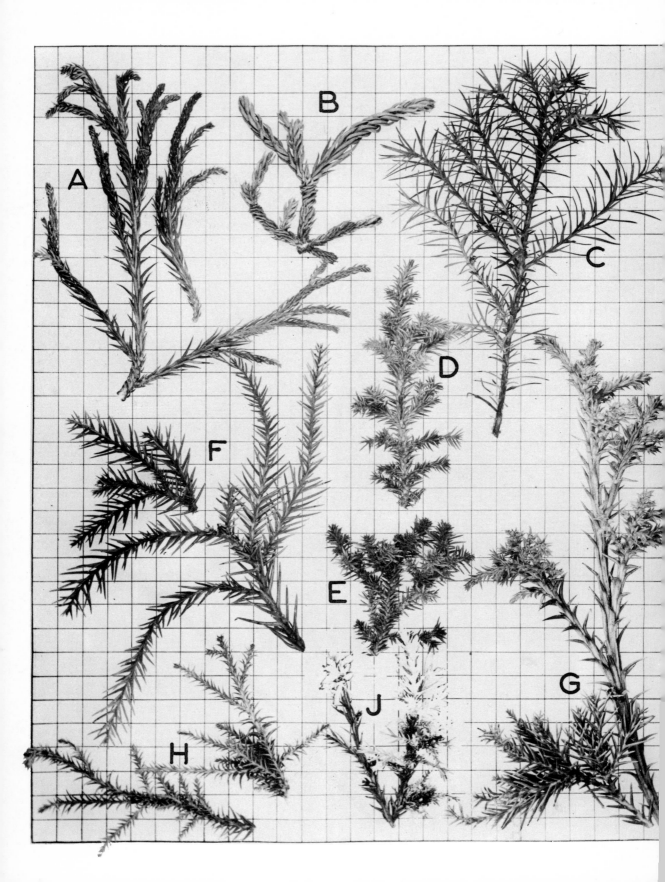

IDENTIFICATION PLATE 7

CRYPTOMERIA JAPONICA 1

A. *Cryptomeria japonica* 'Spiraliter Falcata'. This rather awkward name has priority over the name "*Spiralis elongata*" under which it is occasionally grown. (p. 162)

B. – – 'Spiralis'. The difference between this form and 'Spiraliter Falcata' is very clear in the photograph. The amount of twist on the foliage varies, according to the season. (p. 162)

C. – – 'Elegans Compacta'. This form is doubtless derived from the tall form 'Elegans' and it becomes a large bush in time. The wholly juvenile, very regular foliage is very soft to the touch and turns a deep purple in winter. There is also a form which is indistinguishable in summer but turns yellow-green in winter. (p. 157)

D. – – 'Vilmoriniana'. Makes a globose bush of dense, light-green foliage which bronzes slightly in winter. (p. 163)

E. – – 'Compressa'. Makes a denser and more regular bush than 'Vilmoriniana' (above) and the blue-green foliage turns deep purple-brown in winter. (p. 156)

F. – – 'Globosa' (not to be confused with 'Globosa Nana' on Plate 8). The complete regularity of the foliage distinguishes this form from 'Lobbii Nana' at all times, and in winter it is unmistakable by its rust-red foliage. (p. 158)

G. – – 'Monstrosa'. The three types of foliage carried by this form are shown in the photograph. It grows to 3 m. (p. 160)

H. – – 'Nana'. Note the thinness of the long shoots. Colour: light green, hardly bronzing at all in winter. A very similar form, 'Pygmaea', turns a red-bronze in winter. (p. 161)

J. – – 'Knaptonensis'. The dazzling white growing tips borne in dense, tufted clusters do not show up in the photograph against the white background, but this very distinctive form cannot be confused, save with 'Nana Albo-spica'—in which variety the growth is much more regular and the growing tips creamy-white in colour. (p. 158)

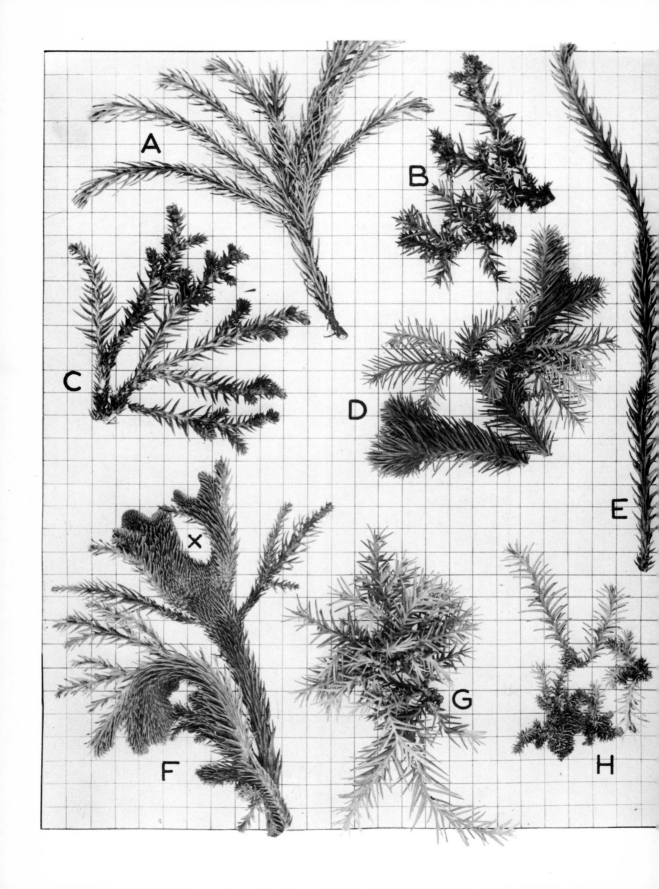

IDENTIFICATION PLATE 8

CRYPTOMERIA JAPONICA 2

A. *Cryptomeria japonica* 'Globosa Nana'. Forms a large, spreading, rounded bush with branchlets sweeping down to the ground. (p. 158)

B. – – 'Bandai-Sugi'. Usually seen as an irregular, congested little bush, but will build up in time to 2 m. The difference between the strong, coarse shoots by means of which it increases in size, and the more prevalent congested, almost monstrous growth can be clearly seen. (p. 155)

C. – – 'Jindai-Sugi'. Forms an upright to conical bush or diminutive tree with regular habit of ascending branches and foliage with no trace of monstrosity and with all growing tips "nodding". Colour: light green, retained in winter. (p. 158)

D. – – 'Kilmacurragh'. Forms a large, rounded bush with clusters of fasciations here and there all over the plant. This monstrosity is not so pronounced as in 'Cristata' (below) and the habit of the plant is quite different. (p. 157)

E. – – 'Viminalis'. The long, snake-like main branches will often extend for several years without developing side branches, but eventually a whorl of these will develop into a curious cluster of short shoots. Colour: light green. (p. 163)
   A very similar variety 'Araucarioides', has thicker and more incurved leaves and the colour is dark green. (p. 155)

F. – – 'Cristata'. Forms an upright bush or small tree with grotesque fasciations here and there. These are sometimes as big as a man's hand. The cock's-comb-like cristation was cut away at X in the photograph as it was twisted and puckered so as to be impossible to photograph in its entirety. (p. 156)

G. – – 'Lobbii Nana'. The upper part of the photograph is looking down on the capitate cluster of short shoots that frequently develops around the terminal bud of a main branch. The remainder of the bush carries juvenile foliage which is straight and quite stiff to the touch. This form has been widely distributed as 'Elegans Nana'. (p. 159)

H. – – 'Fasciata'. Seldom seen as more than a stunted, little bush. Much of the foliage is of the open type of growth to be seen in the photograph, but here and there the older shoots are covered with minute green eruptions hardly justifying their being called leaves. (p. 157)

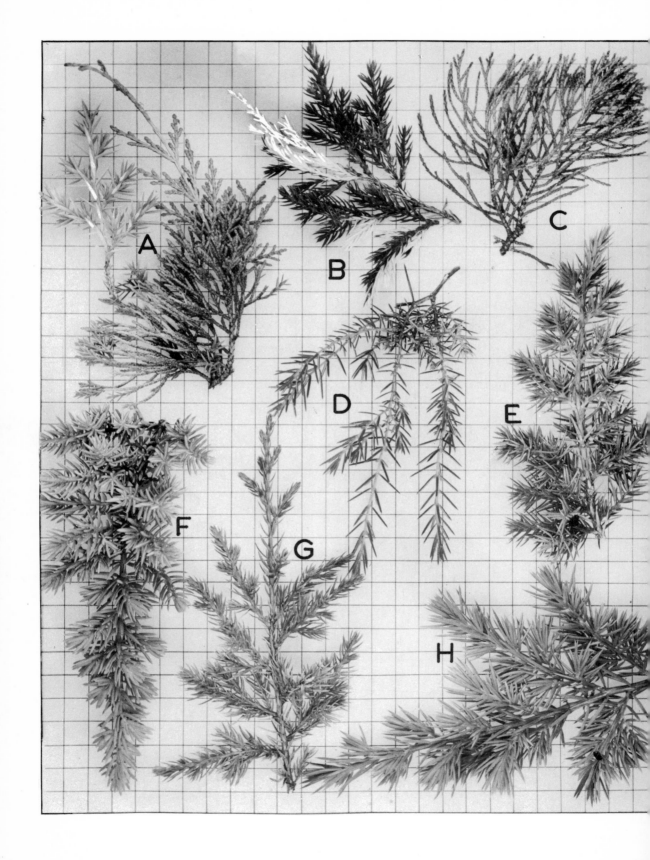

IDENTIFICATION PLATE 9

A. *Juniperus chinensis* 'Aurea'. Usually seen as a columnar tree, golden-yellow most of the year. There is always a certain amount of the juvenile foliage (left) which is lighter in colour than the adult-foliage. (p. 170)

B. – – 'Variegata'. Colour and habit as 'Stricta' (below) but more vigorous, and with bold splashes of creamy white variegation on both juvenile and adult foliage. (p. 175)

C. – – 'Kaizuka'. Deep rich-green foliage and an irregular, upright habit. Leader growth is coarser and more open than in the photograph. (p. 172)

D. *Juniperus rigida*. Usually seen as a graceful small tree. Branchlets strongly pendulous. Leaves very narrow and as sharp as needles. Not a dwarf. (p. 202)

E. *Juniperus chinensis* 'Obelisk'. Forms an irregular, conical to columnar plant, usually with leader not quite upright. Broad, closely set leaves, very glaucous, give a grey look to the whole plant. (p. 173)

F. *Juniperus taxifolia* var. *lutchuensis*. Often grown as *J. maritima*. (Habit completely prostrate, leaves broader than in *J. conferta* and hardly at all prickly to the touch. (p. 210)

G. *Juniperus chinensis* 'Stricta'. Always forms a neat, conical bush when young, with upright branching habit and blue-grey foliage. Retains the dead foliage for several years, so old plants can look rather unattractive. Carries juvenile foliage only, which is soft to the touch. (p. 174)

H. *Juniperus conferta*. Prostrate, spreading habit, but ascending branchlets. Leaves narrower than in F (above) and plant very prickly. (p. 183)

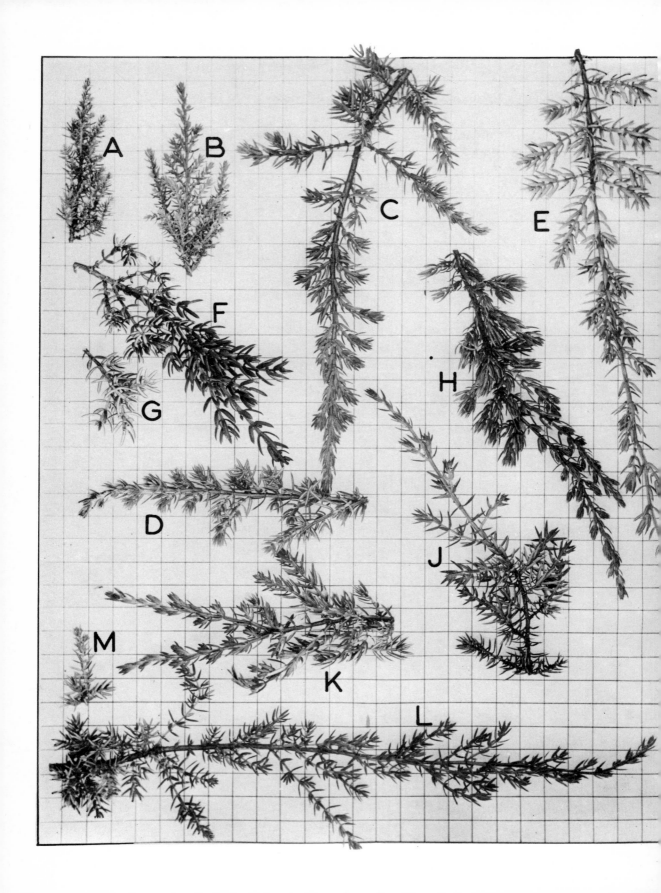

IDENTIFICATION PLATE 10

JUNIPERUS COMMUNIS

A. *Juniperus communis* 'Compressa'. Tiny leaves and narrowly fastigiate habit. Bush usually pointed at tip. Seldom seen over 30 cm high. (p. 176)

B. – – 'Suecica Nana'. Often sold as 'Compressa', but its leaves are larger and the branch system is slightly less fastigiate, so it tends to form a thicker plant, often blunted at tip. Will grow to 1 m or more. (p. 183)

C. – – 'Saxatilis' (upper side of spray). This is the form illustrated by Pallas. It forms a wide-spreading but not recumbent bush. (p. 182)

D. – – 'Saxatilis' (under side of sparay). Note the glaucous leaves (actually, because of the way they are twisted, it is their upper sides) and compare with G. This form is sometimes met with as 'Montana'.

E. – – var. *depressa*. Plants of this group vary in habit from upright-spreading to completely prostrate plants suitable for ground cover, but they all have this broad foliage, frequently bronze-green or brown, and always turned with the glaucous upper surface towards the ground and so not visible. (p. 176)

F. – – Silver Lining'. Quite distinct from 'Saxatilis' and the 'Depressa' groups by its boat-shaped leaves and by the heavy glaucous bloom, especially on the (true) upper sides of the leaves, which are chalk-white. On a mature plant the leaves are twisted so that much of this is to be seen. (p. 182)

G. – – 'Silver Lining'. A small spray held so as to show the chalk-white upper sides of the leaves.

H. – – 'Repanda'. A strong-growing, ground-cover plant. Leaves are dark green, very soft to the touch, and loosely appressed to the shoot. (p. 181)

J. – – 'Nana Aurea'. A prostrate plant and retains its distinctive colouring until late autumn. (p. 181)

K. – – 'Depressa Aurea'. A spreading (not prostrate) plant, loses its lovely golden colour by late summer; has somewhat wider leaves than J, and is a much more vigorous plant (p. 178).

L. – – 'Hornibrookii'. Its tiny leaves belie its energy and capacity to cover the ground. The white upper sides (M) often show up freely at the centre of old plants. (p. 179)

IDENTIFICATION PLATE 11

Juniperus horizontalis, J. recurva, J. squamata

A. *Juniperus recurva* 'Coxii'. Usually seen as a bush or small tree with very graceful, pendulous, soft-green foliage. The leafage needs to be severely thinned to reveal the full beauty of the tree. The name is frequently seen in the botanical equivalent, *Juniperus recurva* var. *coxii*. (p. 200)

    J. recurva itself has smaller leaves, and the form 'Castlewellan' has leaves so small as to give the foliage a "thread-leaf" appearance. Both become large trees in time.

B. *Juniperus squamata* 'Loderi'. Always forms a closely columnar plant with a distinct leader which is erect, but the lateral growing tips "nod" very slightly, as in all *J. squamata* forms. (p. 209)

C. *Juniperus horizontalis* 'Bar Harbor'. Horizontal main branches, ascending branchlets. Dull, dark green in summer, light purplish-grey in winter. Note the narrow foliage. (p. 187)

D. – – 'Prostrata'. This is the form usually supplied in Britain as *J. horizontalis*. Strong-growing leader growth is much coarser than as shown in the photograph. Branchlets are procumbent. (p. 191)

E. – – 'Glauca'. Foliage tips held free. Colour: dark blue-green. Very horizontal habit and a vigorous grower. (p. 189)

F. *Juniperus squamata* 'Glassell'. A very slow-growing bush with tiny, grey-green leaves and a picturesque branch habit. A good plant for a trough garden if some of the leaves are trimmed away to expose the trunk and branches. (p. 209)

G. *Juniperus horizontalis* 'Wiltonii'. Very prostrate, dense and slow-growing. Colouring as 'Glauca' (above), but note the neat foliage pattern. (p. 191)

H. *Juniperus squamata* 'Meyeri'. Usually a strong-growing bush or small tree. Foliage blue-grey—the bluest form of any juniper. (p. 209)

J. – – 'Wilsonii'. Usually a rounded to spreading bush with all growing tips strongly re-curved (turned downwards) and leaves often twisted to show much of the glaucous upper sides (K). (p. 210)

L. *Juniperus recurva* 'Nana'. A wide-spreading low bush with long, recurved growing tips and green foliage. (p. 202)

IDENTIFICATION PLATE 12

JUNIPERUS PROCUMBENS, J. SABINA, J. SARGENTII

A. *Juniperus procumbens* 'Nana'. Forms a wide-spreading, mat-like plant. The leaders tend to rise at the tips, and the short branchlets at the centre of the plant are ascending. (p. 200)

B. *Juniperus procumbens*. The long white smudges at the back of the leaves which are characteristic of this species can just be seen in the photograph (see arrow). They are smaller and more difficult to see in the form 'Nana'. (p. 198)

C. *Juniperus sabina* 'Cupressifolia'. A very prostrate form. Note the preponderance of scale-like, appressed foliage. (p. 203)

D. – – 'Tamariscifolia'. Forms a wide-spreading plant much less prostrate than 'Cupressifolia' (above) and it bears mainly awl-shaped leaves which in the best form are glaucous white above, giving an attractive grey appearance to the whole plant. (p. 205)

E. – – 'Variegata'. Forms an upright to spreading bush with irregular splashes of white variegation, the amount of which seems to vary from year to year. (p. 205)

F. – – 'Hicksii' Forms a bush with an ascending spreading branch system and greyish-blue acicular foliage which becomes purplish in winter. (p. 204)

G. *Juniperus sargentii* (formerly regarded as a geographical variety of *J. chinensis*). A spreading, mat-forming species useful for ground cover. The incurved but loosely held leaves give a characteristic cord-like look to the shoots. The foliage has a very disagreeable odour of camphor when bruised. (p. 206)

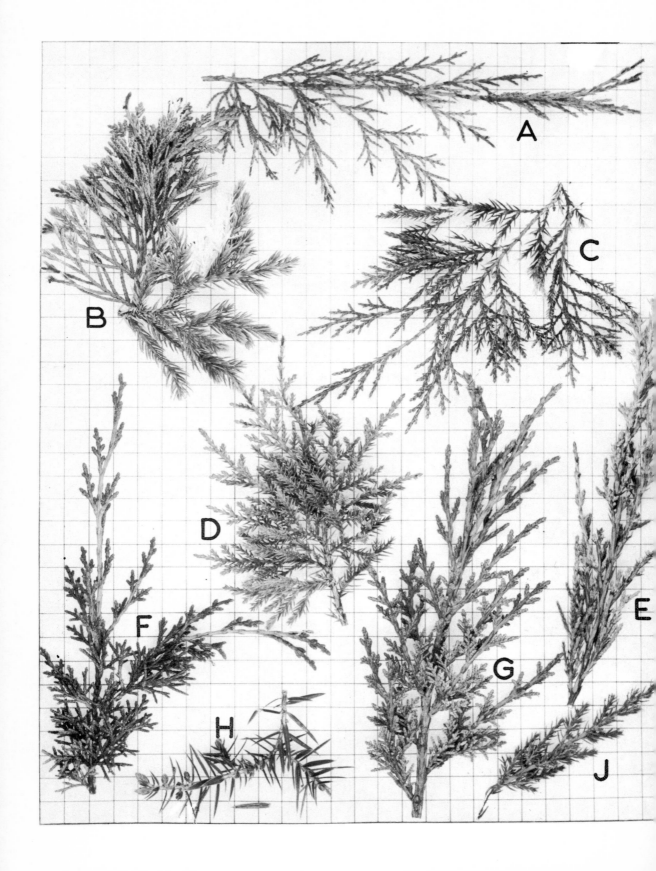

IDENTIFICATION PLATE 13

JUNIPERUS—MISCELLANEOUS

A. *Juniperus* × *media* 'Hetzii'. Forms a more upright plant and stronger-growing than 'Pfitzeriana' (below) and the foliage is a light grey-green.

B. *Juniperus davurica* 'Expansa Variegata'. A wide-spreading, sturdy-looking plant with long cord-like terminal shoots. The green form was at one time called *J. chinensis* 'Parsonsii'. 'Expansa Variegata' carries bold splashes of creamy-white variegation here and there on both the juvenile and the adult foliage. The form 'Aureospicata' bears mainly juvenile foliage and the variegation is golden-yellow. (p. 184)

C. *Juniperus* × *media* 'Pfitzeriana'. This popular form makes a vigorous, spreading plant with main branches ascending at 45°. Most of the plant bears semi-juvenile foliage, but a few shoots carry acicular (awl-like) leaves very glaucous above, towards the centre of the plant. (p. 195)

D. *J.* × *media* 'Pfitzeriana Compacta'. There are several colour and growth habit variants of 'Pfitzeriana'. This form is much more compact and carries almost entirely juvenile foliage. (p. 197)

E. *Juniperus virginiana* 'Skyrocket'. Difficult to mistake, as it is about the most narrowly columnar plant in existence. Many cultivars of this species have similar foliage and differ only in habit and/or colouring. (p. 214)

F. *J.* × *media* 'Globosa Cinerea'. The difference between this form (p. 194) and 'Blaauw' (below) (p. 192) consists in the foliage, the habit (note the narrower branch-angle of 'Blaauw') and the colour.

G. *J.* × *media* 'Blaauw'. See note under F. above.

H. *Juniperus drupacea*. Distinct from all other junipers by reason of its wide leaves. It forms a small upright tree. (p. 185)

J. *Juniperus virginiana* 'Tripartita'. Forms a spreading shrub with several strong-growing main branches rising at an angle of 45–60° and bearing juvenile foliage. It is sometimes confused with *J.* × *media* 'Pfitzeriana'. (p. 215)

IDENTIFICATION PLATE 14

PICEA ABIES

A. *Picea abies* 'Pumila Nigra'. Forms a wide-spreading bush with main branches rising at a steep angle. Colour: very dark green. (p. 245)

B. – – 'Clanbrassiliana Elegans'. Forms a dense, globose plant, with foliage uniform in size all over the bush (p. 225).

C. – – 'Gregoryana'. Forms a dense, globose little plant with shiny globose buds and short, stiff needle-like leaves. (p. 231)
   'Echiniformis' has similar buds and habit, but the leaves are much longer, fewer and wider apart. (p. 229)

D. – – 'Veitchii'. The photograph is of a side branch. At the top of the bush the growth and buds are indistinguishable from 'Gregoryana' (from which 'Veitchii' possibly represents a partial, and 'Parsonsii' a complete, reversion).

E. – – 'Nidiformis'. Forms a spreading bush, often with a conical depression at its centre—faintly suggestive of a nest, hence the name. The foliage has a "wiry" appearance and feel. (p. 239)

F. – – 'Procumbens'. Another wide-spreading, flat-topped variety. Note the strongly tapered outline to the spray. (p. 242)

G. – – 'Dumosa'. The radiating terminal shoots is a characteristic feature. Sometimes seen as a large plant. (p. 228)

H. – – 'Nana Compacta'. Seldom becomes more than a low, flattened globose bush. (p. 238)

J. – – 'Ohlendorffii'. Upright, conical habit with ascending main branches and foliage yellow-green in summer. (p. 240)

K. – – 'Diffusa'. Makes a beeskip-shaped bush with rich, mid-green foliage. One of the best garden forms. (p. 227)

L. – – 'Pygmaea'. Usually a squat, unshapely bush with the growth vigour of the shoots and the size and arrangement of the buds very irregular. (p. 246)

M. – – 'Repens'. A wide-spreading, flat-topped variety. The dominance of the leading growth over the laterals is characteristic. (p. 250)

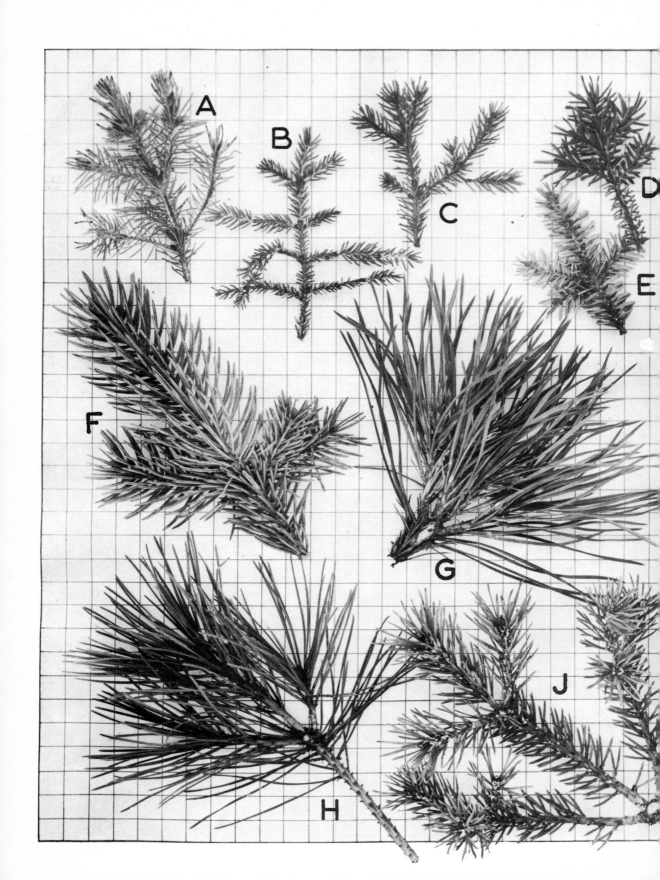

IDENTIFICATION PLATE 15

Picea and Pinus

A. *Picea glauca* 'Albertiana Glauca'. The popular Noah's Ark Juniper, forming a trim conical plant with soft green foliage and narrow, needle-shaped leaves soft to the touch. (p. 252)

B. *Picea orientalis* 'Nana'. Short, round needles with blunt tips. Colour: a rich glossy mid-green. (p. 260)

C. *Picea mariana* 'Nana'. Always forms a trim little bush, densely furnished with its neat foliage, which is a glaucous grey-blue. Unmistakable on account of its colour, which is the bluest of all the small-leafed spruces. (p. 257)

D. *Picea omorika* 'Nana'. Forms a dense and usually conical bush, eventually a small tree. The foliage is dark green above and (E) very glaucous beneath. The leaves are sufficiently twisted to give an attractive two-tone effect to the plant. (p. 258)

F. *Picea pungens* 'Glauca Prostrate'. Because of its attractive foliage and wonderful blue colouring, the prostrate cultivariant of this (and of the various named clones) form magnificent plants for the large rockery. (p. 262)

G. *Pinus sylvestris* 'Globosa Viridis'. Forms a large globose bush very densely clothed with its long, much twisted foliage. (p. 274)

H. *Pinus densiflora* 'Umbraculifera'. Forms a round-topped plant, eventually a small tree. The foliage is a rich mid-green. (p. 264)

J. *Pinus sylvestris* 'Beuvronensis'. The length of the needle will vary considerably according to the vigour of the plant, being always more on an open ground plant than on a specimen on semi-starvation diet in a pot. (p. 272)

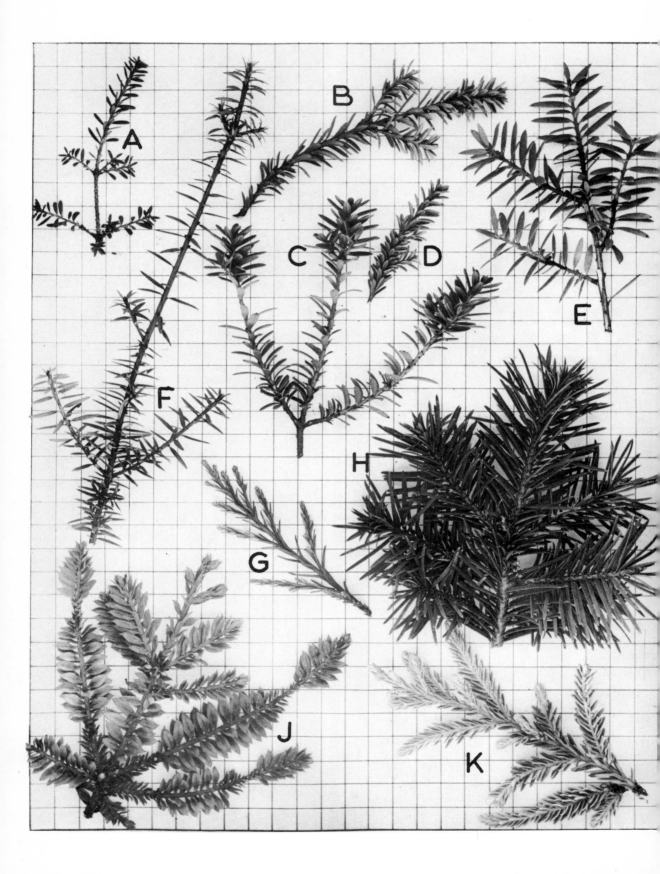

IDENTIFICATION PLATE 16

Podocarpus, Pseudotsuga, Sequoia, Sequoiadendron

A. *Podocarpus alpinus*. Will form a larger plant than its tiny leaves would indicate. (p. 277)

B. and C. *Podocarpus nivalis*. Will remain a low bush in Britain. It varies a good deal in size and shape of leaf. The colour form 'Bronze' (D) has very small leaves of a bronzy-yellow colour. (p. 278)

E. *Podocarpus totara*. Has leaves varying between light yellowish-green and light brown, and larger than those of *P. acutifolius*. (p. 278)

F. *Podocarpus acutifolius*. Has sharply pointed leaves standing off stiffly from the shoot at right angles, a brownish-green. (p. 277)

G. *Sequoiadendron giganteum* 'Pygmaeum'. This contradiction in terms will become a large bush in time, with foliage similar to the species but smaller in all its parts. (p. 284)

H. *Pseudotsuga menziesii* 'Fletcherii'. Dense, grey-green foliage and a flat-topped spreading habit. A very fine dwarf conifer. (p. 280)

J. *Sequoia sempervirens* 'Prostrata'. The width and shape of the leaves distinguish this form, which is sometimes met with under the name 'Cantab'. The colour is an unusual one, a soft grey-brown. (p. 283)

K. – – 'Adpressa'. The young growth in summer is creamy-white. Always an outstanding plant. (p. 282)

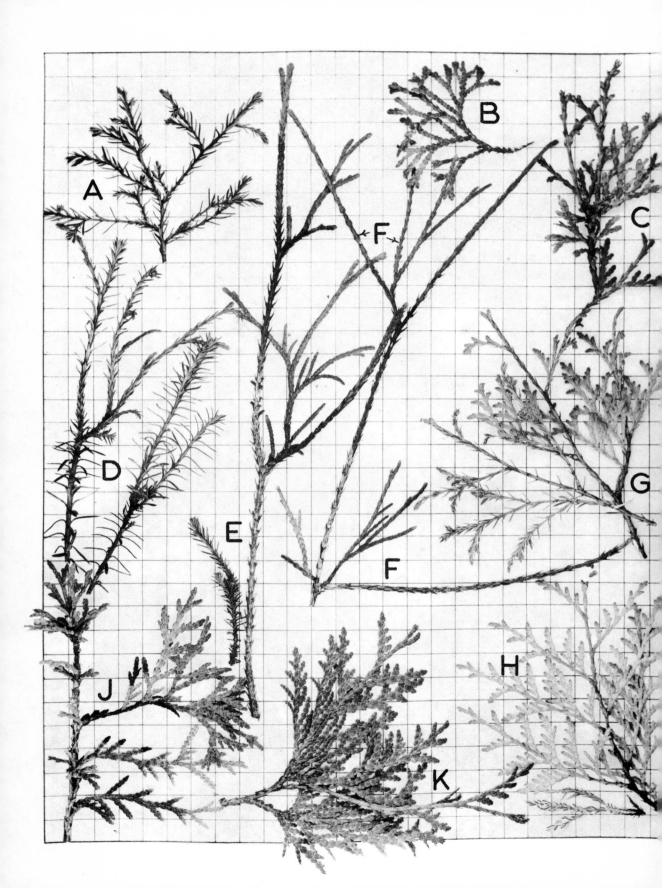

Thuja occidentalis 1

A. *Thuja occidentalis* 'Ericoides'. The fixed juvenile form. Very soft foliage, dull green in summer and medium brown in winter. (p. 299)

B. – – 'Recurva Nana'. This form and 'Dumosa' (C) are frequently confused. They both form flattened/globose plants and have flattened foliage in curved sprays, but whereas 'Recurva Nana' has only this type of growth, 'Dumosa' also carries some straight, thread-like upright shoots on which the foliage is neither flattened nor recurved. (p. 297, 305)

D. – – 'Ohlendorffiii' (syn. 'Spaethii'). Forms a low, rounded bush with two types of foliage, clearly distinguishable in the photograph. (p. 303)

E. – – 'Tetragona'. An uncommon form which also carries the same two types of foliage. It forms an upright and open plant consisting mainly of coarse, upright branches distinctly tetragonal in cross section with few side branches, and usually a small amount of juvenile foliage near the base of the bush. This latter (as the photograph clearly shows) is quite different from that of 'Ohlendorffii'. (p. 304)

F. – – 'Filiformis'. A thread-leaf form with many of the branches thin and pendulous. The foliage is noticeably glandular, has the usual *Thuja occidentalis* smell when bruised and always one or two of the terminal shoots are flattened. (p. 300)

G. – – 'Rheingold' and H. 'Ellwangeriana Aurea'. Golden forms which are frequently confused. The former is a dwarf form and makes a rounded or squatly conical little bush always carrying a good deal of the juvenile foliage. The latter will reach to several metres high and (except as a young plant) carries very little juvenile foliage. (p. 298)

J. – – 'Little Gem' forms a neat, rounded bush with much flattened, rich-green foliage. The little growths all along the old wood which are characteristic of this form can be clearly seen in the photograph. (p. 302)

K. – – 'Pumila' (often confused with 'Little Gem') also forms a globose bush but the flat, regular foliage is quite different and there need be no confusion. (p. 304)

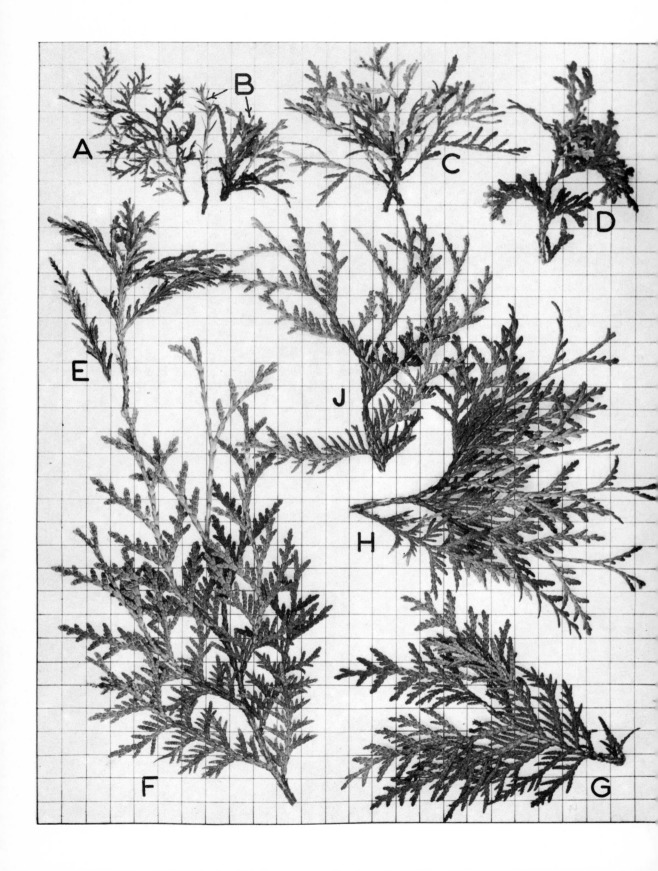

IDENTIFICATION PLATE 18

Thuja occidentalis 2

A. *Thuja occidentalis* 'Sphaerica'. Usually seen as a globose little bush, but will reach to 1·5 m in time. The neat, daintily curled foliage is characteristic. (p. 306)

B. – – 'Caespitosa'. Forms a small, hemispherical bun with congested, flattened foliage and always a small amount of juvenile foliage (arrow). (p. 296)

C. – – 'Hetz Midget'. Forms a low, squat or globose bush with foliage in scale with the diminutive size of the plant. (p. 301)

D. – – 'Pygmaea' (syn. "*plicata pygmaea*"). Forms an open, erratic bush with very much flattened foliage. Colour: dark bluish-green. (p. 305)

E. – – 'Bodmeri'. The normal foliage is altogether absent and the leaves are folded and appressed to give an exaggerated tetragonal cross section, leading shoots being frequently much coarser than in the photograph. (p. 296)

F. – – 'Woodwardii'. The large, flat, mid-green sprays are held vertically in a dense globose bush up to 1·5 m or more. (p. 307)

G. – – 'Umbraculifera'. The summer foliage is the bluest-green of any, and darkens in winter time. Young twigs orange-brown. (p. 306)

H. – – 'Globularis'. A globose variety with bright green foliage (p. 301)

J. – – 'Globosa'. Forms a dense, globose bush, the foliage being a light-green, almost a grey-green. (p. 301)

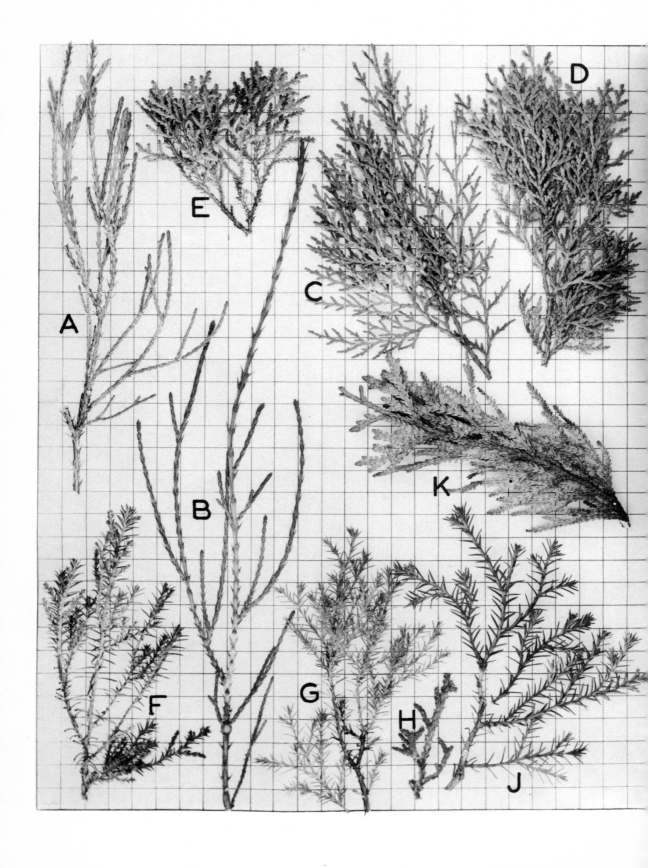

Thuja orientalis, Thujopsis

A. *Thuja orientalis* 'Filiformis Erecta' is a thread-leafed form with branching in all the main part of the bush strongly erect. The thread-leafed forms of this species can be distinguished from the *Chamaecyparis pisifera* 'Filifera' group by the free-standing leaf tips and from similar forms of *Thuja occidentalis* by the absence of glands or the pungent smell of the bruised foliage. (p. 310)

B. – – 'Flagelliformis' becomes a small tree with ascending main branches and pendulous branchlets. Strong, leading shoots are much coarser than shown in the photograph. Colour: light, yellowish-green. (p. 311)

C. – – 'Sieboldii'. Makes a globose or avoid bush, eventually to 2 m. The dainty, lace-like foliage is golden-yellow at first, becoming green later in the year. (p. 313)

D. – – 'Aurea Nana' is always seen as an ovoid or bee skip-shaped bush, reaching to 1 m only after many years. Colour: Golden-yellow in spring and summer, becoming green later. (p. 308)

E. – – 'Minima' (syn. "*minima glauca*"). Makes a tough-looking little bush, with semi-juvenile foliage quite rough to the touch. It turns a dull brown in winter, when it often looks to be dead. (p. 312)

F. – – 'Meldensis'. Forms an upright to globose bush with dark green juvenile foliage that is quite firm to the touch. (p. 312)

G. – – 'Rosedalis' (syn. "*rosedalis compacta*"). Makes a similar plant but the foliage is very soft and supple. Colour: in spring it is a butter-yellow, in summer a soft, pale green and in autumn it turns a dull purple-brown. (p. 313)

H. – – 'Athrotaxoides'. A very rare, monstrous form. (p. 308)

J. – – 'Juniperoides' (probably syn. "*decussata*"). Has the largest foliage of this group and is readily distinguishable by its winter colouring, which is a beautiful purple-mauve, heavily overlaid with a white glaucous coating, like a ripe grape. (p. 311)

K. *Thujopsis dolobrata* 'Nana'. Forms a low, spreading bush with very much flattened foliage. The photograph shows the glaucous underside of the spray. (p. 316)

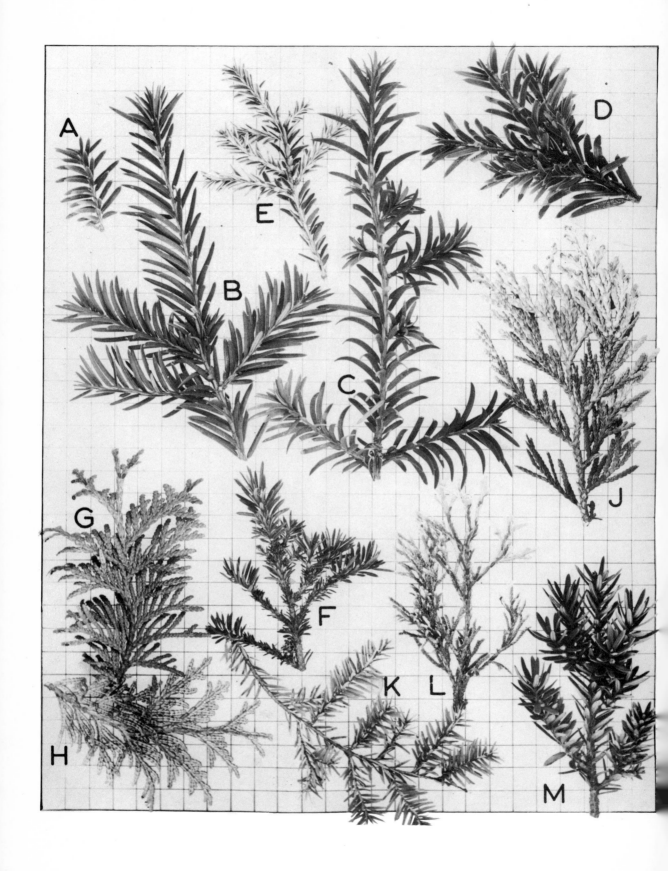

IDENTIFICATION PLATE 20

THUJA KORAENSIS, THUJA PLICATA, TAXUS, TSUGA

A. *Taxus baccata* 'Procumbens'. A prostrate, spreading form usually with the main stems rather bare of leaves. Note the parallel-sided, bluntly pointed leaf shape. (p. 289)

B. – – 'Repandens' and 'Cavendishii' (C) are both wide-spreading forms with dark green foliage. The difference in the leaf-shape is clearly to be seen in the photographs. (p. 286)

D. – – 'Decora'. Makes a dense little plant with lustrous, dark green foliage, often somewhat bronzed. (p. 287)

E. – – 'Adpressa Variegata'. The lighter part of the foliage in the photograph is a clear golden-yellow. (p. 285)

F. – – 'Nutans'. Forms a congested little plant with dark green, very irregular foliage. (p. 288)

G. *Thuja koraiensis*. Much flattened foliage, very glaucous white beneath (H). (p. 294)

J. *Thuja plicata* 'Stoneham Gold'. Slow-growing form with dark-green typical foliage, golden-yellow at the growing tips. (p. 315)

K. *Tsuga canadensis* 'Pendula'. Leader growth is much more vigorous than is the small spray shown. (p. 322)

L. *Thuja plicata* 'Rogersii' (syn. "*aurea rogersii*"). Usually seen as a dense little bush with all the growing tips a bright orange-yellow, but it will become an upright bush to 15 m in time. (p. 315)

M. *Taxus cuspidata* 'Nana'. A dense, spreading bush, becoming large eventually, with dark green foliage with broad, blunt-ended leaves. (p. 293)

though it had been squeezed between sheets of glass and so an actual spray from a plant of the variety illustrated may when held in the hand appear to be more congested than it does in the photograph. No attempt has been made to illustrate every variety; only those forms are included in which some peculiarity of foliage enables a picture of a small spray to have some recognition value. Other forms, where the variation is in habit, size, colour and so on are not shown in the plates.

DEFINITIONS

Before commencing my descriptions I wish to define a few of the words I shall use. For this there is good precedent, for not only do Acts of Parliament (those models of light reading) usually have an "Interpretation Clause" containing definitions of words to be used in the Act, Humpty Dumpty himself told Alice, "When I use a word it means just what I choose it to mean—neither more nor less."

Very well then, when I use the following words they mean just what I say in the following definitions—neither more nor less!

Note: In the first three definitions no attempt at mathematical precision can be made. The proportion relates to the main dimension; normally this is the height but in the case of prostrate forms it will be the spread. We are, of course, saddled with the names compacta, nana and pygmaea as part of the older cultivar names and these may or may not follow my definitions.

Compact Probable growth one-fifth to one-half of the type (Arboreal).

Dwarf Probable growth one-twentieth to one-quarter of the type.

Pygmy Probable growth less than one-twentieth of the type.

Cultivar An abbreviation of "cultivated variety". In many cases plants which have a "correct" name as a botanical "varietas" or "forma" are in this chapter regarded as a cultivar where they are in cultivation and have a distinct garden value.

Cupressoid Having the cross-section of the stem approximately square or circular, as in the familiar case of *Cupressus macrocarpa*. See "Thujoid" below.

Entre-nœud The inter-nodal distance, or length between each leaf or joint where axillary buds have developed or could develop. Where the entre-nœud is abnormally long the plant has a loose-jointed appearance; where it is unusually short it results in a slow-growing, congested form. It is irregular in such plants as *Cryptomeria japonica* 'Bandai Sugi'.

Frondose Having the branchlets and leaves developed in one plane, so as to give a fern-like appearance to the spray.

Glaucous Appearing to have a whitish coating similar to the "bloom" of a grape; not necessarily easily rubbed off. Not used by me to describe merely a blue or grey-green colour (although often so used in garden literature).

Juvenile foliage See page 143.

DEFINITIONS: TYPOGRAPHY

Lateral pair (of leaves) If a leaf spray be laid flat on the table: That pair of leaves which come from the sides of the shoot, i.e. parallel to the table top.

Facing pair That pair of leaves of which one leaf faces upwards and one downwards towards the table. (Note that lateral and facing pairs alternate.)

Reversion The appearance of vigorous, normal and typical growth upon a plant that is a dwarf form as the result of some internal disturbance in the plant's make-up which has reduced its vigour, e.g. a variegation or a witch's broom.

Thujoid Having the cross-section of the stem much flattened in the plane of the spray as though it had been gone over with a domestic flat-iron. See "Cupressoid" above.

TYPOGRAPHY

Botanical Names Except where bold type is used, these are printed in italics, the botanical categories "varietas" and "forma" being abbreviated to var. and f., e.g. *Juniperus communis* var. *saxatilis*.

Cultivar Names These are normally printed in normal type (i.e. not italics) and always with single quotation marks and initial capitals.

Bold Type Bold type is used for both botanical and cultivar names in side headings or where they introduce a variety not appearing under a separate heading.

Wrong Names Where obsolete or illegitimate names have to be quoted to clear up a point of confusion, they are printed in italics, within *double* quotation marks and without initial capitals, to make the illegitimacy as clear as possible, e.g. "*forsteckiana glauca*".

DIMENSIONS

Dimensions are usually given in metrical units and for those more used to feet and inches the following approximate table may be useful.

IN	MM	IN	MM	FT	CM
1/25	1·0	1	25	1	30
1/20	1·25	2	50	2	60
1/16	1·50	3	75	3	90
1/12	2·0		CM		M
1/10	2·5	4	10	4	1·2
1/8	3·0	5	12·5	5	1·5
1/6	4·25	6	15	6	1·8
1/4	6·5	7	18	7	2·1
1/3	8·5	8	20	8	2·4
1/2	12·5	9	23	9	2·7
		10	25·5	10	3·0
		11	28	20	6·0

27 *Abies amabilis* 'Spreading Star'. The mother plant at Arboretum Blijdenstein, Hilversum, Holland. 1·3 m high by 5 m across.

ABIES

The *Abies*, or Silver Firs, form a fairly large genus of forest-sized trees which have given rise to relatively few dwarf forms. They can be distinguished from their nearest relatives the *Picea* from the fact that the leaves when they fall leave disc-like leaf scars, whereas those of the latter species leave small, prominent, peg-like projections.

The *Abies*, like certain other genera, have two distinct forms of growth, the leader growth on which the leaves are radial, and lateral growth on which the leaves are pectinate, or at most semi-radial. This lateral growth, as has been explained in Chapter 1, has little or no capacity for developing true leader growth but it can extend in a horizontal direction and by propagation from lateral branches prostrate forms of distinct garden use can be produced. As the whole plant in such a case consists really of a single branch the growth is always extremely one-sided, but as many of the firs have attractive foliage such plants can be of great garden value when used to clothe a bank or in a prominent position on a large rockery. Some few of these had been named before the new Rules of Nomenclature put a ban upon latinized names and these are with us under the cultivar names 'Prostrata', 'Horizontalis' and 'Pendula' (this last is a misnomer as they are not truly pendulous forms), but in future any cultivars produced in this way (they are one form of "cultivariant") should be simply named by the generic name and specific epithet followed by the cultivar name 'Prostrate' to indicate the cultivariant status.

104

28 A young plant of *Abies lasiocarpa* 'Compacta'.

Abies alba. The Common Silver Fir has not produced for us any true dwarf forms, but there are several compact forms which are attractive as young plants, although they will get too large in time for most situations. The following have been named.

– – **'Brevifolia'** with leaves short and broad, **'Compacta'** a densely branched globose or squatly pyramidal form with dark green glossy leaves, **'Nana'** a similar form. Of these only 'Compacta' is to my knowledge obtainable in Great Britain. **'Microphylla'** and **'Tortuosa'** appear to be lost to cultivation.

– – **'Pendula'** is a true pendulous form making a tree 10–15 m high, and the prostrate forms described by Hornibrook were doubtless cultivariants resulting from the selection of graft scions of side growth. As already suggested, such plants should merely receive the cultivar name 'Prostrate'.

Abies amabilis. The Red Silver Fir, a tree to 75 m high has given rise to no truly dwarf form, unless a plant described by Hornibrook under the cultivar name **'Compacta'** was such, and even this seems lost to cultivation.

Because of its handsome foliage, cultivariants of the **'Prostrate'** type form magnificent plants where they have room to spread. One such is the clone **'Spreading Star'** of which the mother plant is in the Blijdenstein Pinetum at Hilversum in Holland.

▲ 29 *Abies balsamea* 'Prostrata' at Wansdyke Nursery, Devizes, Wilts. View looking down at plant.

▼ 32 A young plant of *Abies procera* 'Prostrate'. (Formerly *A. nobilis prostrata*.)

▲ 30 *Abies balsamea* 'Nana'. Detail of foliage.

◀ 31 *Abies balsamea* 'Hudsonia'.

▼ 33 *Abies concolor* 'Glauca Nana'. A young pl at Wisley.

Abies balsamea. Whilst few truly dwarf forms of *Abies* have been reported (and fewer still brought into cultivation) this species has distinguished itself by giving us several forms which are among the best dwarf conifers we possess.

The Balsam Fir is usually a tree 20–30 m high, but on the higher slopes of the White Mountains, New Hampshire, U.S.A., near the tree-line, it is reduced to a low, variable but always more or less prostrate form having foliage of the same deep glossy green but with leaves shorter and wider than the type and with the habit and leaf arrangement variable, and of this form we have at least three clones in cultivation.

– – f. **hudsonia.** The botanical name *hudsonia* having been the earliest to be used it strictly speaking covers all these forms, but in English cultivation we can distinguish the clone **'Nana'** which forms a globose bush and carries its foliage completely radially, **'Prostrata'** a form in cultivation although rarely met with which has prostrate branches and *completely* pectinate foliage, and a third form (the most common) with a globose to cushion-forming habit, with foliage that is semi-radial, to which we can properly continue to give the cultivar name **'Hudsonia'.**

The difference between 'Nana' and 'Hudsonia' can be clearly seen if a twig of last year's growth be snapped off and looked at from the broken end, and the upper side of the twig of 'Prostrate' is quite clear of leaves, so that these forms are easily distinguishable. The rich glossy foliage and their indestructible hardiness make all of these forms most desirable garden plants.

Abies cephalonica. The Greek Fir with its glossy-green, curved, almost radial, foliage would probably produce attractive plants by grafting from a side branch, and it is possible that the plant described by Mr Hillier as **'Nana'** is of this type.

– – **'Meyer's Dwarf'** would appear to be a true dwarf, as Dr F. G. Meyer in *Plant Explorations, 1963* describes it as "dwarf and slow-growing, with very abbreviated parts". I have not seen it.

Abies concolor. The Colorado White Fir, normally a tall tree, has given us one excellent form. Other named forms are **'Conica'** too strong-growing to be classed as a dwarf, **'Globosa'** lost to cultivation and **'Pendula'** a form which from the description given by Hornibrook of the behaviour of his own specimen sounds suspiciously like a cultivariant of the **'Prostrate'** type.

– – **'Compacta'** is a dwarf, compact shrub of irregular growth, with stout, stiff, short (2·5–4 cm long), very glaucous leaves. It is very rare, but worth searching for.

– – **'Wattezii Prostrate'.** The cultivar 'Wattezii' is a form of the species with creamy-yellow foliage fading to white. In the Pygmy Pinetum there is a young prostrate plant —obviously a cultivariant—which because of this foliage coloration, shows great promise. As 'Wattezii' is always lacking in vigour, this prostrate form should be less rampant than are many of these prostrate firs.

Abies fraseri 'Prostrate' has been described more than once with varying places of origin. It would appear to be merely a cultivariant.

Abies koreana. Although eventually too big for most gardens, young plants of the Korean Fir make excellent garden plants because of their neat habit and attractive foliage and because they bear their long, purple cones freely on quite young trees.

– – **'Compact Dwarf'** is a selected slow-growing form which Dr Boom describes as a compact, horizontal form without a leader and with leaves somewhat shorter than the type, never bearing cones. In this it differs from plants sold in the trade as **'Nana'** which are merely slow-growing forms which cone freely when quite small plants.

Abies lasiocarpa. The Alpine Fir. At the time when Hornibrook wrote his second edition, the Cork Fir of Arizona was by many regarded as a separate species (*A. arizonica*), but it is now generally listed merely as a variety of the Alpine Fir.

– – **'Compacta'.** Because of what is stated above, Hornibrook gives two descriptions of compact forms—his *A. arizonica* var. *Compacta* Grootend, on page 22 and his *A. lasiocarpa* var. *compacta*, Beissner on page 27, but the descriptions are so close that they were obviously descriptions by different observers of the same plant. A strict application of the Rules of Nomenclature would require our plant to be called *A. lasiocarpa* var. *arizonica* 'Compacta', but as whatever plant it was that Beissner was writing about cannot now be ascertained (there being no dwarf form of *A. lasiocarpa* —in its typical form—in cultivation) we can properly use the simpler name for a very desirable dwarf form that usually passes in the trade as "*Abies arizonica compacta*".

It is very slow-growing and forms a densely branched squat to broadly conical tree with attractive crowded grey-green foliage (*Ill. 28*).

All the following are merely cultivariants, but make good garden plants where there is sufficient space.

Abies magnifica 'Prostrate' (syn. "*prostrata*").

Abies nordmanniana 'Prostrate' (syn. "*procumbens*")—and

Abies procera (formerly A. nobilis) **'Prostrate'** (syn. "*prostrata*") and—probably distinguishable in colour of foliage—**'Glauca Prostrate'**.

34 Foliage of *Athrotaxis selaginoides*.

ATHROTAXIS

The Tasmanian Cedars are small trees which in this country are seldom seen larger than tall bushes.

There are no recorded dwarf forms, but each of the following species is sufficiently slow-growing to justify its inclusion here and in any representative collection. They are all upright growing and differ mainly in foliage.

Athrotaxis cupressoides has thick, closely appressed leaves giving the shoots a thick, whipcord-like appearance.

Athrotaxis laxifolia bears its leaves slightly spreading.

Athrotaxis selaginoides bears leaves spreading, lanceolate, incurved, acute, rigid and spine-pointed.

109

CEDRUS

The Cedars are a small genus of four or five species all very much alike and distinguished by having branchlets of two kinds—long terminal shoots bearing scattered leaves, and short, spur-like shoots which bear tufts of leaves in false whorls. In this respect they are akin to the larches but being evergreen cannot be confused with that genus, which are all deciduous. The genus has given us several good dwarf forms.

Cedrus atlantica. The Atlantic or Mount Atlas Cedar is normally a tree to 40 m high, differing from *C. libani* mainly in the size of its cones. It has given rise to few recorded dwarf forms, and to the best of my knowledge, none of these is in cultivation.

35 *Cedrus deodara* 'Pygmaea'.

Cedrus brevifolia. The Cyprus Cedar is so commonly grown as a small tree in a container that many persons are under the impression that it is a dwarf species. This is not the case for in the open ground it becomes a tree upwards of 10 m high, of which there is a good specimen on the rock garden at the Edinburgh Royal Botanic Garden. However, in a pot or other container it seems to remain dwarf indefinitely and because of its small leaves, which are nicely in scale, it makes an excellent pot plant.

36 A young plant of *Cedrus libani* 'Nana' at Wisley.

Cedrus deodara. The Deodar has the longest leaves and most graceful habit of all the cedars. It has given the following dwarf forms, but they are all uncommon in cultivation.

– – **'Hesse'.** A very dwarf and dense form which originated in the nursery of H. A. Hesse at Weener, Ems, in Germany.

– – **'Nana'.** A very slow-growing form which forms a compact bush. There is a good specimen on the rock garden at Kew.

– – **'Pygmy'.** An extremely dwarf form with conspicuously glaucous foliage. It was found by Wm. T. Gotelli in a little nursery in California in or about 1943. The original plant is in the Wm. T. Gotelli collection now in the National Arboretum at Washington. Annual growth about 6 mm.

Cedrus libani. The Cedar of Lebanon has given us several dwarf forms which are very popular, partly because of their·very real value as garden plants and partly perhaps on account of the Biblical associations.

– – **'Nana'.** From time to time seedlings turn up in different parts with dwarf, stunted growth and several of these have been propagated and are grown as *Cedrus libani* 'Nana'. As this is a collective name plants from the different clones will not be identical and so plants obtained from different nurseries may show minor variations. If a sufficiently distinctive form turns up it should be given a new cultivar name, this name with adequate description being "published" in accordance with the Rules, but none of the forms that I have seen is sufficiently different from the others to justify this action.

37 *Cedrus libani* 'Pendula' at Belmonte Arboretum, Wageningen, Holland. All truly pendulous forms merely "sprawl" unless stem-trained.

◀ 38 *Cedrus libani* 'Comte de Dijon'. The "type" plant in the National Garden, Glasnevin, Dublin.

▼ 39 *Cedrus libani* 'Sargentii'. A fine specimen at Edinburgh Botanic Garden.

CEDRUS

– – **'Comte de Dijon'** is a clone of 'Nana' originally distributed by the nursery firm Barbier of Orleans in France. This being the case it may be feared that many of the plants grown as 'Comte de Dijon' have no claim to the name at all.

Of the four authentic plants recorded by Hornibrook in 1938 only that in the National Botanic Gardens at Glasnevin, Dublin, can now be traced. It has now become a tree 5 m high by 4 m across, and as will be seen from the picture opposite, the branching system is distinctly horizontal, with a wide-spreading flat branch system. The foliage is radial, the leaves are long, fine and needle-like, 20–25 mm long by about 0·5 mm diam. tapering gradually to a fine point, often curved slightly and occurring singly on the growing shoot; or shorter, 15–18 mm long, even thinner, and occurring in tufts on the spur-like growths which are characteristic of the species, and with somewhat shorter and often unsymmetrical points. Annual growth about 50 mm. This plant should now be regarded as the type plant, and the name 'Comte de Dijon' be withdrawn from all specimens not conforming to the Dublin plant.

– – **'Sargentii'** is a very valuable dwarf and truly weeping form which should not be confused with *Cedrus libani* 'Pendula', which is a large tree. All cultivars of Cedrus must be grafted on to seedlings of the type and this form needs to be trained up as a young plant to the desired height and it will then form a gracious, dome-shaped bush with long curved sweeping branches. It is a most attractive plant for a prominent spot on a large rockery. It can also be grown successfully in a large pot or other container in which it can look most attractive with its long, pendulous branches sweeping down below the level of the top of the pot. Grown in this way it may look its best if kept rather "open" by pruning away some branches entirely. Unless trained up to a leader the plant, being unable to lift itself above the level of the ground, sprawls about in a most ungainly, unattractive way (*Ill. 37*).

40 *Cephalotaxus harringtonia* var. *fastigiata*. A young plant; it becomes a small tree size in time.

CEPHALOTAXUS

A genus of small yew-like trees or shrubs closely allied to *Torreya* comprising five species all from southern or eastern Asia. It shares with *Abies* and other species a reluctance to develop true leader growth from a side shoot and so lends itself to the production of prostrate "cultivariant" forms. It is distinguishable from *Torreya* by the non-spiny pointed leaves with prominent mid-rip above but not furrowed beneath, and by the more numerous bud-scales.

Cephalotaxus fortunei, with its long, handsome, tapered green leaves, produces, in its cultivariant form **'Prostrate'** (syn. "*prostrata*" and "*Prostrate Spreader*") one of the most attractive spreading conifers we have, ideal as Mr Hillier says for ground cover in a shady position either on acid soil or chalk. It will cover a large area in time.

Cephalotaxus harringtonia is a name now used to include several varieties formerly regarded as separate species. The typical form is a large bush with spreading or slightly arching branches, but it is usually represented in gardens by var. **drupacea** which forms a round-headed, upright shrub with light-green, curved leaves much shorter than those of *C. fortunei*.

– – var. **fastigiata** is a very distinct form with a very strongly upright habit and very dark green leaves. It becomes a small tree in time but is very slow-growing. Mr Hillier records a prostrate form in his collection at Winchester.

– – var. **nana** is a dwarf, shrubby geographical form from Japan which I have not seen, but as it is described as "spreading by suckers" it must be quite distinct from the type.

– – **'Prostrate'** is doubtless a cultivariant form of var. *drupacea*, which it resembles in every way except habit.

114

CHAMAECYPARIS

The Chamaecyparis or False Cypresses, which at one time were included in the genus *Cupressus*, are a genus of six species, three or four of which give us most of our dwarf forms. These are the *Chamaecyparis lawsoniana* (The Lawson Cypress), *Chamaecyparis obtusa* (The Hinoki Cypress), *Chamaecyparis pisifera* (The Sawara Cypress) and *Chamaecyparis thyoides* (The White Cypress of North America).

In each of these species we have forms with fixed juvenile foliage, colour forms and variations of habit and vigour of growth. For no apparent reason, in the case of *C. pisifera* custom has developed group names such as 'Filifera', 'Nana', 'Squarrosa', which appear in the cultivar names. The other species similarly occur in groups but because of the bar there now is on latinized names it is not possible to introduce analogous terms into the cultivar names. I do, however, use group names in the tables at the head of each species which will enable readers to identify their plants more easily and help them choose a cultivar for a particular purpose.

Chamaecyparis lawsoniana. Although the Lawson False-Cypress was only introduced to cultivation as recently as 1864 it has given rise to innumerable cultivars, amongst which are several good dwarf forms. These are mainly variations in colour and form, although there are one or two with peculiarities of foliage, and as all these cultivars are seedling mutants the variations are reasonably stable, i.e. they do not "revert", although in some cases the peculiarity becomes less pronounced with age.

All forms have, however, one drawback which is that they seldom if ever will break from the old wood. This means in gardeners' language that they resent heavy pruning, so both formative and restrictive pruning (the former aimed at shaping the tree to our requirements and the latter being done in order to keep it down in size) must be done little and often, and always before it becomes necessary to cut into the old wood. It also means that the species characteristically has little capacity to recover from severe damage. Although most of the forms are hardy, should an exceptionally severe winter or strong gale kill off all the young growth on one side of the tree it will seldom be killed outright but it will never "break again" and recover its shape, as many gardeners proved in the arctic spring of 1963.

Of the colour forms, the white foliaged and variegated varieties are the least tolerant of wind and these should always be given a sheltered spot. Next in sequence are the yellow or golden forms, some of which (notably 'Erecta Aurea') are intolerant of wind, others being more reliable in this respect. As a general rule the colour of all the yellow forms develops best in full sunlight, plants in the shade never achieving more than a pale yellowish-green. The green and blue forms are the most hardy and the most tolerant of shady conditions.

– – **'Albovariegata'.** This becomes a large ovoid or conical bush (not to be confused with 'Argenteovariegata' which is a very tall-growing form) with deep green leaves profusely spotted and blotched with white. With age the plant will reach 2 m and

115

41 *Chamaecyparis lawsoniana* 'Aurea Densa'.   42 *Chamaecyparis lawsoniana* 'Minima Aurea'.

tends to become round-topped. Here and there about the plant there are small sprays consisting wholly of pure white foliage, giving the bush quite a distinctive appearance, but these white growths are very prone to damage by frost. It is an attractive variety which could well be more widely planted.

– – **'Aurea Densa'.** There are three very slow-growing conical golden forms, all raised at Red Lodge Nursery at Chandlers Ford which are very similar—in fact so similar that gardeners have been known to express a wish that they had not all three been brought into cultivation. The others are **'Lutea Nana'** and **'Minima Aurea'.** Of the three, 'Lutea Nana' is the strongest and most loose in growth but I understand from Messrs Rogers & Son that they do not now feel the difference is sufficient to maintain the distinction and that although the mother plant is still at Red Lodge Nursery they do not now propagate this variety.

The other two cultivars, 'Aurea Densa' and 'Minima Aurea' both form very attractive conical golden bushes, the colour being well maintained throughout the year. 'Aurea Densa' tends to form a blunt-topped cone with the foliage quite stiff to the touch when the bush is patted with the hand. 'Minima Aurea' forms a more pointed bush with the foliage softer to the touch and with a tendency to hold its sprays edgewise in places similar to 'Minima'.

These two varieties are, however, so similar that I am sorry for any poor nurseryman who gets his stock of young cuttings muddled, but if perchance later you receive from him the wrong variety there is no need to be worried. For the first five years you

116

43 *Chamaecyparis lawsoniana* 'Ell-woodii'. A good specimen in the Pygmy Pinetum at Devizes, Wilts. Often seen as a broader and more oval bush.

will discern no difference; for the next five years visiting experts will argue with great enthusiasm as to which variety it is you have; for the next five years the consensus of opinion will slowly verge in one direction or the other. In the meantime in either case you will have had a treasure that after fifteen years you would not part with whatever its name. You are unlikely to live to see either variety exceed 1 m high by about half that amount across.

– – **'Caudata'** is rather more than a dwarf as it will reach to 3 m high but it is very slow-growing for some years. As a very young plant it would pass for 'Forsteckensis' but it soon develops an upright habit with curious growth in which the main branches carry long (to 15 cm) leaves closely attached to the stem except just at the ends, which are free-standing and rather distant, and the short side branchlets carry very dense foliage in flat or congested sprays. The leaves in these sprays are much smaller and usually carry some shoots on which they are very small indeed.

The presence of the two such different types of growth gives quite a distinct appearance to this variety which is therefore easily recognized except when very small. The extensions of the long main branches before the side shoots have developed thereon give rise to the "mouse-tail" appearance to which the variety owes its name, and the grouping of the foliage on the short and somewhat infrequent branchlets gives the whole plant a bunched or "tufted" appearance.

– – **'Compacta'** is a slow-growing, dense form with fan-shaped leaf sprays which when young could very well be taken for a strongly growing plant of 'Minima'. It forms a neat, broadly conical plant. The specimen at the foot of the rockery at Wisley described by Hornibrook as measuring 1·5 by 1·2 m in 1927 has now reached 4 by 3 m and has retained its shape and denseness well (*Ill. 23*).

– – **'Conica'** is merely an incorrect synonym of 'Wisselii'.

117

▲ 44 *Chamaecyparis lawsoniana* 'Dow's Gem'. A young plant in the Wansdyke Nursery, Devizes.

▲ 45 *Chamaecyparis lawsoniana* 'Duncanii' at Castlewellan, Co. Down, N.I. Brought from New Zealand in 1938 by Mr J. Annesley.

◀ 46 *Chamaecyparis lawsoniana* 'Ellwood's Pygmy'. The mother plant in the Pygmy Pinetum at Devizes, Wilts.

▼ 48 *Chamaecyparis lawsoniana* 'Filiformis Compacta'.

▼ 47 *Chamaecyparis lawsoniana* 'Forsteckensis'. The "tight" form. Any "tighter" plant is the result of pruning.

– – **'Dow's Gem'.** This variety has been distributed in Great Britain as "Dow's Variety" and "Noble's Variety". It is a low-growing bush of the "Knowefieldensis" group with strong, coarse, very open, thujoid foliage with a heavy white bloom on the underside of the leaf. It appears as though it will become an attractive large bush, but at Devizes it has not withstood the frost so well as some forms of the Lawson cypress.

– – **'Duncanii'.** This is an attractive form originating in New Zealand and only just becoming available in this country. The picture opposite shows the only mature specimen I know of in the British Isles (at Castlewellan in Co. Down, N. Ireland) and gives a good idea of the plant, which would form a fine specimen on a large lawn where it has room to develop into a plant 5 m across. The foliage is particularly graceful and attractive.

– – **'Ellwoodii'.** There is no need to describe this ubiquitous variety which for all its popularity even with the Departmental Stores, is a most useful plant. A fairly quick grower with blue-green juvenile foliage and upright-oval outline, it has no real competitor in its class. Its value for landscape planting can be seen from the picture on page 117. If a young plant is carefully restricted to a single stem (in other words if grown as a "cordon") 'Ellwoodii' will form a narrow columnar plant as architecturally effective as the Irish Juniper, a tree 3 m high by no more than 30 cm across being quite practicable. Three variations of 'Ellwoodii' have been introduced. The first, **'Kestonensis',** is merely a slow-growing form of 'Ellwoodii', having the same upright habit and identical foliage. The second, **'Ellwood's Pygmy'**, is probably merely a cultivariant. I do not know the origin of this form, but the mother plant at the Pygmy Pinetum is obviously a very old plant and is only about 45 cm high and is wider than it is high. Young propagations retain this bushy characteristic, especially if any tendency to form a leader be checked at once. It is a most attractive form which should be better known. Finally there is **'Ellwood's White'** which is a white variegated sport from "Ellwoodii". It appears to be very slow-growing and the oldest plants I have seen (at Messrs F. J. Grootendorst's Nursery at Boskoop in Holland) are small compact bushes without any of the columnar tendency of 'Ellwoodii'.

– – **'Erecta Argenteovariegata'.** This is a very old variety which seems to have been lost sight of. This is a pity as it is an attractive one. Its habit is very similar to the well-known 'Erecta viridis' but it is slower in growth and the whole plant is liberally splashed with large patches of a clear white variegation, making it a most attractive plant. Like all the "erecta" forms it tends to become bare near the ground in time, so should be planted somewhere where its feet will be hidden.

– – **'Erecta Aurea'.** Slow-growing and attractive when young on account of its habit and bright colour. It is not very hardy and with age becomes a large bush to 3 m, frequently seen much the worse for damage by snow.

– – **'Filiformis Compacta'.** There are two cultivars one meets with under this name, both being, as one would expect, plants with thread-like foliage. The correct name for

119

a form with multiple stiff and erect branches is **'Erecta Filiformis'**, whereas the true 'Filiformis Compacta' is a low, globose bush with very fine cord-like branches and tiny dark blue-green leaves, in which the branches seem barely strong enough to bear their weight and flop about in all directions, giving the bush the appearance of a wet mop. It is occasionally found under the name "*globosa filiformis*".

This cultivar need never be confused with *Chamaecyparis pisifera* 'Filifera' as the foliage is very much thinner and a blue-green, nor with any of the thread-leaf forms of *Thuja* which are all much coarser and stiffer and have the characteristic rank odour if the foliage is bruised (*Ill. 48*).

– – **'Fletcheri'.** This well-known columnar variety has semi-juvenile foliage not dissimilar from 'Ellwoodii' but it is always a lighter and greyer green in colour. When it was first introduced it was hailed as a wonderful subject for rock gardens, but since then it has shown its ability to romp away rapidly to a height of 5 m or more so it is too big for inclusion in this book, were it not for the following circumstances. In the second edition of his classic work on dwarf conifers Murray Hornibrook refers to small round cushions or buns (probably a cultivariant) under the cultivar name **'Fletcheri Nana'** (I think his reference to "*Keston variety*" here was a mistake). I have not come across this variety but the name 'Fletcheri Nana' should be kept for any such low, round cushion or bun forms that may be produced from 'Fletcheri' by suitable selection of propagating material.

From time to time slow-growing forms of 'Fletcheri' with the normal upright habit are put on the market but these are usually unstable forms which sooner or later revert to the typical plant. In the Pygmy Pinetum I have a small plant purchased from a nursery who assured me that they had had it in stock for several years, which has not significantly increased in size since it was purchased. I have yet to learn what it is capable of doing in this respect, but I propose the name **'Fletcher's Compact'** for this and all other plants which vary from normal 'Fletcheri' only by being significantly closer and slower growing.

Of recent years 'Fletcheri' has been setting fertile seed and some of the resulting seedlings appear to be extremely dwarf forms. If these prove themselves as desirable garden plants they will probably be propagated and named by their enthusiastic raisers, but I do hope that we are not in for a spate of names for seedlings that are barely distinguishable apart.

– – **'Fletcher's Pillar'.** (New name.) An extremely fastigiate form which presumably arose from a sport of 'Fletcheri'.

– – **'Fletcher's White'.** There is now on the market a variegated form of 'Fletcheri'. It carries a nice bold variegation of creamy-white and there is a good plant in the Nisbet collection at Wisley. Plants appear to grow rapidly and this form may turn out as big a plant as the 'Fletcheri' from which it was derived as a sport.

I have recently received from Holland young plants of a golden form under the

49 *Chamaecyparis lawsoniana* 'Fletcheri'. This variety is too tall-growing to be classed as a dwarf.

50 *Chamaecyparis lawsoniana* 'Ellwoodii'. One of the original plantings at "Nyewoods", Chilworth, Southampton.

name **'Yellow Transparent',** a name which seems to me much more appropriate for a gage plum than a conifer.

– – **'Forsteckensis'.** This popular and well tried variety (often met with under its wrong spelling "*forsteckiana*") is indispensable in any collection (*Ill. 47*).

In its best form it produces a globose or broadly conical bush never over 60 cm high with main branches very densely set, main branches short and all its growth very congested. It increases in size by sending out longer tips of normal foliage. These will eventually thicken up but the bush can be kept to any desired size and with foliage almost unbelievably congested and moss-like by the systematic removal of these longer growths.

There is, however, a much looser form in cultivation which forms a much larger plant. Hornibrook expresses the opinion that this is the result of propagation from the stronger branches referred to above, but I incline to the view that it is a separate clone. Of this variety there is a wonderful old specimen in Goatcher's Nursery at Washington in Sussex which is (I write from memory) over 2 m high and wider than it is high. This form is just as attractive as the slower-growing one but not, of course, suitable for use in the same position in the garden. The form occasionally met with under the name **'Tilgate'** appears to be the same.

From time to time variegated branches appear on plants of 'Forsteckensis', but I have never yet come across a case where the variegation has been "fixed".

51 *Chamaecyparis lawsoniana* 'Gimbornii'. Dark green, usually tipped with mauve.

52 *Chamaecyparis lawsoniana* 'Lycopodioides'.

– – **'Gimbornii'.** This forms a dense, compact, broadly conical or oval slow-growing little bush seldom seen more than 1 m high. The main branches are thick, stiff and erect and the branchlets short. The foliage is a glaucous blue-green with the tips of the growing shoots purplish-blue during most of the year. Otherwise it is very similar to 'Nana Glauca' in colour and habit.

This cultivar originated as a seedling on the von Gimborn Estate at Doorn, Holland. The mother plant reached a height of nearly 2 m but was unfortunately killed outright by the very severe winter 1962–3.

– – **'Knowefieldensis'.** I am not altogether satisfied that I have been able to locate the true plant, but as grown in the Pygmy Pinetum it is a wide-spreading, flat-topped plant of the 'Tamariscifolia' type, but differing from all the forms I have seen under that name. In this form the foliage is very thin and fine—a deep, rich green above and only slightly glaucous beneath. The leaves are very small, densely set and appressed for most of their length, only the tips being free (and that not *noticeably* so as they are in 'Nidiformis' and 'Tamariscifolia'). They are borne in flat, parallel-sided sprays about 2·5 cm wide, on side shoots regularly set about 2 cm apart and all emerging at a constant angle of about 45° and regularly decreasing in length towards the dominant terminal shoot. The resulting triangular outline at once distinguishes this form from 'Nidiformis' and from 'Tamariscifolia' it is distinct by its regular, crowded, overlapping growth. I believe that the form sometimes met with under the name "*tabuliformis*" is the same as 'Knowefieldensis', as described above.

– – **'Krameri'.** This is a globose, shrubby form not more than a metre high with its main branches set horizontally, partly twisted and pendulous. The branch system is very irregular and contorted, the final growth cord-like.

– – **'Luteocompacta'.** I have no real business to bring this variety into this book as it is by no means a dwarf form, but if it is prevented (by pruning) from forming a leader it will become a large roundish bush with the main branch system horizontal and spreading and the branchlets tending to become pendulous with the leaf sprays twisted on the branch. The leaves are small, pointed and appressed, a golden-yellow colour in full light to yellowish-green in shade. The colouring is very similar to the well known 'Stewartii' and grown in the way suggested it would make a wonderful specimen on an open lawn.

– – **'Lycopodioides'** is hardly a dwarf form as it makes a conical shrub eventually 5–6 m high, but its curiously twisted foliage makes it an interesting plant when young. It might perhaps best be described as a thread-leafed form in which the threads are curled and twisted in all directions, somewhat in the matter of *C. obtusa* 'Coralliformis' from which it can at once be distinguished by the pointed leaves with their free-standing tips. There is a large specimen in the Happy Valley Gardens at Llandudno, North Wales.

– – **'Minima'.** There is a great deal of confusion between 'Minima' and **'Nana'** (with their respective colour forms). This has been largely contributed to, I fear, by Hornibrook's statement to the effect that the rather horizontal arrangement of the leaf sprays in 'Nana' always distinguish it from 'Minima' which, according to him, bears its branches turned rather edgeways. I have never met a large plant which would be 'Nana' by this criterion when approached from one point of the compass which would not equally be 'Minima' when seen from a different direction and I think the fact of the matter is that this is not where the distinction lies. 'Minima' has its trunk very short or missing entirely and has its place taken by a series of more or less vertical main branches of approximately equal length, giving the bush a broadly globose outline, whereas 'Nana' will always be found to have a well-defined central

53 *Chamaecyparis lawsoniana* 'Nana'. Showing central trunk and branching habit.

54 *Chamaecyparis lawsoniana* 'Minima' in Mr A. H. Nisbet's collection at Gosport, Hants.

55 *Chamaecyparis lawsoniana* 'Nana Albospica'.　　56 *Chamaecyparis lawsoniana* 'Pygmaea Argentea'.

trunk and much more horizontally-held *main* branches. This gives 'Nana' much more tendency to become a broad, squat pyramid as it ages. An old plant can have a surprisingly thick trunk nearly to its summit. So that, although there may be some truth in what Hornibrook says as to the arrangement of the leaf sprays this is not a very reliable criterion. On the other hand, the leaf sprays of 'Minima' have a neat, rounded outline and give the whole bush a "well-groomed" look, whereas in 'Nana' the leading shoots project beyond the laterals, making the leaf sprays much more broken in outline and this gives the bush a somewhat less neat and tidy appearance.

Both 'Minima' and 'Nana' are green forms, the former especially being quite a yellow-green in the summer, but both are much more commonly met with in their blue-green forms, **'Minima Glauca'** and **'Nana Glauca'** respectively, and there are also the following colour variations.

– – **'Minima Argenteovariegata'.** This is 'Minima' with a fairly bold and attractive creamy-white variegation. It is a very rare plant, the small specimen at the Pygmy Pinetum being in fact the only one I have ever seen.

– – **'Minima Aurea'.** See page 116 under 'Aurea Densa'.

– – **'Nana'.** See page 123 under 'Minima'.

– – **'Nana Albospica'** is a very slow-growing, dwarf, conical form, dense in growth.

124

57 *Chamaecyparis lawsoniana* 'Rogersii'. Colour: blue-grey.

The main branches are short and horizontal; the branchlets short and thin. The leaves are small, white at the growing points, elsewhere pale green. This variety pays for planting in rich soil as it is only when it is growing strongly that it has the "white appearance to the whole plant" described by Hornibrook. This plant seems to have laboured under a variety of names including "*albospica nana*", "*nana alba*", "*albospicata*" and possibly others ('Albospica' is not a dwarf form). I prefer the name I have selected from the synonymy because it brings it into an appropriate alphabetical position.

– – **'Nana Albovariegata'.** This form appears to be lost to cultivation, and to judge from the description given by Hornibrook it is no great loss.

– – **'Nana Argentea'** is described as a dwarf, broadly ovoid shrublet with ascending branches tightly pressed together but having their tips pendulous or recurving. Foliage greyish-green, silvery-white at the growing tips. It is a very uncommon form, which I have not seen.

– – **'Nana Argenteovariegata'.** This is evidently a case of someone naming a plant too soon, for it is not a dwarf form. It is a densely growing pyramidal plant with pure white-tipped foliage appearing as though lightly covered with snow. Forms with white variegated or white-tipped foliage turn up in the seed beds occasionally, and I fancy that more than one of these has strayed into cultivation.

125

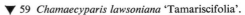
◀ 58 *Chamaecyparis lawsoniana* 'Nidiformis'. These two varieties are very similar and are often confused.

▼ 59 *Chamaecyparis lawsoniana* 'Tamariscifolia'.

– – **'Nidiformis'** (syn. *C.* × *nidifera*). I follow Dr Boom in treating this as merely a cultivar of *C. lawsoniana*, as the theory of its being a hybrid between that species and *C. nootkatensis* is not borne out by an examination of the plant itself.

It forms a low, spreading plant of the 'Tamariscifolia' type (for which cultivar it is often mistaken) vaguely suggesting a large birds' nest (hence the name) with radially spreading and horizontal or arching main branches and decurving branchlets. The foliage looks at a glance to be coarser than that of 'Tamariscifolia' and bears blue- or grey-green foliage a little glaucous above and very glaucous beneath, much flattened

126

(1·5 mm wide); the leaves very crowded, the lateral pair standing off at the free tips at 45°, the facing pair smaller, appressed, in shape a 45° triangle (variable), seldom glandular. The growth is in wide sprays in which many of the side branches twist out of the plane of the spray and almost all the ultimate shoots curve, some up, some down, as though the spray had been gone over with a flat-iron when wet, and in drying each little shoot had curled as it felt inclined. It was doubtless this and the fact that a lack of dominance of the main branch tip over its side branches produces a round-ended spray that suggested to Hornibrook a likeness to an ostrich plume.

I received from Mr Nisbet cuttings of a plant growing in his collection labelled "*hybrida*" which is very close to 'Nidiformis', differing therefrom in being slower growing and perhaps a little more prostrate and in having its leaves much less closely spaced along the shoot, so that the spray is distinctly more open and lace-like. I cannot at present distinguish between this form and plants sometimes met with under the names "*nidifera compacta*" and "*knowefieldensis glauca*". They may very well all be the same. I am trying to get together as many of these forms, including the different clones of 'Tamariscifolia', with the intention of growing them together at the Pygmy Pinetum so that they can be compared.

– – **'Pygmaea Argentea'** is a dwarf form of the 'Nana' type, of very slow growth, forming a small globose or squatly conical bush with its main branches upright. The foliage is dark green, pale creamy-white at the tips and very densely set. When the plant is growing strongly the foliage is almost white in early summer and the whole bush then has the appearance of having been turned upside down when wet into a barrel of flour. It is alleged to be synonymous with **'Backhouse Silver'** but there is an element of doubt about this.

– – **'Rogersii'** (syn. "*nana rogersii*") is a glaucous blue, globular variety with thread-like foliage raised from seed by Rogers and Sons of Red Lodge Nursery, formerly at Southampton but now at Chandlers Ford, Hants. It will grow to 2 m in time. The colour is similar to the well-known tall variety 'Alumii' but the blue is not quite so intense and it seems to become less marked as the plant ages. It is not one of the 'Nana' group, so the simpler name is preferable (*Ill. 57*).

– – **'Shawii'** forms an upright-oval little bush with neat, grass-green foliage, but in my opinion it has no great character. It might aptly be described as a dwarf edition of the well-known tall cultivar 'Pottenii'.

– – **'Tamariscifolia'.** In this cultivar the trunk is always entirely absent and its place is taken by a number of main branches which grow upwards and outwards in such a way that although the plant will reach to 2 m high in time the top is always more or less flat and the width is about twice the height. The branching is very irregular and the branches appear to tumble about in all directions. The foliage is a light mid-green, slightly glaucous above, noticeably so below, much flattened as in 'Nidiformis' but wider (2 mm). The leaves are longer and narrower, the lateral pair standing off at 30°

127

▲ 60 *Chamaecyparis lawsoniana* 'Tharandtensis Caesia'. Colour: blue-grey.

◀ 61 *Chamaecyparis nootkatensis* 'Compacta'.

and the facing pair in the shape of a 30° triangle, nearly always noticeably glandular. The foliage is in wide sprays in which the length of side branchlets reduces regularly towards the dominant leader, resulting in a triangular outline quite different to the rounded spray of 'Nidiformis', and although there is much overlapping the spray lies in a flat plane.

It seems probable that there are several forms of 'Tamariscifolia' about and I incline to the opinion that we have several clones in cultivation derived from different seedlings, but the differences between them does not seem to be sufficient to justify separate cultivar names.

– – **'Tharandtensis'** is a mystery plant that seems to have been lost to cultivation—at any rate I have been unable to locate it—and the so-called "*forsteckiana glauca*" sometimes seen on labels always turns out to be a plant of 'Tharandtensis Caesia'.

– – **'Tharandtensis Caesia'.** This could broadly be likened to a coarse, upright-growing form of 'Forsteckensis' with grey-green to blue-green leaves. Small propagations of these two forms are very difficult to tell apart but as soon as they begin to grow the habit and colouring of 'Tharandtensis Caesia' is very distinctive. This cultivar is much the better for having its long shoots pruned well back occasionally. This keeps the bush dense and postpones the degeneration into typical *C. lawsoniana* foliage which is usually the ultimate fate of all these seedling forms. I have found it unsatisfactory on soil that had been dressed with lime.

128

– – **'Wisselii Nana'** is a charming little extremely slow-growing cultivariant from the well-known tall cultivar 'Wisselii'. A few plants are about in private collections, greatly prized by their proud owners, but I do not think it is at present obtainable in the nursery trade in this country. Cuttings from 'Wisselii' taken from low down on the tree, where weak shoots develop from buds from old wood should give rise to plants of 'Wisselii Nana'.

'Wisselii' itself, after having hung about for several years will run up to 5 m and worse in a very short time, so is no use on a rockery, but where there is room for a fairly large bush it can be used with great effect by taking a young and well-branched plant and cutting the leader right out so as to encourage the branches to develop, repeating this treatment with any strong vertical shoots to encourage sub-laterals. Grown in this way 'Wisselii' forms a large plant as wide as it is high and consisting of a mass of spire-like shoots. I should like to see an old plant on a big lawn that had been so treated.

Chamaecyparis nootkatensis. This is a species of tall tree with dull green thujoid foliage without any white glaucous marking on the underside. The leaves on the main axis are equal in length, appressed with free tips. It has given us the following dwarf forms:

– – **'Compacta'.** This forms a dense pyramidal bush to about 2 m high with typical foliage. It is very hardy, but not particularly outstanding, as a garden plant. In America there is a glaucous form sold as **'Compacta Glauca',** but of this form I only have small plants. It seems to be a blue-green form of 'Compacta' with the same habit of growth but of a much more interesting colour.

According to Dr Boom "*nana*" is merely a collective name intended to cover all these dwarf forms.

Chamaecyparis obtusa. This species comes from Japan, where it forms a large tree. The foliage is distinguished by its obtuse (blunt ended, i.e. not pointed) leaves with white, waxy, X-shaped markings beneath. The foliage is thujoid and the leaves are in pairs, alternately lateral and facing, the lateral pair much larger than the facing, both pairs appressed to the stem with only the blunt tips free. The species has given rise to numerous dwarf garden forms. These are probably all seedling mutations so are not liable to reversion. Nature normally preserves her species by making her freaks sterile, but just occasionally she lets one by and it is to just such an occurrence that we owe a number of most interesting and extremely dwarf forms of *C. obtusa*. For several years before the First World War a large plant of 'Nana Gracilis' in the Red Lodge Nursery, at that time near Southampton, set viable seeds although this dwarf form is usually sterile. The nursery foreman, one George Gardner, sowed these and from them raised a very large number of seedlings. The value of these was not at first realized but when Hornibrook was writing his second edition a number of these seedlings were selected for naming and given such names as 'Minima', 'Caespitosa',

▲ 62 *Chamaecyparis obtusa* 'Caespitosa'.

▲ 63 *Chamaecyparis obtusa* 'Coralliformis'. Dark green with thread-like foliage and red-brown stems.

◄ 64 *Chamaecyparis obtusa* 'Chilworth'. A small plant, but the tree-like habit and the horizontally held, recurved, light-green sprays are characteristic.

'Laxa', 'Intermedia', etc., and these have since been propagated and are now in fairly easy supply, although alas, not always under their correct names. A number of the plants that were not selected were grown on and sold over the years to collectors in this country and in America and some of these have been given names based upon personalities in the Red Lodge Nursery or local place names such as 'Verdonii', 'Bassett', 'Chilworth' and so on. These are occasionally met with in private collections, but they do not appear to have hitherto been validly published, and some are not in circulation, not having at the time been regarded by the raisers as sufficiently distinctive to justify recognition as separate cultivars. I give a description of all the forms I consider worth separating. It is quite a long list—perhaps too long—and I suggest that a very good case ought to be made out before it is added to.

CHAMAECYPARIS

My descriptions of all these attractive little forms have been taken from the mother plants at Red Lodge Nurseries and have been kindly verified for me by Mr Verdon, the present proprietor, or his able assistant Mr R. D. Bunce.

Mr Gardner, who when I last saw him had just celebrated his 100th birthday, seems, as well as his skill, to have been favoured with more than his normal share of luck, for he it was who also sowed some seeds from a golden form of *Thuja plicata* growing in the same nursery and from the sowing raised the three excellent cultivars 'Cuprea', 'Rogersii' and 'Stoneham Gold' described under that species.

Some of the very tiny forms of *C. obtusa* are frost tender and liable to sun scorch in summer, so are plants for the cold greenhouse or a frame, but save for this all are reasonably hardy and easy to manage, and many of them give (at least to the European eye) a subtle suggestion of what is Japanese to any garden.

– – **'Albospica'** is a slow-growing, compact, conical form reaching to 2 m high, densely branched, the young shoots at first creamy-white, changing later in the year to pale green.

– – **'Bassett'** is the first of the Red Lodge seedlings, less well known than some. It is not unlike 'Juniperoides' but forms a much taller plant, with ascending branches, and the foliage is a darker green.

– – **'Caespitosa'** is another of the Red Lodge introductions, one of the smallest. It forms a tiny, dense bun of very dark-green, cup-like sprays with tiny, tightly appressed, scale-like leaves. It is one of the smallest conifers in existence. Not unlike it for size is **'Minima'** (at one time distributed as "*tetragona minima*"), but in that variety the foliage is of a very light green, the cup-like cupressoid sprays are absent and in their place there is a close mass of ascending branches and branchlets tetragonal (i.e. four-sided) in cross-section. It is, if anything, even slower growing and smaller than 'Caespitosa', and usually forms a denser, hemispherical cushion, a twenty-year-old plant being still but a few inches high (*Ill. 74*).

– – **'Chilworth'** is another of the forms we owe to Mr Gardner's green fingers. It has not become so well known as some of the forms but is sufficiently distinctive to justify its becoming better known than it is. It forms an upright and quite "tree-like" plant with light green, tiny leaf sprays which are recurved. It is a form which should appeal to "Bonzai" addicts.

– – **'Contorta'** forms a slow-growing, conical plant, eventually to 2 m, with dense foliage which is twisted and contorted in what, to my eye, is not a particularly attractive manner. It is possible that this type of growth is due to the presence of a virus or some similar derangement of the plant's normality as it will occasionally throw out strong, uncharacteristic growth.

– – **'Coralliformis'** is usually seen as a low, rounded bush in which the normal frondose sprays are entirely absent and instead the foliage is thread-like and cupressoid. The

▲ 65 *Chamaecyparis obtusa* 'Ericoides' (syn. 'Chabo Yadori'). See *Ill. 81*.

◄ 66 *Chamaecyparis obtusa* 'Crippsii'. Not a dwarf form. Rich golden-yellow.

branches and branchlets tend to grow twisted and occasionally monstrous and this constitutes the main attraction of the plant. It should not be confused with 'Lycopodioides' as its foliage has no trace of the coarse, bloated appearance of that variety, nor with *C. lawsoniana* 'Lycopodioides', as it lacks the pointed, free-standing leaf tips of that variety, although the twisted growth is very similar. As a young plant it is rather weedy-looking and insignificant but it fills out in a few years, especially if any lanky growth is shortened back regularly.

I must confess to being unable to distinguish **'Tsatsumi'** from 'Coralliformis' but I am told that it makes a smaller and more bun-like plant with finer, denser and less twisted foliage.

– – **'Crippsii'.** This variety is really too big for inclusion here. It is the well-known golden-yellow conifer of gardens, but if it can be given sufficient room, or used as a background plant it is excellent and I have seen it very effectively grown as a broad bush (presumably by cutting out the leader at about 60 cm). Grown in this way it was most attractive, both colour and branching habit being in its favour.

– – **'Ericoides'.** The only plant rightly entitled to this name is a dense little bushlet with light green, truly juvenile foliage but with the tips of the branchlets here and there all over the bush showing small amounts of the characteristic and unmistakable adult *C. obtusa* foliage.

It should not be confused with 'Sanderi' although this is frequently done.

132

67 *Chamaecyparis obtusa* 'Filicoides' in Jan van Gelderen nursery, Boskoop, Holland.

– – **'Filicoides'** is a fairly strong-growing variety often seen as a small and rather open tree, but it can (by systematic pruning back of all strong shoots) be grown as an attractive bush. It is characterized by the development of side shoots from the axial buds of the lateral leaves only, so has flat, fernlike sprays. This peculiarity of foliage is quite unique to this cultivar, so 'Filicoides' is unlikely to be confused, except with very similar foliage on *Thuja occidentalis* 'Spiralis'. This latter can at once be distinguished by the acrid smell of the bruised foliage characteristic of that species.

This plant, as suggested above, needs a fair space for its proper development, but there is a very attractive tiny form with similar foliage much smaller in all its parts for which I suggest the name **'Pygmy Fernspray'.** There is a very nice plant of this variety not far from the foot of the rockery at Wisley. This rare form has long been known under the unsuitable name "*compacta*", or the descriptive (but now illegitimate) name "*filicoides compacta*". It is very difficult to propagate, a fact which may rule out the possibility of its being a cultivariant of 'Filicoides', but one which will make it always difficult in supply.

– – **'Flabelliformis'** forms a globose, later upright, plant with short, fan-shaped sprays. The leaves are tiny, a light green with a glaucous bloom. 'Flabelliformis' resembles 'Juniperoides' but has bluer foliage.

– – **'Gracilis'** is a very strong-growing variety not to be confused with 'Nana Gracilis' (below). It is not a dwarf form.

– – **'Hage'** is a very dwarf form with dark-green foliage very similar to 'Nana', but the tips of the leaves sometimes yellow-brown in winter. It can be met with under various names, such as "*hagei*" and "*Hage variety*", occasionally with Hage spelled Hague, and many plants distributed under this name in England are not of this variety.

133

68 *Chamaecyparis obtusa* 'Juniperoides'.

69 *Chamaecyparis obtusa* 'Intermedia'. Intermediate between 'Nana' and the so-called "tennis-ball" cypresses.

70 *Chamaecyparis obtusa* 'Juniperoides Compacta'. Large specimens tend to be a little looser, with growth pendulous at the outside edge of the plant.

– – **'Intermedia'** is one of the Red Lodge forms, which as its name indicates is a pygmy form intermediate between 'Nana' and the very minute "tennis-ball" cypresses. It is, in my opinion, the smallest form that can be considered practicable for the open garden, except in sheltered districts. The foliage is a very dark green.

– – **'Juniperoides'** is another very dwarf globose form with dark-green foliage in open and rather "wiry"-looking, fan-shaped, decurving sprays. Not to be confused therewith is another form **'Juniperoides Compacta'** which, as the name would suggest, is generally similar in appearance but of more compact growth. The foliage is a yellow-green and the tiny, confused leaf sprays are down-cupped, with the tips drooping.

– – **'Kosteri'** is one of the most attractive forms of all. It might be regarded as intermediate between 'Nana' and 'Pygmaea' but it is quite distinctive because every spray of the plant is twisted, one lateral turning down and the lateral opposite turning up. This gives the plant a most distinctive appearance and it is quite characteristic of this variety which is therefore one of the easiest to recognize. Left to itself it forms a rather

134

71 *Chamaecyparis obtusa* 'Kosteri' in the Royal
Nurseries, Merriott, Somerset. Untrained plants are
more spreading.

72 *Chamaecyparis obtusa* 'Lycopodioides'.

sprawling bush not unlike 'Pygmaea' but I consider that it is best grown with a central stem trained up as a leader. If this be done the horizontal branches spread out in layers like a wedding cake and the attractiveness of the foliage is seen at its best. The layer-like effect referred to can be accentuated with a little discreet thinning out of the foliage.

– – **'Laxa'.** This was one of the biggest of Mr Gardner's batch of seedlings from 'Nana Gracilis'. It was referred to by Hornibrook as a loose, open-growing plant intermediate between 'Nana' and 'Nana Gracilis', but Messrs Rogers who raised it tell me they have lost the variety and do not know who had it. A plant in the alpine house at Wisley, about 50 cm high, corresponds well with Hornibrook's description, with its dark-green, open sprays, and could well be the original seedling.

– – **'Lycopodioides'.** This is an interesting dwarf form which forms a globose shrub when young and eventually a tall, open shrub to 2 m. The main branches are ascending and rather few and irregular. The branchlets are thick and often cockscomb-like at the tips; the leaves are irregular, dense and set all round the branches. The foliage is dark green and the monstrous growth give the whole plant a curiously bloated appearance.

The variety tends to form a rather open and gaunt tree but this can be checked by pruning back strong growth when young. There is also **'Lycopodioides Aurea'** which is slower growing and in which the young growth in spring and summer is a clear

135

74 *Chamaecyparis obtusa* 'Minima'. A fine old specimen at Wisley.

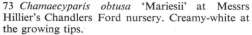

73 *Chamaecyparis obtusa* 'Mariesii' at Messrs Hillier's Chandlers Ford nursery. Creamy-white at the growing tips.

butter-yellow. Beissner refers to a number of monstrous forms under Japanese names but these are apparently no longer in European cultivation.

– – **'Mariesii'.** This is a very attractive, slow-growing dwarf form which makes a conical bush to about 1 m high, characterized by the leaves being yellowish-white to milk-white in summer, rather more yellowish-green in winter. The foliage is very thin and the bush tends to be open and sparsely covered unless checked by shortening the strong growing tips.

The best plant I know of this variety is in Messrs Hilliers' nursery at Chandlers Ford. The stock plant in the Nursery Trial Grounds at Boscoop in Holland measures 1·25 m high by 1 m across. It was badly damaged in the winter of 1962–3.

In the National Botanic Garden at Glasnevin, Dublin, there is a low bun-shaped plant which answers exactly to Hornibrook's description of **'Nana Argentea'.** It is the only plant of this variety that I have met and would appear to be identical with *C. obtusa* f. *nana albovariegata* Beissn. 1891, described as a very dwarf white-variegated form.

– – **'Minima'.** See page 131 under 'Caespitosa'.

– – **'Nana'.** This cultivar raises a nomenclatural problem of the greatest difficulty.

In his Second Edition Hornibrook gives a very good description of the true 'Nana' and states that it can be readily distinguished from 'Nana Gracilis' (apart from the difference in habit and the extreme slowness in growth of 'Nana') by the colour of the foliage, that of 'Nana' being very dark and dull green whilst that of 'Nana Gracilis' is a lustrous, deep green. He could well have added a reference to the difference in the way the sprays are held—those in 'Nana' lying more or less horizontally, each little spray curved downwards in one direction and upwards in the opposite direction,

136

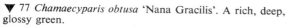
▲ 75 *Chamaecyparis obtusa* 'Nana'. Detail of leaf-spray.

76 *Chamaecyparis obtusa* 'Nana' (TRUE). An old specimen in Arboretum Trompenburg, Rotterdam. ▶

▼ 77 *Chamaecyparis obtusa* 'Nana Gracilis'. A rich, deep,
glossy green.

▼ 78 *Chamaecyparis obtusa* 'Nana Compacta'.

somewhat in the manner of a horse-saddle (this is well brought out in the illustration on page 137) whereas the sprays of 'Nana Gracilis' are usually flat and are held up rather stiffly at random in every direction. Hornibrook states that the true 'Nana' is very rare, but goes on to say that most of the specimens to be found in cultivation under that name are in reality 'Nana Gracilis', but with this I disagree, for (at any rate in the English nursery trade) the plants that are usually supplied as 'Nana', whilst admittedly of much the same colouring as 'Nana Gracilis' are definitely of a slower-growing clone, without the tendency to form an upright plant which characterizes 'Nana Gracilis'.

I see that Mr Hillier claims that **'Nana Densa'** quoted by Hornibrook as a synonym is a distinct plant, so we cannot use that name. In the bad old days to coin the name "pseudo-nana" would have been the easy way out, but because of the ban now put upon latinized names we are in a dilemma; the rules require a fancy name in non-Latin form, but this bright green form has been so widely distributed as 'Nana' that were I to propose a new fancy name I feel sure it would just not be used. In the 1960 Edition of *Die Nadelgehölze*, Krussmann mentions **'Nana Compacta'** which he describes as a bright green dwarf form, growth dense and rounded but with young shoots protruding here and there. This description so far as it goes meets our plant and the illustration on his page 103 could very well be an older specimen of it than I have ever seen. The legitimacy of the name 'Nana Compacta' would depend on whether it was published prior to 1st January 1959, but subject to this I propose this name for the bright-green plant of the colour of, but much slower growing than, 'Nana Gracilis', now being sold in this country as 'Nana'. That name should, in future, be strictly restricted to the true 'Nana', which is the dark, dull-green form described by Hornibrook. It is still not at all common, but is obtainable, with a little searching.

– – **'Nana Aurea'.** This is a more vigorous plant than 'Nana', reaching to 2 m with age. The fan-shaped foliage sprays are golden-yellow on the outside of the bush and yellowish-green away from the light. Krussmann in *Die Nadelgehölze*, has a very good photograph of this form.

– – **'Nana Gracilis'.** This is a very attractive strong-growing form reaching 2–3 m high in time, making a pyramidal bush with rich, lustrous green, healthy-looking foliage and a somewhat rugged and picturesque outline.

It is too well-known to need much description and should be in every garden where there is room for it. It is often supplied instead of 'Nana'.

– – **'Nana Lutea'** seems (rather unfortunately on account of its similarity to 'Nana Aurea') to be the legitimate name of a very nice, new, golden form raised by the Dutch nursery firm Spek of Boscoop. Like so many of these dwarf forms it is loose and open when grafted, but on its own roots it forms a neat, compact little bush with leaf sprays about equivalent to 'Intermedia' but of the clear golden-yellow of *C. lawsoniana* 'Lutea Nana', and the colour is well maintained throughout the year.

79 *Chamaecyparis obtusa* 'Repens' in the Nursery Trial-grounds at Boskoop, Holland. 'Pygmaea' is similar in habit, but less vigorous and different in colour.

– – **'Pygmaea'.** This is one of the most desirable forms and an old, well-grown plant always draws attention to itself. It forms a low, spreading bush always much wider than high, with the flat fan-shaped sprays lying closely one above the other. The difference between this cultivar and **'Pygmaea Aurescens'** is mainly one of colour, but in the Pygmy Pinetum the latter is definitely the stronger grower of the two, and it occasionally throws out strong horizontal shoots quite unlike the fan-shaped sprays of 'Pygmaea'. During the greater part of the year 'Pygmaea' is quite green and 'Pygmaea Aurescens' is brownish-green; in the autumn and winter 'Pygmaea' takes on a slight bronze colour whereas 'Pygmaea Aurescens' turns a rich copper-bronze. There should be no difficulty in telling them apart, but 'Pygmaea Aurescens' is not infrequently labelled 'Pygmaea'.

This is a variety that seems to be particularly susceptible to the influence of root-stock vigour when grafted. At the Westonbirt Arboretum near Tetbury in Gloucester-shire there is a plant labelled 'Pygmaea' which is of an upright, pyramidal shape about 2·5 m high, although cuttings taken and rooted from this plant form the normal prostrate plant. There is a plant of similar shape at Messrs Waterer's nursery at Knap Hill, Surrey, which I should imagine is another grafted plant.

– – **'Repens'.** This is another prostrate form much the same in habit as 'Pygmaea'

139

▲ 81 *Chamaecyparis obtusa* 'Sanderi'. Often wrongly called 'Ericoides'. See *Ill. 65*.

◀ 80 *Chamaecyparis obtusa* 'Tetragona Aurea'.

but very much stronger and coarser in growth and always green in colour, with no trace of bronze.

– – **'Rigid Dwarf'** (syn. "*rigida*"). This is a distinct form, of upright growth and of a stiff and rigid appearance. The main branches sweep up to a nearly vertical position, the foliage is dark green and the leaf sprays hang down like the bent fingers of one's hand held palm downwards.

– – **'Sanderi'.** This is a mystery plant. It was first described in this country as *Juniperus sanderi* and later as *Chamaecyparis obtusa* 'Ericoides'.

It is normally seen as a low round bush (although there was at one time at Bedgebury a plant 2 m high) and it bears juvenile foliage stouter and stiffer than any of the other recorded juvenile forms. In summer its foliage and branchlets are a wonderful glaucous sea-green and in winter they take on the bloom and colour of a blue plum. It is not particularly hardy and should be given shelter from wind during the winter. Whatever its true taxonomic position it certainly has no title to the cultivar named 'Ericoides' which belongs to quite a different plant. Mr J. W. Archer of Farnham and others insist that it is a Juniper because of the smell of its foliage, but until something can be proved as to this it should retain the name I have given it here.

– – **'Spiralis'.** This is an upright-growing form with a stiff habit; the sprays are cup-shaped and curiously twisted around the smaller branchlets: a very distinct and outstanding form, but not a particularly attractive one.

140

– – 'Tempelhof'. A compact, broadly ovoid to pyramidal bush eventually reaching 2·5 m. The leaf sprays are fan-shaped, green to yellowish-green, often with a brownish tint (similar to 'Pygmaea Aurescens'), especially during the winter.

– – 'Tetragona Aurea'. This, when well grown, is one of the most beautiful dwarf conifers we have. It is usually seen in gardens as a small or medium-size bush, but it would seem to respond considerably to the selection of propagating material, because whilst there is, for example, in Mr G. L. Pilkington's garden at Grayswood Hill, Haslemere, Surrey, a plant of this variety about 6 m high, I have seen minute and obviously old and slow-growing bushlets only a few centimetres high. It is distinct from all other forms both in its habit and its colouring. The growth in a good plant is very congested, the main branches being long and gracefully curved, densely set and closely packed with secondary branches from the axils of both facing and lateral leaves, giving the tetragonal cross section to the twig from which it gets its name.

The colour in full sunlight is a rich bronze-gold but it only needs a relatively small amount of over-shading from nearby trees or buildings for this to be reduced to a poor yellowish-green. On the other hand, in full shade it develops a dark, rich, blue-green which is quite attractive. The plant is not a particularly easy one to grow; it tends to throw its strength into the main leading growths and become bare at the base and in the interior of the bush. This characteristic seems to be accentuated by the susceptibility of this variety to drought in the summer and to wind scorch in the winter, both conditions apparently encouraging it to shed some of its foliage. It can be kept dense by regular shortening of strong shoots.

The alleged 'Tetragona' (i.e. the green form of the above) is a mystery plant. In his Second Edition Hornibrook tells of its introduction from Japan and of its having been subsequently lost by the importer, and throws down a challenge to his readers to search for this form. Ever since it has been a sort of horticultural "Holy Grail" but even so it has never to my knowledge turned up, although I myself have on at least three occasions triumphantly returned home with cuttings from a green plant, only to find that when the resulting plants were set out in full sunlight they developed the normal golden colouring. There seem three main possibilities, these being:

(a) That there is no such plant, but the propagations received in 1871, having been at first kept in cold frames and other sheltered spots, remained green but by 1875 they had been planted out in the open and allowed to develop their proper golden colour.

(b) That the gauntlet thrown down by Hornibrook still lies for one of us to pick up, and

(c) That it is synonymous with 'Filicoides'. This is Mr Hillier's theory, first put forward I believe in his lecture on Dwarf Conifers at the International Conference of the Alpine Garden Society in 1961.

My difficulty about this theory is that the foliage of 'Filicoides' never develops a tetragonal cross section, nor have I ever seen a golden form of 'Filicoides' propagated from '*Tetragona Aurea*'. My own feeling is that (a) is the most acceptable theory and I believe that Rehder must have felt so too for he drops the suffix Aurea when describing our 'Tetragona Aurea'. But this I feel is taking a very great risk unless and until someone can *prove* that the green form has never existed, and, of course, a negative statement is very difficult to prove, so it would therefore seem best to leave the names as they are and let the doubt remain as to whether the green form will ever turn up. A form which came to me from Messrs Duncan & Davies Ltd of New Plymouth, New Zealand, under the name **'Kojolcohiba'** is very similar to 'Tetragona Aurea' in foliage, but Mr Trevor Davies tells me that it is a strong grower and forms a conical plant with steeply ascending branches. So far, in the Pygmy Pinetum it gives promise of being a much better "doer" than 'Tetragona Aurea', being less sensitive to sun and wind.

82 *Chamaecyparis obtusa* 'Tonia'. A variegated sport from 'Nana Compacta' or 'Nana Gracilis'.

– – **'Tonia'.** This is a variegated sport from plant of 'Nana Gracilis' which originated in the nursery of William Hage & Co. of Boscoop in about 1928. Plants I have seen are much weaker in growth and with a smaller leaf spray than 'Nana Gracilis'. The variegation is uncertain and spasmodic, and apparently young plants may make several years' growth before any white patches appear. These are a clear white contrasting well with the dark green normal foliage, but I consider the plant more a horticultural curiosity than a thing of beauty.

142

CHAMAECYPARIS

Chamaecyparis pisifera. This is another Japanese species of tree-like proportions which has given us a number of garden forms. Within the species we find true dwarfs, thread-leaf forms and forms with fixed juvenile and semi-juvenile foliage, but whilst these last retain their juvenile foliage they do not all remain dwarf, some of them being prepared to grow to a height of 9 m or more in this country. As a tree of this size with juvenile foliage is quite attractive they have their garden value but they cannot be regarded as dwarf forms. They do, however, stand heavy pruning, so can be kept within bounds to some extent.

As the group names appear in some of the cultivar names but not all, I give below a table of these so that they can be readily found in the alphabetical descriptions that follow:

THE SQUARROSA GROUP   Fixed Juvenile Foliage

Leaves resemble the seed-leaves; long, free-standing, decurved; no distinction between facing and lateral pairs of leaves.

'Boulevard' (syn. 'Cyano-viridis')
'Ericoides'
'Squarrosa Argentea Compacta'
'Squarrosa Dumosa'

'Squarrosa Intermedia' (syn. 'Dwarf Blue')
'Squarrosa Lutea'
'Squarrosa Minima' (syn. 'Pygmaea')
'Squarrosa Sulphurea'

THE PLUMOSA GROUP   Fixed Semi-juvenile Foliage

The free-standing part of the leaf is shorter and closer to the stem. Leaves are folded along the mid-rib and there may be some slight difference between the facing and lateral pairs. A definite branching system is more or less in evidence.

'Plumosa Albo-picta'
'Plumosa Argentea Nana'
'Plumosa Aurea'
'Plumosa Aurea Compacta'
'Plumosa Aurea Nana'
'Plumosa Compressa' (met with under a variety of names)

'Plumosa Flavescens'
'Plumosa Nana Aurea'
'Plumosa Pygmaea'
'Plumosa Pygmaea Aurea'
'Plumosa Rogersii' (syn. "*plumosa aurea rogersii*")

THE FILIFERA GROUP   Thread-leaved Foliage

Main branches often have 5 to 6 pairs of leaves (or more) without branchlets and with extended entre-nœud; branchlets usually develop in clusters and the foliage tends to the cupressoid form.

'Filifera' (Not a dwarf form)
'Filifera Aurea' (Not a dwarf form)
'Filifera Argenteovariegata'
'Filifera Aureovariegata'

'Filifera Gracilis'
'Filifera Nana'
'Gold Spangle'
'Golden Mop' (New name)

143

▲ 84 *Chamaecyparis pisifera* 'Aurea Nana'.

◀ 83 *Chamaecyparis pisifera* 'Boulevard' (syn. "*cyanoviridis*").

THE NANA GROUP   Dwarf and Pygmy Forms

'Aurea Nana'	'Nana'
'Compacta'	'Nana Aureovariegata'
'Compacta Variegata'	'Nana Variegata'

– – **'Aurea Nana'.** This is a very slow-growing and dwarf form which forms a conical or roundish bush having foliage of a rich golden-yellow colour, but otherwise typical of *C. pisifera*. It should not be confused with 'Plumosa Nana Aurea' described later. It is occasionally sent out as "*aurea compacta*".

– – **'Boulevard'.** This is quite a new-comer, and seldom does a fresh introduction amongst garden conifers make such a rapid advance in popularity. It is assumed to be a form of *C. pisifera* with juvenile foliage and is often sold under the name "*squarrosa cyanoviridis*", but the name 'Boulevard', from the American nursery which introduced it into cultivation, has priority.

Whether or not it is a form of *C. pisifera* (which is at least doubtful) and whether or not it is a dwarf form (which is more than doubtful) it is deservedly popular for its attractive foliage and wonderful colour which, when well grown, is a beautiful and outstanding silvery blue-grey, and as it seems to stand heavy pruning it should be possible to keep it within bounds in a given situation for a good many years.

144

5 *Chamaecyparis pisifera* 'Compacta Variegata'.

86 *Chamaecyparis pisifera* 'Nana'. Note the much denser type of growth.

In soils containing lime the true colour fails to develop and instead the plant assumes an unattractive dirty brown, but whatever the soil the colour always seems to be better in shade and although it seems thoroughly hardy the plant will give of its best colour when grown in a cold house, especially during the winter months.

It is now freely available in the trade and is deservedly popular.

– – **'Compacta'.** There is considerable confusion in the nomenclature of the truly dwarf forms, due perhaps in part to the fact that Hornibrook failed to distinguish between 'Compacta' and the very much closer and tighter-growing **'Nana'.**

'Compacta' forms a fairly compact, low-growing, bun-shaped bush bearing wholly adult foliage; mostly in compact, tightly packed sprays which are somewhat recurved, but occasionally it sends out much stronger growth, which does not develop the normal, congested foliage until the next growing season, and by this means the plant increases in size, whereas 'Nana' is a very much smaller plant with smaller, tighter and altogether more congested foliage, consistently remaining one of the lowest and smallest dwarf forms we have. In both cases the colour is dark green.

– – **'Compacta Variegata'.** Having established the distinction between 'Compacta' and 'Nana' we can now justify the use by Hornibrook of this name for a sport from 'Compacta' with a fairly bold variegation in light yellow or white flecks or splashes. In habit the plant is looser than the green form and in time it will form a bush 1·5 m high by 2 m or more across. There is no general golden sheen over the whole plant. This variety is usually offered in the trade as 'Nana Aureovariegata', a name belonging to another plant described below.

– – **'Ericoides'.** Hornibrook gives a full description of this variety, which he states to have been very rare in cultivation at the time he wrote, any plants offered under this name by nurserymen invariably turning out to be *C. thyoides* 'Ericoides', and this situation seems still to apply. See also page 154.

145

87 *Chamaecyparis pisifera* 'Filifera Nana'.

– – **'Filifera'.** This cultivar is not a dwarf form but has given its name to a useful group of garden forms with thread-like foliage.

– – **'Filifera Argenteovariegata'.** This is a form with a creamy-yellow variegation in bold splashes all over the plant which is fairly strong-growing, forming in time a large bush 1–1·5 m high. It is an attractive form and should be more widely planted than it is. **'Filifera Aureovariegata'** is very similar but with the variegation a slightly deeper yellow. You would, however, need to have the two plants growing side by side to be sure of the difference.

– – **'Filifera Aurea'.** This cultivar, like 'Filifera', is not a dwarf and will form an erect plant 4–5 m high, but there is a most desirable low-growing form which maintains a wonderful golden colour throughout the bush. It is considered by the purists a little out of character on a rockery but is very effective in a group of dwarf conifers or when grown as a specimen bush in the open.

In the case of the green variety a dwarf form has been distinguished by the suffix 'Nana', but I do not think that this has ever been validly done for the golden form and it is, of course, not now permissible, so I propose the cultivar name **'Golden Mop'** for the low-growing, denser form of the cultivar 'Filifera Aurea'. It is quite stable in cultivation.

146

– – **'Filifera Gracilis'.** This is a very attractive and uncommon form with foliage an unusual and attractive yellowish-green. Its foliage is slightly more slender and regular than in the other 'Filifera' forms and it remains a dense little bush that should be seen more frequently than it is. It is occasionally offered as **'Filifera Flava'** which was described as of a sulphur-yellow colour and appears to have been lost to cultivation.

– – **'Filifera Nana'.** This is merely a low-growing form of 'Filifera', with the same garden use as 'Golden Mop' already described, and differing only in colour, which is deep green.

– – **'Gold Spangle'.** This, I understand, arose as a sporting branch on a plant of 'Filifera Aurea'. It bears foliage intermediate between the thread-leaf form of that cultivar and the typical leaf and of the same bright golden-yellow colour. It is not a dwarf form, but it can be kept down by hard pruning to the size of a large bush and, so grown, can be very attractive.

– – **'Nana'** has already been described on page 145.

– – **'Nana Aureovariegata'.** This, as quite correctly described and named by Hornibrook, is a form of 'Nana', making the same very dense bun-shaped cushion but with a wonderful golden sheen all over the plant. It looks its best in sunshine and is a most desirable variety, reliably dwarf and slow-growing, but apt to revert to the green form in patches. These should be cut away at once.

– – **'Nana Variegata'.** This variety, not mentioned by Hornibrook, is a form of 'Nana' with a small white and not very effective variegation. It is often incorrectly sold as "*nana albo-variegata*".

It is possible that all these forms have a common origin and that the forms of 'Compacta' were derived from the 'Nana' forms by the selection of coarse-growing wood for cuttings, and this theory is perhaps borne out by the fact that the variegated forms are variable and that intermediate forms can often be found in different parts of the same bush. For this reason, care should be taken by pruning and the selection of propagating material to preserve the types I have described and especially the typical, tight-growing forms of 'Nana'.

– – **'Plumosa'.** With this cultivar and its golden form **'Plumosa Aurea'** we have nothing to do in this book as they are both forms which will reach to 10 m, but the former has given its name to a large group of dwarf forms in the nomenclature of which, unfortunately, there is a great deal of confusion.

The word "Plumosa" is used in this connection to indicate a semi-juvenile type of foliage intermediate between the "Squarrosa" forms with their long, free-standing foliage and the adult type, and it has no connection with the botanical term "plumose" (which means "feather-like") for which I prefer the word "frondose" (i.e. like the frond of a fern).

In most of the "Plumosa" forms the leaf is much shorter and is pressed close to or attached to the stem for part of its length with only the tip standing free, and the branching system shows a definite pattern, with a tendency for the laterals to lie in the same plane, giving just the suggestion of being frondose. Unfortunately, care has not always been exercised in the naming of these forms and there are several named as "Plumosa" in which the foliage is actually much nearer "Squarrosa".

– – **'Plumosa Albopicta'.** This is a slow-growing form which makes an upright bush eventually to about 2 m, with exceptionally small leaves. These are dark green with numerous small areas of white which give the whole plant a speckled appearance.

It is attractive, especially as a young plant, but as the variegation is quite ineffective seen at a distance it should be planted close to a path or in a spot in which it would be observed from close at hand. The variegation is retained throughout the year, but is brightest in the spring and summer.

– – **'Plumosa Argentea'.** This is a variety which I do not know. It is described as similar to 'Plumosa' but with the branchlets developing silvery-white and green leaves, changing to green in their second year.

– – **'Plumosa Aurea Compacta'.** This forms a slow-growing globose (later sometimes upright) bush ultimately to 1·5–2 m. The foliage is a golden-yellow and is much nearer to "Squarrosa" than "Plumosa". Each leaf has two strongly-marked bands of white on the underside.

It is extremely difficult to distinguish between young propagations of this and 'Plumosa Rogersii' described later, but the white marking on the underside leaves of the latter is slightly less prominent and it will soon throw up a leader and begin to assume its characteristic conical shape, whereas 'Plumosa Aurea Compacta' soon develops into a rounded little bush.

– – **'Plumosa Aurea Nana'.** This is just a slow-growing form of the larger plant, presumably derived from it by selection of weak-growing cutting material. It bears rather small and typically "plumosa" foliage, which in the early summer is a beautiful golden-yellow. It is somewhat variable in the trade; some forms later turn to a dull green but the best form retains its golden colour throughout the year.

– – **'Plumosa Compacta'.** This is a green seedling form raised by den Ouden which I have not seen, but as it grows to 2 m it is hardly within the scope of this book. The name should not be used for a dwarf form of any kind.

– – **'Plumosa Compressa'.** This is probably the smallest form of *C. pisifera*. It was raised from a sporting branch of 'Squarrosa' by Van Nes of Boskoop.

It is a most popular and attractive and slow-growing little plant, bearing both "Squarrosa" and "Plumosa" type foliage of diminutive size which seems to vary in colour in different situations and seasons.

In its young state it looks like a tight, glaucous-green moss, and by a little systematic "clipping" in early summer with a pair of nail scissors it can be induced to form a small bun of an almost unbelievably solid appearance and tightness of foliage, but normally, older plants show variation of foliage and colour. Because of this variability, propagations have been made from time to time of likely branches, and to these have been given a wonderful variety of names. It would appear that as these names become more complex they became more difficult to memorize and more

148

▲ 88 *Chamaecyparis pisifera* 'Plumosa Albopicta'. The variegation is only effective when seen from close to the plant.

▲ 89 *Chamaecyparis pisifera* 'Plumosa Aurea'.

◄ 90 *Chamaecyparis pisifera* 'Plumosa Rogersii' (syn. "*plumosa aurea rogersii*").

▼ 91 *Chamaecyparis pisifera* 'Plumosa Compressa'. A fine specimen in the Slieve Donard Nurseries, Newcastle, Co. Down, N.I.

easy to quote differently next time, for one meets every possible combination of the words *"nana"*, *"compacta"*, *"aurea"*, *"glauca"* and others. I once received a nice little plant labelled *Chamaecyparis pisifera "plumosa flavescens aurea compacta nana"* which seemed to me to be carrying the joke a little too far.

This plant is susceptible to frost injury. In the spring as soon as new growth commences the dead growth should be cut out and usually a season's growth will close over the gap.

– – **'Plumosa Flavescens'.** This is quite a distinct and attractive form which is seldom met with. It forms a conical or globose bush never over 1 m high and its cultivar name (which means "yellowish" or "turning yellow") is quite descriptive of the foliage, which is smaller in the leaf and neater than in any other of the 'Plumosa' varieties, and at first is sulphur-yellow at the growing tips. It turns green by the autumn.

– – **'Plumosa Nana'.** This, according to Hornibrook was a sub-globose form which has been lost to cultivation but **'Plumosa Nana Aurea'** is quite a distinct and very uncommon variety which forms a low, compact, bun-shaped cushion. The leaves are much more of the "Squarrosa" type than "Plumosa" and are strongly recurved, a rich golden-yellow. A twig taken from the plant could be mistaken for 'Plumosa Aurea Compacta' or 'Plumosa Rogersii' but the low, slow growth and the bun-shaped habit of the plant make it distinct. Propagation material came to the Pygmy Pinetum from the Westonbirt Arboretum near Tetbury, Gloucestershire, where is the only sizeable plant of this variety that I know. It is not an easy plant, as it needs full light to develop its golden colour, yet is scorched easily by the sun.

– – **'Plumosa Pygmaea'.** On the rock garden in the National Botanic Garden at Glasnevin in Dublin there is a very old specimen about 1·5 m high bearing this name, and although I have not been able to trace it in any of the literature, I am assuming that because of its age it must have been published at some time or other and therefore be legitimate. The plant could be roughly described as a green form of 'Plumosa Rogersii'. Young plants form the same conical-shaped bush and it is an attractive plant which should be better known, having the great advantage that it seems to be thoroughly wind resistant.

In the same Botanic Garden there is a plant labelled *"plumosa aurea pygmaea"* or *"plumosa pygmaea aurea"* (I forget which), but as it is barely distinguishable from the green form for part of the year and indistinguishable therefrom for the remainder I consider that it is not worth perpetuating the distinction.

– – **'Plumosa Rogersii'.** This is a very popular form which forms a conical plant with golden-yellow foliage which is much nearer "Squarrosa" than "Plumosa" and which retains its colour all the winter.

Unfortunately it is a little wind tender, especially in the spring, so should be given a sheltered spot. This form is frequently sold as *"plumosa aurea rogersii"*, but there is no need for the *"aurea"*, and to avoid confusion in future this should be dropped.

150

Chamaecyparis pisifera 'Squarrosa Dumosa' at
Wansdyke Nursery, Devizes, Wilts.

93 Chamaecyparis pisifera 'Squarrosa Intermedia'.

– – **'Squarrosa Argentea Compacta'.** We now come to the last group—those with fixed
juvenile foliage—but again we have no business with the cultivar that gives its name
to the group because in spite of its juvenility of leaf it grows to a large tree. The slow-
growing form has probably been obtained by bud selection from the arboreal form
and remains a medium size bush, with attractive silvery-grey foliage.

– – **'Squarrosa Dumosa'.** This is a most attractive and truly dwarf form which forms
a dense, globose bush that I have never seen over 1 m in height, with fairly large-
leafed foliage which in summer is a quiet grey-green but which in winter takes on a
most attractive metallic-bronze appearance, giving the whole bush the suggestion of
the beauty of old pewter. It should be much more widely known than it is.

– – **'Squarrosa Intermedia'.** This is a very popular form, of which Hornibrook gives a
very detailed description. When properly grown it is seen as a low, rounded bush with
tightly packed congested foliage of the "Squarrosa" type but smaller in leaf than in
any of the other forms. But from time to time (it seems prone to do this more some
years than others) it throws out longer shoots with much more open foliage. If it is
desired to keep the bush small and dense-looking these should be cut away, but it
is by means of these longer shoots that the plant increases in size and they normally
develop the congested type of foliage the following year. But occasionally strong
coarse growth bearing adult foliage appears and this should be cut out as soon as it
appears, for if this is not done it will in a very short while become a lusty young tree
and the character of the plant will be lost entirely. It is not at all uncommon to find
plants labelled 'Squarrosa Intermedia' in collections which have gone to the devil

151

▲ 95 *Chamaecyparis pisifera* 'Squarrosa Minima'.

▲ 94 *Chamaecyparis thyoides* 'Andelyensis' (syn. "*leptoclada*").

◄ 96 *Chamaecyparis thyoides* 'Andelyensis Nana'.

▼ 97 *Chamaecyparis pisifera* 'Squarrosa Sulphurea'. The colour is sulphur-yellow in spring and summer.

152

in this way and are now tree-like plants with only a little of the 'Squarrosa' foliage here and there near the base to remind the visitor of "what might have been".

This variety was distributed by certain continental nurseries at one time as "*Blue Dwarf*" until its true identity was established.

– – **'Squarrosa Lutea'.** This is not a particularly good "doer" as, like many golden forms, it dislikes frost, sun and wind, but it is worth finding the right home for it because when it is happy it forms a most attractive, globose little plant. Its leaves are, I think, the longest of any 'Squarrosa' form and they are of the most wonderful golden-yellow colour throughout the year. **'Squarrosa Aurea'** appears to be a strong-growing, erect form of similar colouring but hardier constitution.

– – **'Squarrosa Minima'.** Hornibrook dithered a little between this name and "*squarrosa pygmaea*" but finally came down in favour of the present name. It is very similar to 'Intermedia' (and may indeed be a cultivariant of it) but as grown in this country it forms a slower-growing, denser and dwarfer plant with a much more neat outline than 'Intermedia' and smaller foliage, but it needs to be watched for reversion.

– – **'Squarrosa Sulphurea',** as its name indicates, is a variety with sulphur-yellow foliage. It forms a dense, conical plant and in spring and early summer is very outstanding because of its colour, but this turns to green later in the year and by winter the plant has only its neat outline and soft-looking foliage to distinguish it.

Chamaecyparis thyoides. This is a tree-like species from North America which has given us several attractive dwarf forms. In the type, the twigs are slender and bear triangular, sharply pointed leaves. The side twigs alternate, forming short, erect, fan-shaped sprays which are held irregularly, i.e. not in flat thujoid sprays as in other species in this genus. Most of the leaves are marked on the back with a resinous gland.

In nature it frequently is found growing in marshy ground or swamps, so the dwarf forms will presumably feel most at home in such conditions.

– – **'Andelyensis'** (syn. "*leptoclada*"). This well-known variety is not, strictly speaking, a dwarf but it is so very slow-growing that it can be used without much immediate concern regarding its ultimate height.

It slowly forms a tall, pointed column with upright branches bearing mainly adult foliage and coning freely. It was much planted years ago but now that we have other columnar forms available it is less in demand.

– – **'Andelyensis Nana'.** This is similar to the preceding cultivar but is a dwarf shrub, broader than high, with erect branches and bearing mostly juvenile foliage.

These forms are somewhat unstable. I have had a batch of cuttings of 'Andelyensis' in which one cutting grew up into the typical arboreal form, and 'Andelyensis Nana' will occasionally throw up a strong leader and lose its globular shape. This may be why the very small forms **'Nana'** (which would appear to have carried at least

153

predominantly adult foliage) and **'Pygmaea'** described by Hornibrook appear to have been lost to cultivation.

– – **'Ericoides'.** The plant which is widely grown under this name and alleged to be a fixed juvenile form of this species forms a regular very close-growing, compact, pyramidal bush, eventually to about 1·5 m high. The colour is a dark grey-green in summer, turning to deep purplish- or violet-brown in winter. It forms an attractive bush but is apt to be damaged by cold winds.

One occasionally comes across this plant labelled "*Chamaecyparis pisifera ericoides*" or even "*Thuja orientalis ericoides*", the taxonomic position of all these juvenile forms being still a little uncertain.

98 *Chamaecyparis thyoides* 'Ericoides'. Dark green in summer, plum-purple in winter.

CRYPTOMERIA

Cryptomeria japonica is the solitary occupant of this species. In nature it is a very tall tree but it is extremely variable from seed and has given us some of our best dwarf conifers. These vary considerably and an assorted group of *Cryptomeria* cultivars can be so diverse as to give rise to considerable surprise that they are all cultivated forms of a single species.

They are (with the exception of the white-tipped forms) very hardy, but most forms colour in the winter, the colour varying from a slight bronzing to a rich, reddish-bronze or purple. In some cases the winter colour provides a valuable means of distinguishing between varieties.

– – **'Araucarioides'.** This shares with 'Viminalis' the same general habit of growth—the few, long, main branches, the long side branches and the absence of branchlets, but the branching is a little more normal than in the case of that variety, so there are not the tufts which characterize 'Viminalis'. The leaves are thicker and more distinctly curved forward and are a *dark* green.

There is a large plant of this variety in Silkwood at the Westonbirt Arboretum, near Tetbury, Glos., also one at Hillier's Nursery at Chandlers Ford, Hants.

– – **'Athrotaxoides'** is very close to 'Araucarioides', if not identical with it. I have never seen it, but as they originated in the same garden my guess is that we here have merely a duplication of names.

– – **'Bandai-Sugi'.** This is a popular garden variety. It is usually seen as a low globular bush, but with age it can reach to 2 m high. The foliage is very congested and irregular, all the branches being thick and the leaves thick, broad and tapered. The entre-nœud is most erratic, some of the branchlets being of fairly strong growth with stiff, straight foliage pointing forward at an angle of 30°, very slightly incurved; other shoots being very short with short, closely-set leaves, some not more than 3 mm long. It should not be confused with 'Monstrosa Nana' in which the monstrous foliage occurs in distinct tufts at the ends of the longer shoots and in which the whole growth is coarser. The colour is green with a slight reddish hue in winter.

99 *Cryptomeria japonica* 'Bandai-Sugi'. Older plants are more irregular in outline.

155

100 *Cryptomeria japonica* 'Compacta' at the Royal Botanic Garden, Edinburgh. It is not a dwarf form.

101 *Cryptomeria japonica* 'Cristata'. Becomes a small tree in time.

– – **'Compacta'.** This is merely a compact form of the type with stiff, short, straight leaves. It is sometimes found in cultivation under the name of "*lobbii compacta*", a name which has served a turn for several plants.

– – **'Compressa'.** This is one of two pygmy globular forms very popular in gardens, the other form being 'Vilmoriniana' (described later). They both have short, densely set, neat, juvenile foliage and both form dense, globular bushes.

They are of about equal garden value and are often confused with each other, but they differ in that the leading shoots in 'Compressa' never project above the general surface of the bush as they do in the case of 'Vilmoriniana' (giving that variety a somewhat less neat and tidy appearance); in that the leaves in 'Compressa' are slightly more decurved than they are in 'Vilmoriniana' (giving the shoot a more rosette-like appearance looked at from the end), and in that 'Compressa' colours to a rich red-bronze in the winter compared to the much less pronounced colouring of 'Vilmoriniana'. Finally, the foliage on the interior of the bush is blue-green in the case of 'Compressa' and yellow-green in 'Vilmoriniana'.

– – **'Cristata'.** There are several forms in cultivation characterized by abnormality in parts of the foliage.

The form commonly grown under this name forms a fairly tall, upright bush or

156

▲ 102 *Cryptomeria japonica* 'Kilmacurragh'. The mother plant mentioned by Hornibrook.

103 *Cryptomeria japonica* 'Elegans Compacta'. A strong grower; very soft to the touch. ▶

low tree to 3 m high with some of its foliage quite normal but developing monstrous foliage here and there, the cristations occasionally being as large as a man's hand. The plant mentioned by Hornibrook as growing at Kilmacurragh, Rathdrum, Co. Wicklow is of quite a different type and for this I propose the cultivar name **'Kilmacurragh'**. In this cultivar the normal foliage is juvenile and the whole bush is covered with fasciated shoots. The original plant is still at Kilmacurragh (having now reached the height of 6 m) to serve as our type plant and there are specimens in the National Botanic Garden at Glasnevin, Dublin, the Royal Botanic Garden, Edinburgh, and in the Pygmy Pinetum at Devizes.

– – **'Elegans Compacta'.** This is merely a compact form of **'Elegans'**, which is the fixed juvenile foliage form of the type. The foliage is very long (to 20 mm) and thin and the leaves and branches are often gracefully curved. The whole plant is soft to the touch and it colours to a rich purple in winter. It forms a graceful, prosperous-looking bush to about 2 m. It is probable that the more correct name for this form would be 'Elegans Nana' but as this name has been widely used in the English nursery trade for another cultivar (see 'Lobbii Nana') I prefer 'Elegans Compacta'. It would in any case appear to be a cultivariant of 'Elegans', as plants of different vigour can be found, but I hardly think additional cultivar names are justified. I have received from New Zealand, under the name **'Elegans Aurea'**, a form which in winter turns a yellowish-green instead of the usual plum-purple, but what its ultimate size will be I cannot yet estimate.

– – **'Fasciata'.** This is a collectors' piece—more a curiosity than a thing of beauty. It forms a low stunted bush with some healthy-looking foliage but with the old wood studded with a curious, moss-like, leafy excrescence (one can hardly call it growth) which gives the bush an unhealthy appearance. There has been a good deal of uncertainty as to the correct name of this form and it has been going around under such parlour names as "*Nyewood Form*" and "*Clark's Mossy*".

157

104 *Cryptomeria japonica* 'Globosa Nana' in Arboretum Trompenburg, Rotterdam, Holland.

– – **'Globosa Nana'** is an attractive dwarf form which bears normal foliage but the trunk is entirely missing and it consequently forms a globose bush. It is densely set with branches and the branchlets are pendulous. It is rather slow in getting going as a small plant, but eventually forms a bush 1–2 m high by as much or more across, and it would form an attractive lawn specimen.

Why Hornibrook should have chosen this name when he described the cultivar in 1923 is unknown, but it was rather unfortunate for it has left the way open for the name **'Globosa'** to be since used for a different cultivar. I have not seen large plants of 'Globosa' but it would appear that it is going to form a smaller plant than 'Globosa Nana'. The plants I have seen are low-growing, much wider across than they are high. The juvenile foliage is generally similar to that of 'Lobbii Nana' but without any trace of monstrosity; but the outstanding feature of 'Globosa' to my mind is the awful colour that it turns in the winter. This is a most unattractive bright red, the colour of a rusty tramp steamer.

– – **'Jindai-Sugi'.** This popular variety forms a compact, conical bush with erect and spreading branches. The foliage is very regular with a short entre-nœud with short, stiff, straight leaves pointing forward at a narrow angle. The colour is a nice soft green which is retained all the year.

– – **'Knaptonensis'.** Hornibrook tells us that this originated as a Witch's Broom on a plant of 'Nana Albospica' (described below) and, as one would therefore expect,

158

▲ 105 *Cryptomeria japonica* 'Knaptonensis'. A fine specimen growing out of doors in a sheltered spot.

106 *Cryptomeria japonica* 'Jindai-Sugi'. ▶

when true to type it consists of a congested mass of irregular shoots. These are a glistening white, but it shows a tendency to revert to the looser, dirty creamy-white of the mother variety.

It is an extremely attractive plant when well grown, but as it dislikes wind and frost it is really a plant for the cold greenhouse.

– – **'Lobbii Nana'.** There is a low-growing variety in circulation with juvenile foliage which is shorter than in 'Elegans Compacta' and with its leaves stiff and straight. The growth is dense and congested and occasionally fasciated shoots develop on larger plants, or the leading shoot will terminate with a closely-packed, capitate cluster of buds. It turns a dull brown in winter.

I do not think it is either 'Kilmacurragh' nor 'Montrosa Nana' but my plants of all these forms in the Pygmy Pinetum are not sufficiently mature to remove all doubt. Dallimore and Jackson 1948, 255 describe 'Lobbii Nana' as "of dwarf habit with dark-green leaves" which fits our plant so far as it goes (which is not very far). It has sometimes been circulated in England as "*elegans nana*" and it is probably identical with plants on the rockery at Kew labelled 'Lobbii Nana', the origin of which is not on record.

It has no logical claim to the inclusion of either of the words Elegans or Lobbii in its name, but pending more information on the behaviour of mature plants I think the Kew plants should have the benefit of the doubt (*Ill. 108*).

159

▲ 107 *Cryptomeria japonica* 'Monstrosa'. An old specimen in Arboretum Trompenburg, Rotterdam.

▲ 109 *Cryptomeria japonica* 'Monstrosa'. Detail of foliage.

◀ 108 *Cryptomeria japonica* 'Lobbii Nana' on the rock garden at Kew.

▼ 110 *Cryptomeria japonica* 'Monstrosa Nana'. Note the tufts at the end of the branches.

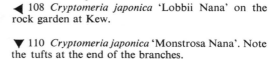

– – **'Monstrosa'.** This is hardly a dwarf form as it forms an upright columnar or round-topped bush to 2 m or more high, but there is another form **'Monstrosa Nana'** which is similar in habit but smaller in all its parts, seldom exceeding 1 m in height.

111 *Cryptomeria japonica* 'Nana' ('Pygmaea' differs little, save in its winter colour).

In both, the growth is very erratic. Some long shoots appear bearing long, stiff, straight leaves pointing forward at 50°, these being succeeded by bunches of short, curved, congested branches bearing short, curved leaves, these appearing in the form of tufts here and there over the surface of the bush. In 'Monstrosa' the needles are up to 20 mm long but in 'Monstrosa Nana' they are never more than about 12 mm in length.

– – **'Nana'.** The cultivar names 'Nana' and 'Pygmaea' have been running neck and neck for many years. Hornibrook plumped for 'Pygmaea' (which he unfortunately proceeds to support with what appears to me to be an excellent description of 'Lobbii Nana') but 'Nana' now seems to be in favour.

As we have two cultivars in cultivation very similar but distinguishable, I have conveniently assumed that those early writers, the cunning old rascals, knew all the time that there were the two plants to need the two names, and in the absence of any indication in the descriptions as to which was meant by which, I use 'Nana' for the form that is much the commoner of the two today. 'Nana' therefore is a dwarf, congested, slow-growing form to about 1 m high. The main branches are very thin and erect, the branchlets are horizontal with the tips pendulous. The leaves vary in length. On main branches they are up to 15 mm long, at first appressed to the stem but the free part curving quickly out to an angle of 50°, but elsewhere they are short to very short, accentuating the thinness of the branches.

This variety remains green in winter or at most turns a dull metallic green, but an otherwise barely distinguishable and uncommon variety, **'Pygmaea'**, turns a rich reddish-bronze.

161

112 *Cryptomeria japonica* 'Spiralis'. A young plant.

113 *Cryptomeria japonica* 'Spiraliter Falcata' in the National Pinetum at Bedgebury in Kent.

– – **'Nana Albospica'.** I prefer this name to the many others (*"argenteovariegata"*, *"albovariegata"*, *"albospicata"*), under which it has from time to time laboured, because it can fairly be described as a white-variegated form of 'Nana' in which the whole of the young growth is a creamy-white which gets duller with age, eventually becoming a pale green.

This cultivar is somewhat hardier than 'Knaptonensis' derived from it and will normally stand outside during a winter, the older foliage turning a pink-bronze.

– – **'Spiralis'.** There are two quite distinct forms with the foliage twisted spirally round the branches. The present form is known in specimens of tree-like dimensions, but the garden variety (which may have been derived from the larger tree as a cultivariant) is normally seen as a low congested little bush, unmistakable on account of the thick, incurved and twisted foliage.

– – **'Spiraliter Falcata'.** This variety forms a much taller, upright bush and carries longer and thinner branches than in 'Spiralis' and they all tend to twist and curve. It bears much thinner, narrower leaves, rather irregular in size. There is a good specimen of this form in the National Pinetum at Bedgebury, Kent. It is occasionally met with under the name of *"spiralis elongata"*. These two spiral forms are quite distinct, even as small plants, and mechanically-minded persons familiar with the

115 *Cryptomeria japonica* 'Viminalis', showing the tufts that are characteristic of this variety. ▶

◀ 114 *Cryptomeria japonica* 'Vilmoriniana'. A fine specimen of this popular plant in the Royal Botanic Garden at Edinburgh.

screwthreads in question will understand exactly why our nursery nickname for 'Spiralis' is "Whitworth" while for 'Spiraliter Falcata' it is "B.S.F.".

– – **'Vilmoriniana'.** This is one of the most popular dwarf conifers. It forms a compact, roughly globular bush never seen more than about 1 m high by as much through with a very neat foliage with closely packed recurved leaves. The differences between this cultivar and 'Compressa', the only one likely to be confused with it, are given under that variety.

– – **'Viminalis'.** I prefer to retain this name, first suggested by Hornibrook in 1923 and now in general use, in place of the name "*lycopodioides*" suggested by Carriere in 1885. It forms a large bush 2–3 m high and as much through, rather sparsely furnished with long, slender, snake-like main branches with few or no side branches, such as there are being in whorls, as can be clearly seen in the picture. The foliage is a light green.

This form would appear to be identical with **'Selaginoides'** and possibly also **'Dacrydioides'** and **'Kewensis'.** The identity of all these varieties (if they differ) needs sorting out, but the present confusion is no major tragedy as none of them can be regarded as more than a horticultural curiosity. They all become large plants, without much garden value or beauty.

163

116 *Cupressus arizonica* 'Compacta'.

117 *Cupressus macrocarpa* 'Nisbet's Gem' (syn. "*minima*"). The larger plant is beginning to put on coarse growth.

CUPRESSUS

The true cypresses form a genus of a dozen species, only two or three of which can be regarded as hardy in the British Isles. At one time the genus included all the species now known as *Chamaecyparis*, and many nurserymen still use the name *Cupressus* in the wider sense. In this they are perhaps less influenced by conservatism and reluctance to change than by a conviction that the old name is better known by the public and so is a better commercial proposition than the new name, which so many customers regard as an irritating tongue-twister.

Cupressus arizonica is normally a tall, pyramidal tree with glaucous grey foliage, but it has given us one good dwarf form.

– – **'Compacta'** forms a dense, conical or ovoid bush, very slow-growing, with typical foliage of an attractive grey-green. In the true plant the foliage is very congested, but a looser form is frequently supplied in its place.

Cupressus macrocarpa, well-known as the fast-growing 'Cypress' (at one time so popular for hedges and shelter planting but now being rapidly ousted by the by-generic hybrid *Cupressocyparis × leylandii*) has given rise to several very minute seedling forms. These are not garden plants at all. In most cases they are not hardy out of doors in a hard winter, but they are sought after by collectors and are usually a point of interest to visitors, partly I think because most of them know the species well in its usual, arboreal form and are so surprised to see such a tiny representative thereof

164

Cupressus macrocarpa 'Woking'.   119 *Cupresses macrocarpa* 'Pygmaea'.

a few inches high growing in a pot, such a striking contrast to all the other *Cupressus macrocarpa* trees they know.

Mr R. S. Corley of High Wycombe, who has studied these forms very closely, has kindly allowed me to give extracts from his article in *Gardeners' Chronicle* of 5 May 1962.

– – **'Nisbet's Gem'** (syn. "*minima*" Hort.) is the hardiest of the group. It was raised by Mr R. Menzies at the Golden Gate Park, San Francisco and sent by the late Mr Noble to Mr A. H. Nisbet, and by him distributed to the trade in England. It forms at first a low, rounded bush with neat, congested and mainly juvenile foliage, and as it is much easier to propagate than the other forms it will always be in easier supply. When I last saw the original plant in Mr Nisbet's garden recently it had put on some very coarse growth and was in danger of losing character.

– – **'Pygmaea'** is the only form referred to by Hornibrook in his Second Edition. He tells us that the mother plant was raised from seed in 1929 by a Mr Marcham of Carshalton Nursery and passed into the possession of Mr W. Bentley, of Quarry Wood, Burghclere, Hants. It subsequently became part of the collection of Mr G. L. Pilkington, of Grayswood Hill, Haslemere, Surrey. Mr Pilkington grew it in the open ground for several years, but disaster overtook it during the drought of 1960, and when it was sent to the Pygmy Pinetum for hospital treatment it was in a very bad way indeed. It was then a spreading little tree about 45 cm high and about the same in width, although over thirty years of age. I popped it at once into the congenial atmosphere and warmth of the mist-propagator here and for a time two small areas each about the size of a walnut continued green, but slowly even these went back and eventually there was nothing to be done except give the plant honourable burial here in Devizes. Fortunately it had been propagated and Mr Corley himself has a plant 20 m high by 30 cm across, and if he continues the generosity he so rightly records of its previous owner it should soon be available again in the trade.

It was originally described as having foliage of two kinds, the lower leaves decussate and broadly awl-shaped about 1 mm long, and the upper leaves—towards the growing tips of the shoots—scale-like, appressed, glandular below. Mr Corley describes the plant at thirty years as having rich green foliage, almost entirely adult, with only a vestige of the juvenile foliage remaining on some lower branchlets. The habit of Mr Pilkington's plant was decidedly irregular and most remarkable for its extreme density of foliage, with tightly packed cockscomb-like formations in bosses. Mr Corley's plant, now twenty-four years old, is showing signs of developing the same cockscomb-like growths.

– – 'Woking'. Mr Corley gives also the history of this form, the mother plant of which, at Jackman's nursery at Woking, was an irregular dense column about 60 cm high by 1 m across. This plant unfortunately died in 1958 at the approximate age of twenty years. Mr Corley states: "My own plant of this form is pyramidal with a height of 23 cm, and its leaves are entirely juvenile, broadly awl-shaped, bright green, about 1 mm in length, arranged in four ranks, and densely set on the numerous short branchlets, the annual growth of these being about 2 cm. The branchlets are somewhat ascending and the branchlet tips are recurved or slightly pendulous. This plant, grown in a pot for seven years, has so far shown no signs of becoming arborescent, but the one remaining plant at Jackman's nursery, planted in the open ground, has developed longer leading shoots and assumed a definitely columnar habit, while retaining exclusively juvenile foliage. Whether or not this variety will prove to be a true and constant dwarf remains to be seen, but whatever its ultimate size, it is undoubtedly an interesting variation from the type species." This cultivar is in some collections as "*Mrs Anley's variety*"—a name of no authority, despite the esteem in which the lady herself is held amongst gardeners.

166

DACRYDIUM: FITZROYA

DACRYDIUM

Although this genus includes about sixteen species, all from the Southern Hemisphere, relatively few have been introduced here, and of these only one comes within our range for size.

Dacrydium laxifolium is a prostrate or sub-erect shrub in nature with slender trailing branches, but in cultivation in this country is only seen as a specimen in a pot, although I see no reason why it should not be hardy.

It is interesting as being the smallest known conifer, fruiting specimens no higher than 7–8 cm occurring in the wild, but it has no particular beauty. Even a prize specimen most uninitiated folk would be apt to pass by, thinking it to be some form of heather not in flower. It is a collectors' item.

FITZROYA

The genus *Fitzroya* contains only a single species, but as this was at one time called *F. patagonica*, confusion sometimes occurs.

Fitzroya cupressoides comes from Southern Chile, where it forms a large tree, but in this country it seldom grows beyond a large bush or small tree, except in very sheltered situations.

It is interesting on account of its unusual foliage, which consists of small shiny leaves which, cupressus-like, are attached to the shoots save for a pointed triangular tip which is free-standing and ending in a sharp, tiny, incurved point. It is, however, unmistakable for that genus because the leaves are in whorls of three. The branches are usually thickly furnished with short branchlets and in older plants are pendulous.

It stands pruning, so can be kept down to size and those in search of the unusual could try it as a hedge-plant.

167

JUNIPERUS

This large genus, comprising upwards of 40 species, is a very useful one. Most of the junipers are extremely hardy and tough, they stand hot, dry conditions well and varieties can be safely planted on limy soil or where there is a chalk subsoil. They are, however, prone to damage by aphis, scale and certain rusts.

The junipers are evergreen trees and shrubs, often with thin flaking bark, with finely divided branchlets and two types of leaves, the juvenile or acicular (i.e. needle-like) leaves and the adult, scale-like leaves (sometimes the word "squammiform" is used to describe these) which in the different species sometime occur separately or both may occur on the same tree. Several scales unite to form a berry-like fruit containing one or more seeds. As befits the genus with the largest distribution throughout the Northern Hemisphere it has given us many useful garden forms. These come in every conceivable size, colour and texture, and in shape they range from the completely prostrate form of *Juniperus horizontalis*, through spreading, globose and pyramidal forms to perhaps the most spectacularly needle-like plant known, *Juniperus virginiana* 'Sky Rocket'. As well as green forms of every hue there are golden, glaucous, blue-grey forms and variegated forms and some of the plants take on rich purple hues in the winter.

It is a genus that must have sadly tried the patience of botanists because (particularly on account of the habit that many of the forms have of clothing themselves wholly or mainly with juvenile foliage when young and changing over gradually and leisurely (sometimes incompletely and in some cases not at all) to adult foliage in the mature plant, and its other habit—in species that are characteristically dioecious—of not running invariably true to type) it does not lend itself at all well to study by the normal methods of orthodox botany, which rely mainly upon herbarium specimens and little if at all upon the knowledge and study of living plants.

There are several species of juniper which never become large trees and these can therefore be used in gardens equally as well as the dwarf forms of taller-growing species. The persistent juvenile habit of others is an invitation to use them in their juvenile forms, as many of these are most attractive both in foliage and in habit, which in the early years is often regularly conical.

Juniperus chinensis. The Chinese Juniper. This is a very difficult and perplexing species with many nomenclatural problems.

In 1946 an American nurseryman named P. J. van Melle of Poughkeepsie, N.Y., who was interested in the Chinese Juniper and its cultivated forms, published his findings in the American publication *Phytologia* and the following year these were collected and republished in book form entitled *Review of Juniperus Chinensis*. This was published by the New York Potanical Garden from whom copies can be obtained by writing to Publications Department, The New York Botanical Garden, Bronx Park, New York 58, New York, U.S.A.

120 Dwarf conifers in the Japanese Gardens at Tully, Co. Kildare, Eire.

Briefly, van Melle complains that the original species *J. chinensis* L, was inadequately defined by Linnaeus when he named it, that *J. sphaerica* Lindl. was subsequently quite unjustifiably reduced to a variety of *J. chinensis* and that *J. chinensis* var. *sheppardii* should have been recognized as a distinct species and that in result (what with all the garden forms that have appeared and a whole group of natural and garden hybrids with the prostrate species *J. sabina*) the name *J. chinensis* has come to include, as he puts it, "everything but the kitchen stove—a loose aggregate, incapable of definition in terms of a species".

To overcome this he proposed to limit the use of *J. chinensis*, to resuscitate *J. sphaerica* and to raise *J. sheppardii* to specific status. He also proposed a new hybrid species *J.* × *media* to contain all the more or less bush-like forms in which *J. sabina* blood—or should it be sap?—was discernible by the characteristic savin odour of the crushed foliage. He also separated certain garden forms being grown as cultivars of *J. chinensis* and identified them with another species *J. davurica* and he regarded *J. chinensis* 'Sargentii' as a separate species.

In support of all these suggestions he clearly did an immense amount of work both amongst the literature and herbarium specimens of all these junipers and amongst the living plants, but like persons always tend to do once they have found a tenable theory, he disregarded every contribution from earlier botanical work that did not support his proposals. That many of these early writers were often mere copyists or at best were writing with but limited knowledge of the junipers of which they wrote is only too clear (e.g. many of them as young plants, with predominantly juvenile foliage, are quite unlike the same trees as adults) so he had good grounds for exasperation over much of the literature he was trying to sort out, but in result, van Melle's work has not been fully accepted in the botanical world. When I asked one of the leading

169

taxonomists about it his reply was "Van Melle is probably right, but a lot more work will have to be done on these junipers before we can accept all he says—it will mean scrapping so much in all the books". And that seems to sum up the general attitude.

In these circumstances each subsequent writer has had to make up his own mind how far he will follow van Melle's recommendations. I notice for instance that Mr Hillier accepts the new hybrid *J. × media* but does not agree with the transfer of the cultivars 'Parsonsii' and 'Expansa Variegata' to *J. davurica*, although this latter is now the practice in the nursery trade in Holland, where on the other hand *J. × media* has not "caught on".

To avoid confusing the reader I will not set out van Melle's proposals in full (anyone interested can study his work for themselves) but I should give a word of warning that the nomenclature of this species, or group of species if that is what it ultimately becomes, is subject to review. To make the position of the present book clear, come what may, I here treat van Melle's proposals as follows:

1. Van Melle's main proposals are not accepted.
2. The transfers to his new hybrid species *J. × media* are accepted. (But see my notes on the 'Globosa' and 'Plumosa' forms.)
3. The transfers to *J. davurica* are accepted.
4. Recognition of *J. sargentii* as of specific rank is accepted.
5. Van Melle's differentiation between *J. procumbens* 'Nana' and *J. squamata* 'Prostrata' is completely rejected. I am of the opinion that van Melle could only have had *J. procumbens* 'Nana' to examine and that both the photographs on his plate XII are of that cultivar.

J. chinensis normally comes as an upright or conical tree upwards of 20 m high so that most of its geographical varieties and cultivated clones are outside the scope of this book, but the alleged hybrids with J. sabina are usually regarded as dwarf forms and so are included under *J. × media*. *J. chinensis* usually bears adult and juvenile leaves on the same plant, the former small, usually in pairs, closely flattened to the branches and blunt at the apex: the latter being usually ternate (occasionally in opposite pairs), 5–10 mm long, awl-shaped and sharply pointed; very densely set on the plant. The species is dioecious (that is to say the male and the female flowers are borne on separate plants).

– – '**Aurea**'. This, as Hornibrook points out, in time grows too large to be regarded as a dwarf conifer, but being of slow growth it should be retained as long as possible on account of its wonderful colour, this being a brilliant golden-yellow during the spring and summer if the plant is grown in full sunlight, but it becomes less outstanding by winter. It is never in very easy supply in the nursery trade as it is a very difficult plant to propagate and to rear satisfactorily, but once it forms a good leader of adult

▲ 122 *Juniperus chinensis* 'Japonica'. The foliage is very dense and prickly to the touch.

◄ 121 *Juniperus chinensis* 'Aurea'. Not a dwarf form, worth planting for its colour.

growth it usually gets away well, although it should be clipped over occasionally when young to encourage a dense habit. It bears juvenile and adult foliage in approximately equal amounts.

– – **'Japonica'.** Hornibrook seems to have made a valiant attempt to unravel what is usually referred to as "The Japonica Tangle", this being the confusion amongst several *J. chinensis* forms that had resulted from the free and light-hearted use made of the word "Japonica" both as a specific and as a varietal name by nineteenth century writers on conifers. But in spite of all his trouble I, personally, remain uncertain as to just how many forms he was trying to leave with us. Van Melle, on the other hand, convinced himself that the title could be dropped entirely. This sort of tangle is just the situation where the International Registration Authority can be so valuable because of its authority to end all controversy by giving a pragmatic sanction to the names to be used in the future, but in the meantime we must retain this as a cultivar name to describe a plant usually found in gardens as a fairly low bush with two or three ascending main branches bearing adult foliage at their tips but densely covered throughout the rest of their length with juvenile foliage which is very densely set and extremely prickly. This prickliness is one of the main characteristics and is so pronounced that it is advisable to wear gloves when handling the plant. It is an attractive garden form and capable because of its prickliness of holding its own against animals, red indians, commandos and (nowadays of course) spacemen.

171

It distributes its energy amongst two or three leading branches, so that each plant seems to be more than usually governed in later life by its treatment (intentional or accidental) in its early days, for plants with this type of foliage but with varying habits of growth are to be found.

Another, and perhaps more probable, explanation is that there are several seedling forms in cultivation. At Westonbirt Arboretum near Tetbury in Gloucestershire there is a conical plant with a vertical leader over 2 m high labelled **'Nana'**, and I have seen small plants of other allegedly upright forms under such names as "*japonica erecta*", "*mas Knap Hill*" and the (obviously incorrect) "*sargentii erecta*", but I think the form **'Oblonga'** reported by Slavin in the *Report of the Conifer Conference in 1932* was merely a peculiar plant of 'Japonica', for unless the plant so labelled in the Pygmy Pinetum has been wrongly identified, 'Oblonga' seems indistinguishable from 'Japonica'.

It might be well here to enumerate the various forms of *J. chinensis* to which the word "japonica" has been applied in the past and to which it has no longer any application. Van Melle dismisses Hornibrook's *J. chinensis* var. *veitchii* with the opinion expressed in characteristically pungent phraseology that it "represents no kind of juniper, living or extinct, but only a muddle in Veitch's mind" and it seems clear that we should have no plants so labelled. So also *J. chinensis* 'Stricta', *J.* × *media* 'Plumosa' (and see also *J.* × *media* 'Globosa'), *J. procumbens* and *J. davurica* 'Parsonsii' are all now clearly recognized for what they are and should be dissociated from the word "japonica" in any way whatever.

– – **'Kaizuka'.** This attractive form will grow eventually to tree-size but it is slow-growing and for many years in its early stages is a most desirable plant, having a picturesque, rugged outline with a tendency for its trunk or main branches to be slightly out of upright and this character should not be modified by pruning. In the Arboretum Trompenburg in Rotterdam there are some quite tall specimens, but the best plant I personally know in this country is in the Happy Valley Gardens at Llandudno. I understand it is a very popular plant in the gardens of California in Western United States where it is usually known as "*Torulosa*" or "*Hollywood Variety*". Part of the attraction of this plant is the picturesque effect given by the irregular crowding of the branchlets into dense mop-like clusters which often form cylindrical effects (hence the word "torulose"—not to be confused with the word "tortuose" which means twisted) along the branches. In the best form the foliage is a bright, rich green which will hold its own with the green of *Chamaecyparis obtusa* 'Nana Gracilis', but there are clones in cultivation in which the colour is a much duller, bluish-green. There is a variegated form, **'Kaizuka Variegated'** with a bold white variegation of which I only have small propagations, but it should make a very attractive plant.

If van Melle ultimately gets his way he will have elevated this form into a botanical variety of his proposed species *J. sheppardii*. In that event his proposed *J. sheppardii*

172

▲ 123 *Juniperus chinensis* 'Kaizuka'. Colour: rich, deep mid-green.

◀ 124 *Juniperus chinensis* 'Obelisk' in the Arboretum Trompenburg, Rotterdam.

var. *torulosa* would cover all these colour forms, leaving the cultivar name 'Kaizuka' still available for the bright green form which is the one we want in our gardens.

– – **'Obelisk'.** This is a new and very attractive form which becomes a narrow, pyramidal plant to about 3 m high. The main branches and branchlets are spreading and short and stout, the leaves are very densely set, juvenile, directed forward, slightly decurved with apices very sharply pointed, 10–15 mm long with the underside glaucous. The whitish upper side of the leaves being turned outwards give the plant a distinctive glaucous-grey appearance. The variety was raised by F. J. Grootendorst & Son, Nurserymen of Boskoop, Holland, and the best plants I know are in Arboretum Trompenburg at Rotterdam. The slope to the leader seems to be characteristic of this variety and for formal situations would be a defect.

– – **'Pyramidalis'.** This and **'Columnaris'** are collective names for very old, pyramidal forms in which the foliage is very prickly, this serving to distinguish them from 'Stricta'. Several clones have received cultivar names but they are all too tall-growing to come within the scope of this book.

– – **'San José'.** This attractive dwarf form was found by W. B. Clarke, a nurseryman of San José, California, in 1935, mixed in with a planting of *J. chinensis*. It lies low on the ground and displays a mixture of adult and juvenile foliage and has I understand become extremely popular in California. The foliage is sage green. It was at first called *J. c. japonica* 'San José', which was understandable as it could broadly be described as a low-growing form of 'Japonica', but it can always be distinguished from it by

173

125 *Juniperus chinensis* 'Stricta'. Silvery-grey; not very prickly to the touch.

its lower habit of growth and its softer foliage, which has none of the prickliness of that of 'Japonica'.

– – **'Sheppardii'.** I have not seen this variety, but from the description given by Hornibrook it would appear to be of similar colouring to the popular 'Stricta' but lacking that variety's upright habit of growth, as he describes it as making an irregular and rather floppy bush owing to the suppleness of its branches and their rather top-heavy load of branchlets.

– – **'Stricta'.** This plant becomes too large in time but it serves us well as a garden plant, for in its young stages it forms a regularly conical bushlet with ascending branches and wholly juvenile foliage of a very beautiful, light blue-grey, quite soft to the touch, i.e. not prickly. It remains an attractive plant for some years but eventually its habit of holding on to its dead foliage for several years gives the plant an unhealthy appearance, by which time it is usually best to replace it. It has laboured under a variety of names. Hornibrook refers (p. 102) to two of them, *J. japonica* Carr. (1897) and *J. chinensis* var. *pyramidalis*, Beissn. (1891). In the American nursery trade it is for some inscrutable reason widely distributed as *J. excelsa* "*stricta*"; it also appears as "*Bleak House*" in some collections in the United States, and occasionally in this country it has been sent out as *J.* "*squamata campbellii*".

174

– – **'Variegata'.** This variety, which received its present name some years before Veitch suggested the name "*albovariegata*" quoted by Hornibrook, forms a slow-growing but eventually large, conical bush which is worthy of a better position than the rough corner assigned to it by Hornibrook, as its blue-green foliage (very similar in colour to 'Stricta') with its combination of juvenile and adult foliage, both types being irregularly but often liberally splashed with a creamy-white variegation, can be very effective when seen from close at hand. The plant is especially attractive when its neighbours are green or of some other, contrasting, colour.

In the Royal Botanic Garden in Edinburgh on the rock garden there is a small round-topped bush of entirely juvenile foliage labelled **'Alba Recurva'** with quite a different type of variegation. I cannot trace this name but it seems a very desirable garden plant.

Juniperus communis. This species is widely distributed throughout Europe and North America. It is very variable in habit and there are considerable regional divergencies. It is usually an upright tree but there are many forms that are prostrate shrubs. The species is easily distinguishable from most of the other junipers which give us dwarf forms by its leaves. These are invariably awl-shaped and grow straight out at an angle from the stem, never clasping it as in *J. sabina* and many other species. The branchlets are triangular with projecting ridges and the leaves are in whorls of three. The leaves are stalkless and taper from a swollen base to a sharp point, their upper surface having a single broad band of stomata, their lower side being convex and bluntly keeled.

Because of the geographical distribution of the different forms of this juniper, several of them in the past have been regarded as separate species, and even as recently as 1962 the botanist Franco proposed to recognize this heterogeneity by the creation of four sub-species. His arguments were not, however, altogether convincing and I think the fact of the matter is that the varieties in the wild will not just play the game—individual plants turn up in Ireland or on a mountain in Europe that could very well have been found in America, and vice versa.

I therefore propose to separate the cultivars into the following five groups according to distinctions which will be understood by the gardening public, without having regard to botanical considerations. The lists cover a few forms not otherwise mentioned in the book.

THE HIBERNICA GROUP Upright to columnar forms mostly too tall to be regarded as dwarf forms.

'Bruns' 'Hibernica'
'Columnaris' (syn. 'Suecica Nana') 'Suecica'
'Compressa' 'Suecica Nana'
'Cracovia'

175

JUNIPERUS

THE CANADENSIS GROUP Prostrate and/or spreading forms with thick stems and coarse, wide leaves, all turned towards the ground.

var. *depressa*
'Depressa Aurea'
'Depressed Star'
'Dumosa'

'Gimbornii'
'Nana Aurea'
'Prostrata' Beissn. non Hornb.
'Vase' (syn. 'Vase-shaped')

THE SAXATILIS GROUP Prostrate and spreading forms with thin stems and densely set leaves showing the white upper sides to a noticeable extent.

var. *saxatilis*
'Effusa' (syn. 'Repanda')
'Montana'
'Nana'

'Repanda'
'Sibirica'
'Silver Lining'

THE HORNIBROOKII GROUP Prostrate and spreading forms with very small leaves, many with their upper sides showing.

'Hornibrookii'
var. *jackii*

'Prostrata' Hornb. See 'Hornibrookii'

MISCELLANEOUS FORMS
'Echiniformis'

'Hemisphaerica'

– – **'Compressa'.** In his second edition Hornibrook refers to three dwarf, upright forms of *J. communis*: 'Columnaris', 'Compressa' and 'Suecica Nana'. These we can now safely reduce to two, as his 'Columnaris' was apparently only a redundant name for 'Suecica Nana'.

'Compressa' is the well-known, minute, columnar plant so universally popular, with its steeply ascending branches, pointed apex and tiny leaves, about 5 mm by 1 mm, and an average annual growth of 5 cm or less—a tiny replica of the Irish Juniper. Unfortunately it is not an easy plant, being very prone to damage by wind, frost and red spider.

– – var. **depressa,** the Canadian Juniper, is the common wild juniper of Eastern North America. It is a low, spreading shrub never more than 1 m high and occurs sometimes in large groups, there being a very good illustration in *Cultivated Conifers in North America* by L. H. Bailey, 1933, Plate XXXIX. It thrives in dry, sandy, stony or gravelly soil and is extremely hardy and a rapid, vigorous grower. It is very useful for massing in front of trees or in the wild or moorland garden. The leaves are 8–10 mm by 1–1·5 mm, oval to lanceolate, with a long and finely drawn out transparent tip. These make the plant prickly to the touch. The lower side of the leaf is prominently keeled, yellowish to brownish-green in summer, sometimes touched with darker brown near the tips, and brown in winter, unless grown in full shade. The leaves are in whorls of three and each leaf is sharply curved near its base and twisted so as to face the ground, consequently the white stomatic band $\frac{1}{2}$ to $\frac{2}{3}$ the total width

126 *Juniperus communis* 'Depressed Star' in the Trial Ground at Boskoop, Holland. Other selections in this group are some more, and some less prostrate.

127 *Juniperus communis* 'Depressa Aurea'. The young growth is a lovely butter yellow in early summer. The other yellow form, 'Nana Aurea' is a prostrate plant and retains its colour longer.

177

128 *Juniperus communis* 'Compressa'. The popular miniature, never over 40 cm high.

129 *Juniperus communis* 'Suecica Nana'. Will reach 1 m or more.

130 *Juniperus communis* 'Hibernica' the Irish Juniper.

of leaf (not quite reaching to its base) on the upper side of the leaf is not seen. The leaves at the strong-growing tips are strongly appressed to the stem and the growth is in irregular, flat sprays.

– – **'Depressa Aurea',** as its name suggests, is a form with its leaves and young twigs a rich golden-yellow in early summer. The colour becomes less striking as the year goes on, but it is a very attractive plant.

– – **'Depressed Star'.** As var. *depressa* is a botanical designation it covers several clones which are regarded as cultivars, and 'Depressed Star' is the name suggested by Dr Boom for the clone that has been widely distributed as 'Depressa': a widely spreading shrub with the characteristic foliage of the variety. The other selections that have been named vary mainly in habit. **'Prostrata'** is a completely prostrate form, useful for ground cover. In the opposite direction (from the type represented by 'Depressed Star') **'Dumosa', 'Gimbornii'** and **'Vase'** (syn. 'Vase-shaped') are shrubby forms, increasingly upright, in the order given. Probably all the forms become more spreading with age. 'Vase' colours to a rich chocolate-brown in winter and especially when young is a very attractive form (*Ill. 126*).

– – **'Echiniformis',** is a tiny plant which traditionally is regarded as a form of *J. communis*, but on what ground or authority I cannot say, for it would appear to have

178

▲ 131 *Juniperus communis* (?) 'Echiniformis'. Notice the reverting branch.

◄ 132 *Juniperus communis* 'Suecica', the Swedish Juniper. Less fastigiate than 'Hibernica'.

much more affinity to *J. chinensis*. It is a tiny form with crowded, congested foliage and short branches densely and irregularly covered with tiny leaves. It is a popular exhibit at Alpine Flower Shows where neat, bun-shaped specimens in apparently excellent health can be seen a foot or more across, but such are more a testimonial to the skill of the grower than objects of beauty. As a garden plant 'Echiniformis' is unreliably hardy and not to be recommended. It is very difficult to propagate and not worth the trouble of growing.

– – **'Effusa',** if not identical with 'Repanda' (described below), is not worth separating from that cultivar.

– – var. **hemisphaerica** is a geographical form found wild in high mountainous areas around the Western Mediterranean in Europe and Africa up to 3000 m. It forms a low, rounded bush to 2·5 m high, with straight, oblong-linear, pointed, prickly leaves 4–12 mm long by 1–3 mm wide with a broad (more than twice the width of each green margin) white band above. It is not hardy in Britain so is seldom seen here.

– – **'Hibernica'** is the well-known "Irish Juniper", forming a tall narrow columnar tree with tightly packed vertical branches. **'Bruns', 'Cracovia'** and **'Suecica'** are other fastigiate forms, but they are all too strong-growing for attention in this book.

– – **'Hornibrookii'** is a very popular and at first completely prostrate form, much used on rockeries because of its neat habit and tiny leaves as a young plant, although it builds up in the centre and covers a large area in time. The very young twigs are green

179

133 *Juniperus communis* 'Hornibrookii'. Some forms are very much more prostrate, especially as young plants.

with three semi-translucent ridges, but they soon turn to brown and then the ridges are very noticeable. The leaves, are 5×1 mm (occasionally to 8×1.25 mm), flat below with a very prominent keel, linear/lanceolate, with a broad white stomatic band above. The leaves stand out at a right angle to the stem but are curved near the base, being then straight or nearly so for the remainder of their length. Owing to the way the leaves are twisted many of them show the white stomatic bands, especially is this so near the middle of the plant. The plant is prickly to the touch—in a way that is appropriate to its tiny leaves.

Murray Hornibrook has caused a lot of confusion by writing of 'Prostrata' Beissn. 1896 (which he admits to not having seen), under the apparent impression that that form was a stronger-growing form of the small leaved Hornibrookii group (whereas it is of the Depressa Group, with coarse, wide leaves, all facing the ground). There do, however, seem to be several clones of 'Hornibrookii' in cultivation, as some plants are stronger growing and less prostrate than others. In the Edgbaston Botanic Garden in Birmingham there is a small unlabelled plant with about the habit of growth of the Pfitzer juniper on a reduced scale and on the rock garden at Edinburgh there is a globular bush labelled *J. communis* 'Nana' with leaves of the Hornibrookii type.

There seems to be a need for a study of the various clones in cultivation and scope for a little restrained naming of worthwhile garden forms.

180

134 *Juniperus communis* 'Repanda'. Growth in young plants is more prostrate, and the plant builds up with age.

– – var. **jackii** is a geographical form collected in 1907 from a mountain in California and is not to my knowledge in cultivation in Britain. As it is apparently characterized by the habit of confining itself to two or three long main branches which extend for several feet without lateral growth it is more a botanical curiosity than a useful garden form.

– – **'Nana Aurea'** is a prostrate form never more than 0·5 m high. The main branches are procumbent with drooping tips. The branchlets are set at a wide angle to the main stem. The leaves are silvery-white, striped with green edges above, but golden-yellow to brown-yellow below, this colour being retained throughout the year.

It is very easily distinguished from all other forms, but it is not a very good "doer" so is unpopular with nurserymen and is seldom seen.

– – **'Repanda'** is a very strong-growing, dense, prostrate form, very useful as a ground cover plant. The whole plant is very soft to the touch with no trace of prickliness. The twigs are very supple and have a cross section consisting of three ridges and three grooves. Leading shoots send out their laterals in regular flat sprays but the branching towards the centre of the plant is irregular and twigs stand up at all angles. The twigs are light brown with entre-nœud up to 10 mm, usually much less. The leaves vary in size, up to 10×1·5 mm, and are upcurved so that they lie close to

181

135 *Juniperus communis* var. *saxatilis*. This is the form nearest to the illustration in Pallas, 1788.

136 *Juniperus communis* 'Silver Lining'. This is the plant for which I propose this new name.

the shoot; the underside prominently keeled but with a sunk midrib, the upper side with an ill-defined, broad stomatic band, light grey in colour but largely hidden from view because of the way the leaves are held. 'Effusa' appears to be indistinguishable from this form.

– – var. **saxatilis** is a group in which much confusion exists. The name was first used by Pallas in 1788 and, interestingly enough, was accompanied by a "description" which consisted of a hand-coloured drawing, but clones of it have been grown (and are still found) under the names "*sibirica*", "*montana*", "*nana*", "*alpina*" and sundry combinations of these words. It is a dense and slow-growing, prostrate to procumbent shrub with leading shoots 0–45°, straight or nearly so, laterals in regular flat (or shallow V; sprays. Entre-nœud 3–4 mm, leaves 7–10 mm × 1–1·5 with parallel sides narrowing rapidly to a blunt tip which is drawn out to a long sharp point. The underside is dull green and prominently keeled. The upper side has a wide (over half the total width) irregular band of minute oval stomata, with a very narrow green midrib not extending to the tip. The leaves emerge at right angles from the stem but are incurved to an angle of 50–60°, and as they are twisted in some forms to show much of the white upper surface the plant has a grey-green appearance.

– – **'Silver Lining'.** This is the name which I now propose for a plant which although one of our best garden forms has had an amazing struggle for a place in the nomenclatural sun. It is often regarded as one clone of var. *saxatilis* but it in no way corresponds to the illustration of that variety by Pallas. It had long been grown in Holland variously as *J. nana* and *J. prostrata* and in his second edition Hornibrook combined these into the name *J. communis* 'Nana Prostrata', and although he then expressed the opinion that it was not var. *saxatilis* (var. *saxatilis* is synonymous with his 'Montana' on his p. 110) it has been much grown under that name in Britain.

JUNIPERUS

The name "*minima*" suggested in 1940 has no standing in view of the prior-published name by Hornibrook, and as this was a mere concoction I propose the new name, which is euphonious and very descriptive. This probably is indefensible under the Rules, strictly applied, but if the proposal is acceptable on commonsense grounds the International Registration Authority may be willing to establish this name in view of the excellence and popularity of this desirable form.

It forms a very prostrate plant which is hard and rough to the touch but not prickly, with strong leading growths which nod at the growing tips. Young twigs are distinctly triangular, pink above, green below; older branches brownish-purple. Entre-nœud up to 10 mm, less towards tips of shoot. Leaves 5–8 × 1·5–2 mm, upcurved, but narrow at the base and bluntly pointed; each leaf viewed from above or the side being boat-shaped, rather like a Venetian gondola. The leaves are shiny green below but the whole leaf is covered with a heavy glaucous bloom (easily rubbed off) giving the plant a grey-green appearance which is maintained throughout the year. Above, the leaves carry a very wide band of minute stomata covered with a chalky-white bloom and as many of the leaves are twisted so that this whiteness is seen, especially near the centre of the plant, the general effect is most attractive. It is a fairly strong grower.

– – **'Suecica Nana'.** This is simply a looser and freer-growing edition of 'Compressa'; similarly fastigiate to, but much slower, compacter and tighter than 'Hibernica'. It will make a plant 1·5 m high by not more than 30 cm across, but without some assistance from the knife such old plants usually become a bit irregular in outline towards the top and even as a young plant it is usually blunt-topped in comparison with 'Compressa'. It seems much more wind resistant and hardy than that variety and is, of course, quicker growing, but 'Suecica Nana' is apt to throw out loose, strong growth. This should be cut out as soon as it appears.

I do not feel able to be definite on the point, but in my experience the true 'Compressa' does not make this coarse growth. If this be correct, the presence of such growth on any plant would indicate that it is 'Suecica Nana' rather than 'Compressa'. The coarse growth, if propagated, gives plants of the normal 'Suecica' type.

Juniperus conferta. This is a prostrate, dense, mat-forming species from Japan which makes a useful garden plant. In its native habitat it grows on the seashore, so presumably would be a valuable plant for coastal gardens. It forms a prostrate shrub with brownish bark, thick main branches, and dense, erect branchlets. The leaves are crowded, overlapping, about ½ inch long, awl-shaped and green, each tapering to a sharp point. These points give a distinctly prickly feel to the plant when brushed with the hand and this at once distinguishes it from another prostrate juniper which has long been grown in England as *J. c.* var. *maritima* but which the Japanese botanist Satake has now identified as *Juniperus taxifolia* var. *lutchuensis*.

Each of these plants forms a dense, healthy-looking mat of a rich green and both are particularly useful as being amongst the few shrubs that will hang downwards

137 *Juniperus taxifolia* var. *lutchuensis* (syn. *J. maritima*). *J. conferta* has less prostrate branchlets and narrower leaves and is *very prickly to the touch*.

over a wall or bank after the manner of the Aubrieta. They are very similar in foliage but can be at once distinguished by the feel, *J. conferta* being very prickly to the touch, *J. taxifolia* var. *lutchuensis* being hardly so at all. It is also more prostrate in habit.

Juniperus davurica. According to van Melle, *Juniperus davurica* is a very common and widely distributed species in Eastern Asia, but as far as I am aware it is only found in cultivation in the present form and its variegated counterparts.

– – **'Expansa'.** It has always apparently been assumed (with what justification I cannot say) that our green form is not the typical *J. davurica*, so the plant in cultivation has always been saddled with a varietal name. Hornibrook mentions it in his Second Edition as *J. chinensis* var. 'Parsonsii' without adequate description, but the name I use would appear to be a much more logical one. The plant forms at first a low, flat, spreading bush which for some years may not exceed 30–50 cm in height, but ultimately it builds itself up into a dome-shaped mound 3 m across and up to about 1 m high at the centre.

It is not a prostrate juniper. Individual plants in open, uncrowded situations develop stout and very rigid, horizontally-spreading primary branches which *do not rest upon the ground* but extend themselves horizontally just clear of it. Because of this characteristic, it is important not to plant this juniper too deep and I have noticed

184

138 *Juniperus davurica* 'Expansa' (syn. *J. chinensis parsonsii*). There are two variegated forms.

that when set so that the main branches are touching the ground, the plant does not prosper. It carries a mixture of adult and juvenile foliage, one attractive feature being the prominent development of long, slender, filiform, adult, ultimate branches arranged in more or less dense, rich-looking foliage sprays. The whole plant has a strong and robust appearance looking as though it would be none the worse for being slept on by a cow.

– – **'Expansa Aureospicata'** is similar, with butter-yellow variegation. It is less vigorous than 'Expansa Variegata' and carries mainly juvenile foliage.

– – **'Expansa Variegata'** is similar but with bold splashes of creamy-white variegation here and there over the plant on both adult and juvenile foliage. This variegation is apt to suffer during the winter frosts, but usually appears again with the new season's growth. Both variegated forms are attractive plants.

Juniperus drupacea in nature is a tree 15 m high, but in cultivation is only seen as a very slow-growing, upright tree.

It is an interesting addition to a collection where there is room for it on account of its foliage, the leaves being the widest of any juniper.

185

▲ 139 *Juniperus horizontalis*. The "whip-cord" terminal growths can be clearly seen.

◄ 140 A young plant that has been well cut back after planting to secure a dense, mat-like plant.

Juniperus horizontalis is a species from North America in which numerous forms have been selected and named. They are all more or less prostrate plants and nearly all are vigorous growers and capable of covering a large area. Having been regarded at one time as a prostrate variety of *J. sabina*, at another as a variety of *J. virginiana* and even, by one authority, simply as *J. prostrata* the species is frequently found incorrectly labelled.

The main branches are long, the branchlets very numerous, short and dense. The leaves on the cultivated forms are mainly needle-shaped, often in whorls of three, green or blue-green, frequently colouring to blue or mauve tones in the winter, 2–6 mm long and standing free at the tips, with very sharp points; convex on the underside, with a gland. On mature foliage the leaves are scale-like and loosely imbricate.

186

141 *Juniperus horizontalis* 'Bar Harbor'. This clone as grown in England is grey-green in summer and mauve in winter.

Like all junipers, this species and its varieties withstand hot, dry situations, growing under town conditions and tolerating moderately alkaline soils. They are usually much improved by the shortening of the long main shoots for two or three seasons after planting to induce a dense branch system, and thereafter by an occasional hard pruning.

– – **'Admirabilis'** is similar to 'Emerson' but is a male clone. It has prostrate main branches, with branches and branchlets held well above the horizontal so that even young plants are several inches high. The leaves are all juvenile, a yellowish-green with a heavy grey bloom, especially on the upper sides of the leaves. It is a vigorous plant.

– – **'Alpina'** is a dwarf creeping form 60 cm high by up to 2 m broad, branches at first nearly erect, gradually becoming creeping, leaves exclusively awl-shaped, 3–4 mm long, more or less bluish or greyish, changing into purple in the autumn. It is a rank grower and consequently of limited value.

– – **'Bar Harbor'** as I have it here in the Pygmy Pinetum is an attractive, close-growing variety with thin branches (never over 1·5 mm) and very small leaves tightly appressed, giving the plant a particularly neat appearance. The long main branches are prostrate and horizontal or nearly so at their tips, but the side branches are ascending at

187

142 *Juniperus horizontalis* 'Glauca' used as ground cover. A plant (perhaps a group of plants) forming a solid carpet over 3 m across in the Arboretum Trompenburg at Rotterdam.

varying (mainly steep) angles, and all branchlets turn upwards so as to produce a V-shaped (i.e. not flat) spray. The young shoots are orange-brown, mauve at the growing tips. The foliage is actually a deep grass green but the whole plant is heavily coated with a white glaucous bloom, giving it a rich grey-green (not blue-green as 'Glauca') appearance, which turns to a lovely soft mauve in the autumn.

There seem to be several clones in cultivation under this name in England and I understand that in America the complaint is made that there are as many forms of 'Bar Harbor' as there are nurserymen, so it would be a good thing for an American authority to issue an authoritative and adequate description. It is sometimes confused with 'Glauca', but the form I have described is different from that form in colour, and from all other forms I have seen in the smallness of its leaves and branches and the resulting fineness of growth. A form received as "*Hollywood variety*" appears indistinguishable.

As 'Bar Harbor' is a place name, this spelling should presumably be used.

– – **'Douglasii'**, known in America as the "Waukegan Juniper", is a strong-growing completely prostrate form useful for ground cover, succeeding equally well in sun or shade. It forms a dense, low mat with long, trailing main branches sparsely furnished but with the branchlets densely covered with very closely set, overlapping,

188

free-standing juvenile foliage, so densely set as to give a somewhat tufty look to the plant. The foliage is a bright grey-green, turning a light purple in autumn; always very glaucous.

– – **'Emerson'** is a very prostrate shrub with blue foliage, holding this colour throughout the winter. It is sometimes met with under the names "*Black Hills Creeper*" and "*Marshall*". A very hardy form.

– – **'Filicinus'** is a dense, dwarf, very low-growing shrub with prostrate branches; branchlets light brown; sprays upright, directed forward; leaves blue, purplish-blue in winter. A female form with dainty, lace-like foliage; not reliably hardy.

– – **'Glauca',** as grown in England, is a completely prostrate, mat-forming form with long, straight main branches (2 mm diam.) which at first lie along the ground, although the plant later builds up a little height by super-imposition of later growths. Branchlets are numerous, pointing forwards and rising at a low angle only, well clothed with densely set, closely appressed leaves, giving the "whip-cord" effect mentioned by Hornibrook. In the centre of the plant the leaves on the weaker shoots sometimes carry densely set, awl-shaped, free-standing leaves in four ranks, but more usually have tiny leaves which are closely appressed.

– – **'Glenmore'** is a dwarf form, one of the lowest and slowest of the species, main branches horizontal, held just clear of the ground, branchlets thin, a dull light brown; sprays nearly upright; leaves all juvenile, very closely set, dark green, tips brownish in winter. A female form.

– – **'Glomerata'** is a most distinctive variety, which I have only seen on the rockery at Kew. There as a young plant it was carrying long, often twisted, pinkish-brown main branches, mostly rising at a steep angle and bearing juvenile leaves, nearly appressed. The branchlets were short, mainly vertical or nearly so, with very dense, rich-green foliage and tiny leaves in flat sprays almost suggestive of one of the tiny forms of *Chamaecyparis obtusa*. There is some glaucousness on a few small, juvenile leaves in the interior of the plant. It turns the usual purple-violet colour of this species in winter.

It is clearly a very dwarf form, quite unlike the rampant, spreading varieties so useful for ground cover. If the long main branches were regularly shortened it could no doubt be induced to form an unusual, dense little bush, and I would say this might be the best treatment for this unusual form.

– – **'Grey Carpet'** is a creeping form with long, trailing branches forming low cushions. It differs from 'Bar Harbor' by its more green foliage.

– – **'Humilis'** is a prostrate, dense form 20–30 cm high by 1·5–2 m across. Branches creeping, long; branchlets nearly erect 3–5 cm long; sprays laterally arranged, curving towards each other, tips slightly recurved, leaves scale-like, green.

143 *Juniperus horizontalis* 'Plumosa' carries all its main branches at +45°.

– – **'Lividus'** forms a dense mat of yellow-brown main branches and many side branches pointing forwards, all completely prostrate to the tips. Branches are numerous and very short, seldom rising to 45° even at the centre of the plant (at least when young—I have not seen an old specimen). Foliage is all juvenile, the leaves are very small except on strong-growing main shoots, much resembling *J. sabina* 'Tamariscifolia'. Colour is actually a deep grass green, but a heavy grey bloom all over the plant gives it a greyish appearance.

– – **'Petraeus'.** I have only seen this form as a young plant on the rockery at Kew, where it is forming a loose, straggling plant with prostrate main branches each turned upwards at the growing tips. Side branches rise at about 45°. Stems are thick, the foliage is all juvenile, fairly closely appressed, green to yellowish-green but covered with glaucous coating. The whole plant has a grey look, with a slight tinge of purple at the growing tips.

– – **'Plumosa',** the Andorra Creeping Juniper, forms a flat-topped, spreading shrub, never over 60 cm high but spreading laterally by means of prostrate main branches radiating from the centre of the plant. The branches rise at an angle of about 45° (reminiscent of the "Pfitzer" Juniper) and bear dense, awl-like foliage loosely appressed and arranged in plumes. The foliage is a light grey-green, becoming purplish plum colour in the winter. It is less hardy than some forms of *J. horizontalis*.

190

– – **'Procumbens'** is a very dwarf, prostrate form about 20 cm high by 4 m broad. The branches are irregularly spreading; the branchlets short, erect or procumbent. Leaves are awl-shaped, 4–5 mm long, more or less appressed; at first a soft glaucous green, becoming bluish-green with age.

– – **'Prostrata'** is a prostrate, dense and mat-forming variety, forming a plant up to 30 cm high by 3–4 m across. Main branches are long and stout, prostrate but with tips slightly turned up, the branchlets are numerous and densely set, covering the ground; the sprays are blue-grey with the tips purplish; the leaves are mostly awl-shaped and thin but towards the growing tips are scale-like, a glaucous green. It is one of the best prostrate forms and one that has been in cultivation a long time, but often found wrongly named. Plants supplied in Britain as *J. horizontalis* are usually of this cultivar.

– – **'Pulchella'** is a very slow-growing and dense, compact variety, forming a symmetrical mat-like plant seldom over 10–15 cm high but more than 1 m across, with trailing branches and greenish-grey, acicular leaves. Claimed by the late Mr Robert E. More to be an exceptionally hardy form, withstanding sun, shade and drought.

– – **'Variegata'**, the, Variegated Creeping Juniper, is an attractive and vigorous prostrate form with a creamy-white variegation. It is all the better for an occasional hard cutting back, as the variegation is much more effective in the denser growth thereby secured.

– – **'Viridis'**. A prostrate, densely branched, broad shrub, 50–60 cm high; branches horizontal; branchlets spreading, covering the branches; leaves for the greater part awl-shaped with pointed apex, light green above, sometimes slightly blue bloomy beneath. A female form and distinct from all others by its green colour in summer.

– – **'Wiltonii'** is very flat growing, with trailing branches and foliage a rich silvery blue. Described by the late Robert E. More as "The slowest and lowest growing of all . . . the dwarfest of evergreens; its bright-blue foliage and berries make it a rock-garden gem".

It labours under a variety of names in the American nursery trade, including "*Blue Wilton*", "*glauca wiltonii*", "*Blue Rug*", "*Wilton Carpet*" (Wilton is a well-known make of carpet in England) and "*horizontalis glauca*" and (subject to later confirmation) in England it is sometimes grown as *J. horizontalis* 'Glauca Nana'.

From 'Glauca' it is distinguishable by its slower growth and by its being smaller in every part (the foliage and stems are as fine as in the description given under 'Bar Harbor' above, but from that variety it is quite distinct in its denser growth and completely prostrate habit).

Numerous other forms are to be found carrying names in collections and nurseries in America and further study is required, to determine how many of these are sufficiently distinct to be worth perpetuating.

191

Juniperus × media. This is the hybrid species suggested by the late P. J. van Melle as a convenient way of dealing with a large group of junipers which as he pointed out "constitute a reasonably homogenous group of considerable practical importance". They are all more or less evidently hybrids between *J. chinensis* and *J. sabina*, the evidence of the sabina influence being the characteristic "savin" odour of the foliage when bruised. As would be expected this is stronger in some forms than in others.

As most of the dwarf forms formerly treated as cultivars of *J. chinensis* (and in many books still so regarded) are transferred to *J. × media* this is now an important species in the dwarf conifer firmament, but I would warn my readers that they will probably find them listed under *J. chinensis* in some textbooks on conifers for some time to come.

They group themselves simply as follows:

THE PLUMOSA GROUP Bushes carrying almost exclusively adult foliage, with prominent, vigorous, nodding, leading shoots with short laterals pointing forward and very short sub-laterals, carrying the foliage in dense tufts. As all the growing tips curl over the effect is suggestive of ostrich plumes.

'Blaauw'	'Plumosa Albovariegata'
'Globosa'	'Plumosa Aurea'
'Globosa Aurea' (syn. 'Plumosa Aurea')	'Plumosa Aureovariegata'
'Globosa Cinerea'	'Shimpaku'
'Plumosa'	

THE PFITZERIANA GROUP Spreading bushes with main branches ascending at an angle and arching over so that the tips are pendulous (more so in some forms than others), carrying some juvenile and some adult foliage but mainly a form of semi-juvenile foliage in which the lower half of the leaf clasps the stem closely, the upper half standing off stiffly at an angle.

'Armstrongii'	'Old Gold'
'Blue Cloud'	'Pfitzeriana'
'Hetzii'	'Pfitzeriana Aurea'
'Kosteriana'	'Pfitzeriana Compacta'
'Mathot'	'Pfitzeriana Glauca'
'Nick's Compact'	'Pfitzeriana Nana'

– – **'Armstrongii'** is a low-growing shrub of the 'Pfitzeriana' type but of more compact and lower growth, seldom reaching much beyond 1 m high. The leaves are finer, softer and more grey and scale-like and very sharp. It has been available in America since 1932, but I have not seen it.

– – **'Blaauw'** is a strong-growing and upright variety in which the differentiation in vigour between the leading shoots and the sub-laterals is very pronounced so that the relatively few, strongly-growing main branches striking up at a steep angle give a

144 *Juniperus* × *media* 'Blaauw'. Colour: blue-grey.

characteristically rugged outline to the plant which is most attractive. The colour of the foliage, a rich blue-grey is an additional attraction for the plant. It was formerly known as "*Blaauw's variety*".

– – **'Blue Cloud'** is an attractive variant of the 'Pfitzeriana' type which forms a large bush with glaucous grey foliage, very dense in the centre of the bush but with long twisted "whiskery" shoots thrown out at all angles giving an untidy but picturesque look to the plant.

– – **'Globosa'** and its colour forms have had an interesting and amusing history. They first came on to the western scene as importations into this country and the United States from a Japanese nursery of plants labelled "*Juniperus virginalis globosa*". These were certainly nice, globose plants and came in three colours, green, gold and grey, and they apparently sold well. After a while the fact that there was no *J. virginalis* known to botanists was noticed and it was thereupon assumed that the correct name should have been "*J. virginiana globosa*", so the next few customers received them under this name, and under this name they can still be found. Later it was seen that they were not a *J. virginiana* form at all but were cultivars of *J. chinensis*, so Hornibrook in his Second Edition described them as "*J. c. globosa*", "*J. c. globosa aurea*" and "*J. c. globosa cinerea*".

Finally, it was found that they had not even any moral right to the designation "*globosa*", for the plants remaining unsold, deprived of the careful attention from the knife to which they had been accustomed in their native Yokohama were beginning to develop a habit that was by no means globose.

193

▲ 145 *Juniperus* × *media* 'Old Gold'. Less spreading than the type, and a wonderful colour right through the plant.

146 *Juniperus* × *media* 'Hetzii'. Grey-green and more upright in habit than *J.* × *media* 'Pfitzeriana'. ▶

The present position, therefore, is that 'Globosa' differs from 'Plumosa' only in minor respects. It forms a more symmetrical plant, the branches are much shorter and stand at different angles all over the plant and the foliage is a little lighter shade of green. The true 'Globosa' is rare in cultivation, but the difference between the forms is so slight that both are only needed in a very complete collection.

– – **'Globosa Aurea'** is a synonym of 'Plumosa Aurea', so the name should no longer be used.

– – **'Globosa Cinerea'** is very close to the cultivar 'Blaauw', so much so that, especially in young plants, they are difficult to tell apart. 'Globosa Cinerea' does not, however, throw up quite such strong leader growth and the angle of divergence of side shoots is greater, so it forms a plant of less rugged outline; also the foliage, especially in wintertime, is more a yellow-green than the blue-grey of 'Blaauw'. As in the case of the green forms, these two grey varieties are too close together for both to be needed in the average garden, and my choice would always rest with 'Blaauw'.

– – **'Hetzii'** is hardly a dwarf form since it grows to 3 m high, but where there is room for it to develop fully it is an attractive plant. The foliage is similar to 'Pfitzeriana Glauca' but the habit of growth is much more upright and vigorous. It can always be readily distinguished from 'Pfitzeriana Glauca' by the soft feel of the foliage, which entirely lacks the prickliness of that cultivar.

194

147 A warning to planters of *Juniperus* × *media* 'Pfitzeriana'. The foliage of this plant in the Arboretum Trompenburg at Rotterdam clears the heads of passers!

– – **'Kosteriana'.** There seems to be some mystery about this plant. As I know it, it is almost identical with 'Pfitzeriana' in its foliage but has a very much more prostrate habit, the main branches seldom being above 15°.

I notice that Dr Boom gives this cultivar name as a synonym as *J. virginiana* 'Kosteri', but my plant has a pronounced savin odour to the foliage when crushed. Krussman describes both forms in his recent book; so there is some mystery yet to be solved.

– – **'Mathot'** is similar to 'Pfitzeriana' in growth, but denser; the leaves are all juvenile, in pairs, to 7·5 mm long, with bluish-green bands above, green below. As the upper sides of the leaves are turned outwards the plant has a generally glaucous appearance.

– – **'Old Gold'** is a very attractive form, descriptively named. It forms a much more compact plant than the typical 'Pfitzeriana' and the lovely golden colour goes right through the plant. This clearly distinguishes it from 'Pfitzeriana Aurea', in which the golden colour at its best is limited to the young growth. The colour is retained throughout the winter. This variety should become very popular when better known.

– – **'Pfitzeriana'.** This is a good example of the growth in popularity of a good plant. When Hornibrook wrote his second edition in 1938 he evidently (from the paucity of

195

148 *Juniperus* × *media* 'Plumosa Albovariegata'. The variegation consists of a peppering of small creamy-white patches. *J.* × *media* 'Plumosa Aureovariegata, is slower growing and has a bolder variegation of bright yellow.

his description) had not seen a plant, but now it is one of the most widely planted conifers and is so well known as not to need a description. It is planted by the thousand each year, mainly I expect because of its picturesque outline as a young plant. One excellent use for it is to mask the presence of a manhole-cover on a lawn. This, its vigour and characteristic habit of growth enables it to do effectively in a short while and yet permit free access to the drains beneath on lawful occasions, but I wonder how many planters of this excellent juniper bear in mind its ultimate size? In the Arboretum Trompenburg in Rotterdam, for instance, there is a specimen large enough to afford complete shelter for quite a number of persons during a shower.

Its picturesque habit of growth is due largely to the preponderance of a semi-juvenile type of foliage and its habit of throwing up its strong main branches at an angle of 45°, from which angle the tips of the leader and the principal laterals arch over so that all the growing tips are pendulous. The foliage is a light yellowish-green but owing to the fact that the juvenile foliage (of which the centre of the bush mainly consists) shows the white uppersides, the general effect is that of a grey-green colour.

In America I understand there is a demand for this Juniper trained up in its early days to a central stem and it was evidently one of these plants from which Hornibrook obtained the description "broad, slow-growing pyramid". I have not seen a plant of this form but to anyone familiar with the picturesque character of 'Pfitzeriana' left to its own devices a trained specimen of this kind must appear a monstrosity.

It has given rise to a number of variations, both by way of bud mutations and seedlings, but the plant sometimes distributed as *J. sabina* "*Knap Hill*" is indistinguishable from 'Pfitzeriana'.

– – **'Pfitzeriana Aurea'** has the typical Pfitzeriana growth but with a tendency to a flatter habit, the branches being held at an angle of 30°. The branchlets and leaves are a bright golden-yellow in summer but become yellowish-green by the winter.

149 *Juniperus × media* 'Plumosa Aurea'. The colour is a rich old-gold, intensifying as the winter approaches.

– – **'Pfitzeriana Compacta'** is, as its name indicates, a slower-growing, compact form. In the form I have it bears no adult foliage at all, and in both the predominating semi-juvenile and the juvenile foliage the leaves are much longer (up to 8 mm) than in the typical 'Pfitzeriana'. In America I understand it is distributed under the name "Nick's Compact Pfitzer Juniper". In Holland I have seen another compact form growing under the name **'Pfitzeriana Nana'** with foliage which is a bright grass green, but I do not know whether it is yet in cultivation in Great Britain.

– – **'Pfitzeriana Glauca'** is a form with its foliage varying between silvery-blue and a dull greyish-green. I have seen several variegated forms in nurseries in Holland, and of these one named **'Silver Tip'** is attractively speckled with creamy-white similarly to *J. × media* 'Plumosa Albovariegata' and when it becomes available it should become popular. The foliage of 'Pfitzeriana Glauca' is very prickly, which distinguishes it at once from 'Hetzii' which is quite soft to the touch.

– – **'Plumosa'** is a broad, spreading shrub, seldom seen above 1·5 m high, with long main branches and numerous short side branches all pointing strongly forwards, the sprays being crowded and plume-like, with all growing tips curved gracefully over. There is usually a small amount of juvenile foliage near the base of the plant. Unless otherwise trained in its early days it limits itself to relatively few main branches and when one of these predominates the plant has a lop-sided development which may or may not be an advantage according to the situation. The colour is dark green.

– – **'Plumosa Albovariegata'** is similar to 'Plumosa' with a somewhat lower and more spreading habit and with its foliage liberally peppered with a small creamy-white variegation.

– – **'Plumosa Aurea'** is the most decorative colour-form in this group. It is a strong

197

grower with foliage and branchlets yellow-green in spring, the colour becoming more pronounced through the year until by winter it is a rich golden-bronze.

– – **'Plumosa Aureovariegata'** is a slower-growing form with its deep-green foliage carrying a deep yellow variegation, usually somewhat irregularly.

Where there is room for such a group to be seen from a little distance, a remarkable colour and texture effect could doubtless be obtained from a large group of these 'Plumosa' forms, including 'Blaauw' and 'Globosa Cinerea' for their contributions in colour, and the rich green of the taller-growing *J. chinensis* 'Kaizuka' at the back or centre of the group.

– – **'Shimpaku'.** This is a very small, slow-growing and delightful dwarf form of the Plumosa group, with dull, greyish-green foliage. It is a form much used by the "manufacturers" of Bonzai trees in Japan, but when it becomes available in this country it should become very popular as a garden plant or for use in troughs.

150 *Juniperus procumbens* spreads over a large area.

Juniperus procumbens. This is a procumbent species not always seen in good health. In time it will cover a large area, for plants 1 m high by 7 m across are known. The main branches are stiff, stout and rampant, all growing tips tending to turn *upwards*. The leaves are in threes, linear-lanceolate, sharp-pointed, 6–8 mm long; concave above, with two glaucous bands; convex beneath.

An invariable characteristic of this species is a pair of prominent white smudges on the underside of each leaf, one on each side near its base.

TABLE OF COMPARISON OF JUNIPERUS PROCUMBENS AND CERTAIN RELATED SPECIES*

Species	Habit	Branchlets	Leaves					Fruit
			Length	Point	Habit of Growth	Upper side	Lower Side	
J. procumbens	Low, spreading shrub with stiff, ascending branch-lets, shoots turning up at ends.	Stiff with glaucous ridges.	$\frac{1}{4}-\frac{1}{3}$ in	Spiny pointed.	Adherent except upper part.	Concave. Broad white stomatic band. Green mid-rib not extending to apex.	Bluish-green, with two white spots or smudges‡ from which two glaucous lines run down the edges of the pulvini.	Sub-globose. About $\frac{2}{3}$ in across. 2–3 seeded.
J. recurva	Graceful shrub or small tree. Thin light-brown bark peeling off in strips.	Not glaucous.	$\frac{1}{8}-\frac{1}{4}$ in	Hard; sharp.	Densely overlapping. Curved.	Concave. Whitened. Persisting several years after death.	Convex. Channelled only near base.	Ovoid to $\frac{1}{2}$ in long. 1 seeded. Seed pitted, dark purplish-brown.
J. squamata	Decumbent shrub,* branch-lets thick, always tending to nod at tips.† Foliage much more closely packed than J. procumbens.	Green, grooved.	$\frac{1}{6}-\frac{1}{4}$ in	Finely pointed.	Crowded, overlapping, loosely appressed. Straight or slightly curved. Persisting as dry brown scale.	Two greyish white bands.	Convex. Grooved from base to near apex.	Ellipsoid. $\frac{1}{4}-\frac{1}{2}$ in long. Reddish-brown to purplish-black. 1 seeded.
J. morrison-icola	Shrub or small tree of open habit with ascending, terete branches and all growing tips bending over.	Green, 3-angled.	$\frac{1}{8}-\frac{1}{6}$ in	Lanceo-late, sharp-tipped.	Spreading; densely set and persistent to second year.	Concave; glaucescent.	Grey glaucous. Slightly keeled.	Globose. $\frac{1}{4}$ in diam. Dry, black, glabrous.

* Not true of some varieties.
† Only very slightly so in the fastigiate form J. squamata 'Loderi'.
‡ Not always clearly present in J. procumbens 'Nana'.

199

151 *Juniperus procumbens* 'Nana'. Note the raised branch-tips.

– – **'Nana'** is a slower-growing form with reduced entre-nœud, thicker stems and shorter and wider leaves. It forms a dense mat and is a much more desirable garden plant than the typical form, being particularly useful for ground cover or planting so as to trail downhill over rocks or a tree root.

There is a colour form **'Nana Glauca'** which is described by its name, but I cannot distinguish the form sold under the name **'Bonin Isles'** from 'Nana'.

In these garden forms the characteristic white smudges are not always discernible with the naked eye on every leaf and the plant may have to be searched over until a leaf is found on which they can be seen, and always the marks are much smaller than in the type species. 'Nana' is often confused with *J. squamata* 'Prostrata'. Apart from the presence of the smudges which will always identify *J. procumbens*, the growing tips of all forms of this species tend to turn upwards, whereas all forms of *J. squamata* nod, more or less, according to the variety. See table on page 199.

Juniperus recurva. This species has no claim to be regarded as a dwarf, but var. **coxii** makes such an attractive plant for some years if well grown that it is well worth planting, even although one knows at the time that it will have to come out after ten years or so. After all, gardeners are willing to go to a lot of trouble over annuals and bedding plants knowing that their usefulness will be limited to less than that number of months, so I can see no possible objection to planting a tree on these terms. The name *Juniperus recurva* 'Coxii' is equally "correct".

As its name, Coffin Juniper, indicates it forms a large timber tree in its native land, but when small it is an outstandingly graceful little tree with rich-green foliage and very pendulous branches. It is especially effective when planted to overhang water with its trunk leaning over at an angle.

The leader needs tying up for several years and the lower branches should be cut away and the foliage thinned drastically as the tree grows to bare the trunk and display the graceful habit of the tree.

◀ 152 *Juniperus recurva* 'Coxii'. A plant at the Wansdyke Nursery at Devizes, Wilts.

153 *Juniperus recurva* 'Embley Park', (syn. *Juniperus recurva* var. *viridis*). ▶

– – 'Embley Park' is an attractive garden variety making a wide-spreading bush with densely packed, rich, deep-green foliage. It was first noticed in a derelict rock garden at Embley Park, near Romsey, Hants (at one time the home of Florence Nightingale and now a boy's school), and it was named by Mr Hillier var. *viridis* on the assumption that it had been sent home by the plant collector George Forrest and so was established "in the wild". This is a case where a plant can have two "correct" names and, following the plan of this book, I prefer to use the above cultivar name.

It is a very attractive plant which should be much better known. Save for three plants at Embley Park, the only mature specimen I have seen is in a cottage garden at Headfort, Co. Kells, in Ireland.

154 *Juniperus recurva* 'Nana'. A young plant is much lower and more spreading.

– – 'Nana' is a form which, like the arboreal *J. squamata* var. *fargesii*, indicates a connection between the two species by showing intermediate characteristics, and I place it here because it is generally found under this species, rather than as myself having much conviction on the point. It is a picturesque, low, spreading plant with all its growing points strongly recurved; the leaves are much shorter than in *J. recurva* 'Coxii' but are of similar colouring. It builds up slowly in the centre of the bush, but is always much wider than high. The foliage is not uniike that of *Juniperus squamata* 'Wilsonii', but the plant has a more spreading habit. Also the general colour of the foliage is green, not grey as in that variety and in the diminutive form 'Glassell', for which *J. recurva* 'Nana' is sometimes mistaken, they being very similar in habit as small plants.

Juniperus rigida. This is a somewhat variable species which grows too big in time but it forms an interesting plant or small tree for some years. Its popular name, the Needle Juniper, is well earned and it is not a plant to be handled carelessly or without gloves. On the other hand its specific name is misleading as it is of a graceful, pendulous habit. It would make an interesting lawn specimen.

A procumbent shrub with yellow-brown branchlets and lustrous leaves, deeply concave and whitish on the upper side, which is found wild in the mountain zone of Japan and which has been grown as *J. communis* var. *nipponica* is now understood to be a mountain variety of this present species so should now be labelled **J. rigida** var. **nipponica.**

202

155 *Juniperus sabina* 'Cupressifolia'—a young plant. Note the prostrate habit and adult foliage.

156 *Juniperus rigida*. Close-up view of the always pendulous—and extremely prickly—foliage.

Juniperus sabina is a very variable, spreading or procumbent shrub widely distributed on the high mountains of Europe and Asia, and one in which the numerous named selections are much better garden plants than the type. All forms have a characteristic, disagreeable, pungent odour to the foliage when bruised, and a bitter taste. Both juvenile (awl-shaped) and adult (scale-like) leaves are usually to be found on any plant, both kinds appearing in opposite pairs.

– – **'Arcadia'** is one of the three cultivars (the others being 'Broadmoor' and 'Skandia') selected from many thousands of seedlings raised by the D. Hill Nursery Co., Dundee, Ill., U.S.A. from seed imported from a government forestry station near Petersburgh in Russia in 1933. All three are proving resistant to the juniper blight which is seriously troubling most plants of *J. sabina* in the mid-west and so are proving popular in the United States. 'Arcadia' is of a light grass-green colour and its habit resembles a low-growing form of 'Tamariscifolia', but the leaves are predominantly scale-like and small.

– – **'Blue Danube'** forms a low shrub with spreading branches having their tops curved upwards. The branchlets are crowded, the leaves mainly scale-like but the awl-shaped leaves inside the plant are a light greyish-blue. It is not in my opinion a particularly outstanding form.

– – **'Broadmoor'** is a dwarf, low, spreading, staminate form which looks like a rather neat form of 'Tamariscifolia' when young, but the plant tends to build up at the centre with age. The main branches are strong and spreading horizontally; the branchlets short and reaching upwards; the sprays very short and occurring mainly on the upper side of the branchlets. The foliage colour is a soft grey-green.

– – **'Cupressifolia'.** There is some confusion about this form. The name properly

203

157 *Juniperus sabina* 'Tamariscifolia'. A very old plant planted at the top of a low wall.

belongs to a compact and very low-growing form with almost wholly scale-like and appressed foliage. The branches are mainly spreading horizontally or occasionally upwards but never approaching to upright.

The name is sometimes wrongly applied to **'Erecta'**, which is a tall, loose-growing shrub, also with a predominance of adult foliage but with branches all ascending at a steep angle. It is not a particularly good garden plant and is hardly worth distinguishing from *J. sabina* in its typical form. 'Erecta' should not be confused with **'Fastigiata'**, which is a narrowly columnar form most unlike the typical *J. sabina* and by no means a dwarf form (*Ill. 161*).

– – **'Hicksii'** is a rather strong-growing shrub with branches at first ascending, becoming procumbent as the plant ages. Its foliage is dark bluish-green with a dull mauve tint in the winter and as it is mainly juvenile with the white upper sides of the leaves showing the plant has an attractive greyish-blue tint.

– – **'Musgrave'** is a low, spreading form which closely covers the ground, carrying mostly tightly appressed, adult foliage, but awl-shaped leaves occur here and there over the bush and in the centre of the plant. The foliage is glaucous.

▲ 158 *Juniperus sabina* 'Variegata'. The variegation varies from year to year.

◀ 159 *Juniperus sabina* 'Erecta'. An inferior garden plant. It is the common wild form.

– – **'Skandia'** is a flat-growing form, similar to 'Arcadia' (and of the same origin) but with a somewhat lower habit of growth and foliage slightly more yellow.

– – **'Tamariscifolia'.** This strictly speaking is a botanical variety, as it is found in the wild in Southern Europe, but it is so popular and useful in gardens that I here treat it as a cultivar. It is a low, spreading shrub with branches horizontal or nearly so and branchlets crowded and all lying forward at a narrow angle to the stem. It carries mostly juvenile, pointed leaves in opposite pairs, small and loosely appressed, white above and with a gland on the back of each leaf.

'Tamariscifolia' is a most useful plant, having an architectural quality all its own. It fits into the most formal layout, serving as an excellent foil to stonework. It also looks equally at home on a rough bank, or on the edge of the lawn. In time it will become a large plant, but its regular branching habit allows of quite heavy pruning without the plant losing its character.

Being a botanical variety it is variable and it is worth searching for a good clone. I consider the best form to be one which carries its leaves at a wider angle to the stem so that the white upper sides are more seen, this giving a greyish-blue look to the plant.

– – **'Variegata'** is an upright to spreading shrub with closely set branches and dark green adult foliage irregularly sprinkled with white variegation. It is quite an attractive form which could well be more widely planted.

– – **'Von Ehren'** is an upright, spreading form with light green foliage, with very small, adult leaves. Left to itself it forms a rather loose, open plant with no particular attraction (at least when young), but in America I understand it is in much demand sheered into a dense, globose shrub.

205

▲ 160 *Juniperus sargentii* (syn. *Juniperus chinensis* var. *sargentii*).
A good ground-cover plant.

161 *Juniperus sabina* 'Fastigiata' in Pinetum Schovenhorst at
Putten, Holland. ▶

Juniperus sargentii is a prostrate shrub found by Dr Sargent on the coast of North Japan, very useful for ground cover as it is hardy, very accommodating as to soil and situation and disease-free.

It has been variously described as *J. procumbens*, *J. chinensis* var. *procumbens* and *J. chinensis* var. *sargentii*, and as always in such circumstances can still be found growing under any name it has once carried. The last-mentioned is still recognized by some writers on the coniferae but I follow van Melle in treating it as a distinct species.

J. sargentii forms a low mat-like, spreading shrub with stout prostrate main branches and short ascending branchlets. The leaves are in whorls of three; keeled below, concave with a raised mid-rib above, up to 8 mm long by 2 mm broad and quite free standing on the main branches, but very much smaller, very closely set and loosely appressed on the branchlets and growing tips, giving them a cord-like appearance. The foliage has a very unpleasant smell of camphor when bruised, quite unlike any other juniper I know.

As a species (if species it be) it is somewhat variable and colour and habit variations have been selected as follows:

– – **'Compacta'.** Much more compact in growth with juvenile leaves dark green, very glaucous above, adult leaves light green with a dark green margin.

– – **'Glauca'.** A slow-growing form with glaucous grey-green foliage.

– – **'Viridis'.** A form lacking the glaucous bloom and hence appearing greener than the type.

Juniperus scopulorum. The Western Red Cedar or Rocky Mountain Juniper is a very variable species of which a large number of selected clones have been named in America, although few of them are dwarf forms. The foliage is in a general way similar to *J. virginiana*, a closely related species, but its branchlets are shorter and the foliage is more densely set, more or less tetragonal, 1 mm across; leaves adult, tightly appressed, tips pointed.

– – **'Admiral'** is a broad, pyramidal shrub with grey-green foliage.

– – **'Gareei'** is a dwarf, rounded, compact bush reaching to 1·5 m; branches spreading; foliage whitish-blue.

– – **'Globe',** as its name indicates, is a variety of globose habit: to 2 m high in time, with silvery-grey, juvenile foliage.

– – **'Hall's Sport'** is a semi-dwarf, upright, pyramidal form; very dense and slow-growing, with acicular (juvenile) foliage of a splendid silver colour.

– – **'Palmeri'.** (See 'Repens'.)

– – **'Repens'** Hornb. 1938 (126) is a dwarf form with prostrate branches similar to *J. horizontalis* 'Prostrata', branches spreading; branchlets directed forward, prostrate but with tips slightly turned up, leaves awl-shaped 5 mm long, bluish-green. This has been distributed as 'Palmeri' but the name 'Repens' has priority.

– – **'Silver King'** is a dwarf and spreading form, reaching to 50 cm high by 2 m diam. Densely branched and spreading with more or less filiform foliage of silvery-blue. An American patented variety.

– – **'Tabletop'** is a dwarf shrub to 2 m high by 5 m across with wide-spreading main branches, branchlets thin, pale yellow-brown; leaves very small, closely appressed, conspicuously blue. Female plants bear berries which add considerably to the attractiveness of the plant.

– – **'Welchii'.** With a name like this it should be good, but unfortunately it is not a dwarf form, so I cannot bring it in here. It is described as silvery-grey with "less silver in old age", so it would appear that extreme poverty stares me in the face eventually.

▲ 162 *Juniperus squamata* 'Loderi'. Detail of the foliage.

▲ 163 *Juniperus squamata* 'Meyeri'. The bluest of all junipers, but a strong grower.

◄ 164 *Juniperus squamata* 'Loderi'.

▼ 165 *Juniperus squamata* 'Glassell'. A very old plant in the Pygmy Pinetum at Devizes, Wilts., still less than 20 cm high.

JUNIPERUS

Juniperus squamata is a very variable, shrubby species from Central Asia, usually a low to prostrate shrub, but in some forms capable of being trained up as a small tree. The leaves are always awl-shaped, loosely appressed, overlapping, in whorls of three, not always easy to distinguish from the related species *J. procumbens* and *J. recurva* (see table on page 199). A distinct mark of *J. squamata* in all its forms is the tendency of the growing tips to turn downwards, or "nod".

– – **'Fargesii'** is an upright form of tree size with foliage and habit very similar to *J. recurva* 'Coxii'. It is rare in cultivation but there is a good specimen at Embley Park, near Romsey, Hants.

– – **'Forrestii'**. There is a distinct form in cultivation in Britain with foliage similar to the cultivar 'Wilsonii' but having a more upright habit, intermediate between that form and the fastigiate 'Loderi'. I cannot trace its origin, nor can I vouch for the legitimacy of the name, which may need to be replaced by a "fancy" name under the Code. In America this, or a similar plant, is grown as 'Campbellii', a name to which the same remarks apply. Confusion has been added to by the use of the latter name quite wrongly for *J. chinensis* 'Stricta' by some growers.

– – **'Glassell'** is a dwarf and very slow-growing form with branches ascending at steep, picturesque angles and short, curved branchlets. Foliage is greyish as 'Wilsonii', but much shorter and denser. It is an ideal plant for a trough garden, as its branching habit gives a "Ye olde gnarled apple tree" appearance to the tiniest plant, especially if all its foliage is nipped off except at the growing tips.

– – **'Loderi'** is a semi-dwarf form which forms a dense, columnar bush of the habit of *J. communis* 'Compressa', for a giant specimen of which it can be mistaken at a distance. Foliage is similar to 'Wilsonii'. Even in this fastigiate form the characteristic nodding at the growing tips is discernible. This form is sometimes quite incorrectly distributed as 'Fargesii'.

– – **'Meyeri'** forms a large handsome bush (or if trained as a young plant—a small tree) with strong-growing, luxuriant main shoots and short branchlets, gracefully curling over at every growing tip, quite one of the most beautiful of conifers, or indeed of all plants, when well grown. The foliage is dense and of a beautiful blue-grey. Leaves are long, straight and sharp-pointed, 6–10 mm long by 1·5 mm broad.

As this cultivar has a bad habit found in this species and holds on to its dead leaves several years it tends to develop a half-dead appearance in time. This can be overcome by regular hard pruning (as is advocated for black currants) to encourage strong young main branches and plenty of new wood.

– – **'Prostrata'**. There is some mystery here, and possibly this is actually the type plant of our species. As grown in England it is a low, spreading bush with horizontal branches and branchlets in wide sprays with all growing tips turned downwards. *J. procumbens* 'Nana' frequently passes under this name and I have already mentioned

▲ 167 *Juniperus squamata* 'Pygmaea'.

◀ 166 *Juniperus squamata* 'Wilsonii' in den Ouden nursery at Boskoop, Holland.

the mistake which I consider van Melle made on this point. The table on page 199 should help to distinguish these species.

– – **'Pygmaea'** forms a squat, dense little bush with its main branches standing out stiffly. Foliage is similar to 'Wilsonii', but growing tips less decurved.

– – **'Wilsonii'** is usually seen as an upright to spreading bush, densely furnished with branches and branchlets with all growing tips strongly decurved. The awl-shaped leaves are densely set 5–6 mm long by 1 mm wide, strongly incurved, the upper side with two bluish-white bands with a green mid-rib and narrow green margins; the lower sides green and keeled. Large bushes fruit freely.

Juniperus taxifolia Hooker and Arn. is a Japanese species seldom met with in cultivation which has given rise to a procumbent form which is a valuable garden plant.

– – var. **lutchuensis** (Koidz) Satake in Bull. Nat. Sci. Mus., Tokyo, Dec. 1962, **6**, 192, is a prostrate plant not unlike a *J. conferta* but differing from that species by its flatter leaves (less deeply grooved above, and with the mid-rib sometimes evident) its much more prostrate habit and the lack of prickliness to the foliage when bruised, or pungency when crushed. It has been grown as *J. conferta* "*maritima*" and as *J. lutchuensis*.

It is one of the few conifers that will fall down the face of a rock-wall like an Aubrieta and with its dense growth and fresh, grass-green foliage is a useful ground-cover plant and deserves to be much more widely known.

210

168 *Juniperus virginiana* 'Chamberlaynii' in the Pygmy Pinetum at Devizes, Wilts.

Juniperus virginiana. This species is closely related to *J. scopulorum*, being the equivalent in the eastern North America of that species in the west of the continent. It is clearly distinguishable from *J. scopulorum* in its flowering parts and in its habit of ripening its seeds in the first year, but in the dwarf forms, where we are usually restricted to foliage characteristics, they are often difficult to separate.

From all *J. chinensis* forms it can usually be distinguished by its juvenile leaves being in pairs (very rarely in threes) and by its adult leaves being always pointed, and from *J. sabina* forms by the absence of the true savin odour and taste to the foliage.

J. virginiana is mostly a tall, upright tree, but it is variable from seed and has given us a few shrubby and several spreading to prostrate forms. The leaves are usually adult, but frequently juvenile leaves are present even on old trees. The juvenile leaves are in pairs 3–6 mm long with a sharp point, concave and glaucous above except at margins, green and convex below, pointing forwards. The adult leaves are much smaller and are in four ranks (giving a somewhat tetragonal cross-section to the twigs which are very thin), overlapping, closely appressed (except, occasionally, at apex) with a glandular depression on the back.

– – **'Burkii'** is not a dwarf form, but can be grown as a large bush. It is attractive because of its grey foliage and purplish winter colour.

– – **'Chamberlaynii'** is a vigorous and nearly prostrate form with its branchlets mostly

211

169 *Juniperus virginiana* 'Globosa'.　　　　170 *Juniperus virginiana* 'Nana Compacta'.

hanging below the level of the vigorous, horizontally-held main branches. Strong shoots carry long juvenile leaves clasping the stem save for the free awl-shaped tips 3–5 mm long with a fine point; weaker shoots carry much smaller juvenile leaves nearly appressed. All juvenile foliage is green with a grey bloom (easily rubbed off) which gives a characteristically grey appearance to the whole plant. Usually old specimens carry a small amount of adult foliage in the centre of the plant, this being a dark green with an oval gland on the back of the leaf.

– – **'Globosa'.** This makes a truly globular plant, being probably one of the most naturally globose conifers we have, even large plants having the appearance of having had some artificial help in keeping their neat shape.

A specimen fifty years old in the Arnold Arboretum, Mass., U.S.A., is only 4·5 m high and is an excellent rounded and densely branched specimen. Except in small plants the foliage is mainly adult with small leaves and fine twigs densely set, the leaves being green. It is one of the most attractive forms and has been in cultivation for many years. **'Dumosa'** if it differed from the above is no longer in cultivation.

– – **'Grey Owl'.** This is an alleged hybrid (*J. virginiana* 'Glauca' × *J. media* 'Pfitzeriana') which inherits the habit of one parent and the foliage colouring of the other.

The branches are thin and the growing tips are sometimes tinged with purple in the winter.

– – **'Horizontalis'.** There seems to be some confusion between this name and **'Reptans'.** Hornibrook alleges that they are "quite distinct" and den Ouden follows it in listing them separately. Krussmann in *Die Nadelgehölze*, 1960, in his description of 'Reptans'

171 *Juniperus virginiana* 'Kosteri'. Has a more prostrate habit than *J.* × *media* 'Pfitzeriana'.

more or less repeats Hornibrook's description of 'Horizontalis', giving that cultivar as a synonym and adding that it is a popular variety in German nurseries. Kumlien in *The Friendly Evergreens*, 1954, repeats the story of the finding of a prostrate form on a high cliff on the coast of Maine and calls the variety in cultivation in America **'Horizontalis Glauca'** (adding the vernacular name 'Blue Coast Juniper') and gives a very good colour illustration of a plant that does not answer Krussmann's description of 'Reptans'. Whether the German and the American plants are the same I cannot say. Neither of them appears to be in cultivation in Britain, plants labelled *J. virginiana* 'Horizontalis' being as Mr Hillier says always forms of *J. horizontalis* and plants of *J. virginiana* 'Horizontalis Glauca' turning out to be 'Chamberlaynii'.

It would be necessary to study the two plants, or at least compare living material, to settle this conundrum.

– – **'Kosteri'**. I have referred to this mystery form on page 195, under *J.* × *media*.

– – **'Montrosa'** is a curious form, very slow-growing and with congested foliage. It is a collectors' piece only.

– – **'Nana Compacta'** is a bush up to about 1 m, more or less globose but much less regular in outline than 'Globosa' and bearing mainly juvenile foliage on its crowded branchlets. The leaves are greenish-grey above, green below, turning dull purplish-green in winter.

I believe this to be the plant which Mr Hillier tells of having been purchased by

213

172 *Juniperus virginiana* 'Tripartita'.

173 *Juniperus virginiana* 'Skyrocket'.

Mr Nisbet for 6*d.* and grown by him under the name of "*tripartita nana*". Grown in the open ground it soon becomes much larger than Mr Nisbet's specimen.

– – **'Pendula Nana'** is a very small, slow-growing form with a strongly pendulous habit so that, as described by Mr Hillier (incorrectly, as I believe) under the cultivar name 'Chamberlaynii', it makes an almost prostrate grey-green mat unless trained up in its early days. In the Pygmy Pinetum, Devizes, I have a small plant that was so trained to a height of 30 cm or so and is now planted where it is flowing down over the face of the rockery where in time I think it will make a most attractive specimen. There is a good plant in the National Pinetum at Bedgebury in Kent.

– – **'Sky Rocket'** is not a dwarf form, but as it must be one of the most narrowly columnar trees in existence it can be used with great effect for some years where a strong vertical line is required in the garden picture. It passes as a form of *J. virginiana*, but in a young plant here I notice the juvenile foliage is in threes, so I "hae' me doots". It needs no description—it is too narrowly columnar to be anything else than what it is.

214

174 *Juniperus virginiana* 'Pendula Nana'. A young plant in the Pygmy Pinetum at Devizes, Wilts.

– – **'Tripartita'** is a strong-growing form which forms a large dense bush 2–2·5 m across by nearly as much high. It usually throws several stiff main branches from near the ground level and bears a mixture of adult and juvenile foliage which is green, turning to dull purple in winter. It is not in my opinion a particularly attractive form, but is useful where a fairly large and wide-spreading plant is required, being roughly the equivalent of *J.* × *media* 'Pfitzeriana', but it is more upright and of a stiffer habit of growth.

Larix

This is a small genus of forest trees much in demand for timber production. It has given rise to two or three pendulous forms, but these are not dwarfs and of a few truly dwarf forms that have been recorded from time to time none is in cultivation. As the Larix is one of the few deciduous conifers this is not from a garden point of view a great loss. The leaf arrangement of Larix is similar to that of Cedrus, for which genus plants can be mistaken when in young foliage in early summer.

175 *Libocedrus decurrens* 'Intricata' in Mr H. G. Hillier's collection.

Libocedrus

Various attempts have been made to change the name of this genus, which can be found under the names *Calocedrus* and *Heyderia*, but here I follow the Kew hand list of 1961 in retaining this name.

Libocedrus decurrens is a species which is usually seen as a tall columnar tree of monumental proportions with dense, rich green foliage. The leaves are dark green, in fours, equal in size, pressed close to the branchlets except at the short, pointed tip which is free, those of ultimate branchlets about 6 mm long those on the main shoots about 12 mm long, the latter pair boat-shaped and overlapping the facing pair. It has given us two, or possibly three, dwarf forms.

216

– – **'Compacta'** is a form with foliage of a normal size but with a reduced entre-nœud which results in a compact plant. There is a good specimen at the Westonbirt Arboretum, in Gloucestershire, near the Head Forester's office.

– – **'Intricata'** is a true dwarf, forming a compact, erect little plant with a very dense branching system and very dense foliage which bronzes in winter.

– – **'Nana'** is described as "very dwarf and compact, suitable for the rock garden". Whether it is distinct from 'Intricata' I cannot say.

176 *Microcachrys tetragona* in the alpine collection at Wisley.

MICROCACHRYS

Microcachrys tetragona, the sole occupant of this genus, in its native Tasmania is a low, straggling evergreen bush with long, slender, whip-cord-like branches. It is hardy in Britain but is usually grown in an alpine house, where it soon gets out of hand unless the branches are regularly shortened to encourage a bushy habit which is not natural to the plant.

The tiny leaves are in four regular ranks, giving a tetragonal effect to the shoot and they persist for several years. It will often set its tiny red cones in captivity and is an interesting little plant when well grown, the best specimen I know being in Mr Ingwersen's collection at East Grinstead, Sussex.

PICEA

The dwarf spruces are among the aristocrats of the dwarf conifer world, but unfortunately this is the very group in which the greatest confusion exists as regards identification and nomenclature.

The Norway spruce alone has given rise to eighty dwarf forms (perhaps I should be more correct in saying eighty *names*) and several of the other species add their quota, and they are all very much tangled up.

In 1938 Hornibrook wrote "One could fill a good-sized garden with the dwarf forms of the Norway spruce" and he could with equal truth today add the words ". . . as to the correct names of all of which one's visitor experts will disagree".

One major difficulty is that botanical writers have seldom taken much real interest in these dwarf forms, so some of the earlier descriptions are quite inadequate to identify the plant intended. Another difficulty is that many of these forms are very variable and liable to reversion (especially is this the case where a dwarf form has originated with a Witch's Broom) so that they are liable to be mistaken for closely related forms.

Hornibrook made a valiant attempt to collect together all the then known forms and to provide adequate descriptions and additional names where necessary, but even so it is difficult and often impossible to identify a plant from his descriptions and there are several new forms now in cultivation, so I feel that the only way to sort this group out is to record the characteristics of these cultivars much more thoroughly and systematically than has ever previously been attempted. Opposite there is a replica of the "Survey Sheet" that I am using for this purpose, from which it will be seen that most aspects of the plant are being studied closely, and before another edition of this book is called for I hope to be able to produce a reliable key to all or nearly all of the forms now in cultivation.

In the meantime I am restricting myself to a description of those varieties in which the diagnostic position is reasonably clear, these being most, but not all, of the forms readily obtainable. I am aware that the omissions will disappoint my readers, but a glance at the "Survey Sheet" will show that the task, although neither a difficult one nor one calling for much botanical knowledge is a very tedious one, and to have waited until the elucidation of all the dwarf forms in this genus was complete would have delayed the appearance of this book for a couple of years or more.

In the meantime readers can help considerably in this good work by bringing to my notice the whereabouts of mature specimens (especially of the less common forms) whose age or recorded history gives authority to the names under which they are being grown. Having so much detail recorded from a survey made of any particular plant, I find that it is usually quite easy to say with reasonable certainty whether another plant I am asked to identify elsewhere is that same cultivar or not. This fact augurs well for the ultimate success of the scheme and, in the absence of an established reference collection, by far the most difficult aspect of the work is to locate plants of

SURVEY SHEET FOR PICEA KEY

Species   Cultivar   Location   Date

Age of plant   Origin (if known)   Dimensions   (High) ×   (Across)

HABIT

1 Habit of growth of plant
Pendulous ☐   Prostrate or procumbent ☐
Decumbent ☐   Cushion-shape ☐
Spreading, wider than high ☐   Globose ☐
Broadly conical ☐   Narrowly conical ☐
Columnar ☐

2 General appearance of plant is:
Uniform and regular ☐   Irregular and untidy ☐

3 Growth is:
Open ☐   Dense ☐   Very dense ☐

4 Pattern of branch system
Ascending ☐   Spreading ☐
Noticeably in layers ☐   No clear pattern ☐

5 Angle to the horizontal of the main side branches
Above ☐   Below ☐

DORMANT BUDS

6 Shade
Light ☐   Medium ☐   Dark ☐

7 Colour of bud
Yellow ☐   Orange ☐   Brown ☐
Red ☐   Crimson ☐

8 Colour is:
Bright ☐   Dull ☐

9 Shape of bud
Conical ☐   Cylindrical ☐
Ovoid ☐   Globose ☐

10 Shape of apex of bud
Sharp point ☐   Blunt point ☐   Rounded ☐

Size in mm (largest dimension)   Min   Max
11 Terminal buds ☐ to ☐
12 Minor lateral buds ☐ to ☐

13 Surface texture of buds
Glossy ☐   Sheen ☐   Dull ☐

    Yes   No
14 Whether resinous in winter ☐ ☐
15 Number in terminal cluster ☐

    Yes   No
16 Are lateral buds numerous? ☐ ☐

17 Are the buds prominent when the plant is viewed as a whole?
Very prominent ☐   Noticeable ☐
Inconspicuous ☐   Invisible ☐

BUD SCALES

18 Size relative to size of bud
Large ☐   Medium ☐   Small ☐

Shape of bud scale
19 Pointed ☐   Rounded ☐

    Yes   No
20 Fringed with hairs or resin ☐ ☐
21 Appressed (held close to bud) ☐

MATURE LEAVES

22 Shade
Light ☐   Medium ☐   Dark ☐

23 Colour is: Bright ☐   Dull ☐

24 Colour of leaves
Grey-green ☐   Blue-green ☐
Mid-green ☐   Yellow-green ☐
Variegated ☐   (Describe)

Leaf shape (along itself)
25 Straight ☐   Curved ☐   Other ☐ (Describe)

    Yes   No
26 Sides are parallel ☐ ☐
27 Tapered: base to tip ☐ ☐
28 Tapered: from centre both ways ☐ ☐
29 Top half tapered ☐ ☐

30 Cross section of leaf
Thin and flat ☐   Thick and flat ☐
Square or rhombic ☐   Round like a needle ☐

    Yes   No
31 Mid-rib is prominent ☐ ☐

32 Are leaves stiff to the touch?
Very ☐   Yes ☐   No ☐

Shape of leaf tip
33 Sharp point ☐   Medium point ☐   Blunt point ☐
34 Point symmetrical ☐   Oblique ☐
35 Is tip drawn out? (Describe)

    Yes   No
36 Sharp to the touch? ☐ ☐

Stomatic lines (number of rows)
37 Top of leaf ☐   Underside ☐ (rows each side of mid-rib)

    Yes   No
38 Stomata extend to leaf tip ☐ ☐

Size of leaf (mm)   Min   Max
39 Length ☐ to ☐
40 Width (greatest) ☐ to ☐

Surface texture
41 Glossy ☐   Sheen ☐   Dull ☐

42 Leaf arrangement on shoot
Radial ☐   Semi-radial ☐
Pectinate (in two rows) ☐

Leaf angle to shoot, in degrees
43 At sides, viewed from above ☐
44 Above, viewed from the side ☐
45 Below, viewed from the side ☐
46 Angle of aberrant leaf below each lateral bud (If no such aberrant leaf) ☐

47 Spacing of leaves on shoot
Over-lapping ☐   Close together ☐   Wide apart ☐

48 Leaves on top of shoot:
    Yes   No
Point forward along shoot ☐ ☐
Hide shoot from view ☐ ☐

Shape outlined by tips of leaves
49 Oval ☐   Parallel ☐   Taper ☐
50 Describe arrangement of leaves around terminal bud

FIRST YEAR SHOOTS

51 Upper side: shade
Light ☐   Medium ☐   Dark ☐

52 Upper side: colour
White ☐   Yellow ☐   Orange ☐
Brown ☐   Grey ☐

53 Lower side: shade
Light ☐   Medium ☐   Dark ☐

54 Lower side: colour
White ☐   Yellow ☐   Orange ☐
Brown ☐   Grey ☐

55 Surface texture
Glossy ☐   Sheen ☐   Dull ☐
Hairy (pubescent) ☐   Bare (glabrous) ☐

    Yes   No
56 Are pulvini prominent? ☐ ☐
57 Shoots are: Thin ☐   Thick ☐
58 Shoots feel: Flexible ☐   Stiff ☐

    Min   Max
59 Annual growth in mm ☐ to ☐

    Degrees
60 Angle: shoot to branch ☐ to ☐
61 Describe a typical spray of one, two and three year wood as held in the hand.

Add any special information of help in recognizing the variety and/or distinguishing between it and similar varieties.

219

177 *Picea abies* 'Acrocona'. Not a dwarf form, but interesting for the way it bears its cones, even as a small plant.

unimpeachable veracity to serve as my "types", for even in the best collections there are plants which are clearly different from plants similarly labelled elsewhere.

I have taken Murray Hornibrook's work as a basis. Some of his descriptions clearly relate to the plants I now describe in more detail, but in some cases I shall probably have to fall back upon the balance of probability or a consensus of evidence from several reliable sources, so I endeavour whenever possible to examine several plants of each variety of different ages and in different surroundings, and any readers who can help at all, even if only with regard to a single form, are invited to communicate with me through the publishers or by writing to me direct at The Pygmy Pinetum, Devizes, Wiltshire.

The following descriptions have been compiled from my own surveys and the information follows the same order as on the survey sheet on page 219, a glance at which will make clear the meaning of the occasionally cryptic form of the descriptions. A magnifying glass of × 25 magnification has been used throughout.

In the use of my descriptions several points need to be borne in mind. One is that it is quite impossible to distinguish the various forms during the summer months, from the time the young buds swell and burst until the new dormant buds are well formed in the autumn.

Of the characteristics recorded, some are more variable than others. Habit, for instance, varies considerably with the age of plant; annual growth with its vigour; colour of shoots and foliage is affected by soil and climate; pubescence and other characters vary with the season—so these characteristics must be used with caution. On the other hand, leaf shape; the angle at which the leaf is held to the twig and the side twig to the main shoot; the angle of the main *side* branches to the horizontal; the size and arrangement of the buds, especially in the terminal cluster, and the disposition of the leaves at this part of the shoot are usually stable throughout the life of the plant and so have greater diagnostic value.

The prostrate and procumbent forms have been a particularly difficult group. As always, the older descriptions are too sketchy to carry any certainty and Hornibrook in some cases gave names to plants he had not seen. I have allocated the published names amongst all the different cultivars I have been able to find, according to the best available evidence but I must admit to having been finally reduced to rather arbitrary action in one or two cases, so I am far from claiming to have had the last word on this subject. However, I think my descriptions should be adequate to identify each clone I deal with and if further research requires any changes in the names I have used it should cause no great difficulty. The basis of my choice of name is given in the course of each description.

Picea abies. The Norway Spruce is normally a conical tree up to 50 m high but the dwarf forms are of all sizes down to small bun-like plants never over 50 cm high. Those forms which originated by propagation from a Witch's Broom tend to revert (i.e. throw out strong, healthy normal growth), and seedling variants tend to grow coarse and out of character in time. In both cases the garden value of the plant can be preserved indefinitely by regular and systematic cutting away of all strong growth as it appears.

The dwarf forms group themselves broadly, according to habit, as follows:

Prostrate to Spreading
  'Decumbens'
  'Ellwangeriana'
  'Nidiformis'
  'Procumbens'
  'Pseudo-prostrata'
  'Pumila'
  'Pumila Glauca'
  'Pumila Nigra'
  'Repens'
  'Tabuliformis'

Very small Bun-shaped to Globose
  'Echiniformis'
  'Gregoryana'
  'Gregoryana Parsonii'
  'Gregoryana Veitchii'
  'Humilis'
  'Nana Compacta'
  'Pygmaea'

Globose and Squat
  'Capitata'
  'Clanbrassiliana'
  'Clanbrassiliana Elegans'
  'Diffusa'
  'Ellwangeriana'
  'Globosa Nana'
  'Knaptonensis'
  'Maxwellii'   ?
  'Merkii'   ?
  'Nana'
  'Pseudo-Maxwellii'   ?

Conical and Upright
  'Beissneri'
  'Dumosa'
  'Microsperma'
  'Mucronata'
  'Ohlendorffii'
  'Pachyphylla'
  'Phylicoides'
  'Remontii'

Pendulous
  'Inversa'
  'Reflexa'

221

178 *Picea abies* 'Beissneri'.　　　　　　　　　179 *Picea abies* 'Capitata'.

– – **'Beissneri'** is an uncommon but quite distinctive form which should be better known. My description was taken from a plant 2 m high by 1·25 m across at the Schovenhorst Pinetum at Putten in Holland. Its dense habit and thick, square leaves give a "lusty" look to the bush. The thick leaves clustering round and hiding the terminal bud distinguish it from all forms save **'Barryi'**, which I fancy is a coarse form to which this cultivar may revert. The solitary terminal bud distinguishes it from 'Capitata'. It forms a globose plant when young, becoming broadly conical with age. The growth is very irregular and untidy and very dense; the branching system is ascending, but in no clear pattern; many main branches rise steeply, weaker branches at all angles.

BUDS: Very light yellow-green, flat globose, with rounded tip; 5–7 mm (terminal), 2–3 mm (other), dull. Solitary terminal bud completely hidden by the leaves.

BUD SCALES: Small and shapeless, fringed with resin.

LEAVES: Dark mid-green, parallel-sided, very thick and stout, square in cross section, ending in a sharp point with a drawn-out tip. Three to four or more broken rows of stomatic lines above and below. *Size*: 5–15 mm long and proportionally wide (the width varying with the vigour of the shoot), glossy, arranged radially to semi-radially held at 50/70° horizontally and 30° above. A dense cluster of thick leaves closes round the terminal bud completely hiding it from view. Leaves are set close together near the terminal bud only and are very stiff to the touch.

SHOOTS: Light yellow-brown. Pulvini are very prominent. Shoots are very thick and stiff; annual growth 20–27 mm side shoots at 45–50° to branch.

– – **'Capitata'.** The identity of this variety is fairly clear. The following description was taken from a plant 60 cm high and 1 m across near the top of the rock garden at

222

the Royal Horticultural Gardens at Wisley, and larger plants at Glasnevin agree closely.

'Capitata' forms a globose to spreading plant of irregular, open and lush growth, with branching system ascending and spreading in no clear pattern. Many branches rise steeply and are surmounted with a cluster of short shoots (hence the name) giving the plant an irregular, congested appearance which is characteristic. It is an attractive form which should be better known. It is sometimes confused with 'Beissneri'.

BUDS: Dull medium orange-brown, but with centres sometimes green, ovoid to globose (variable) with blunt point; 3–5 mm (terminal) 2–3 mm (other) glossy, resinous in winter. Number in terminal cluster very variable. Sometimes it is 1–3, but occasionally 4–10 buds are clustered closely around the terminal or sub-terminal bud so closely as to be almost like one large bud. Buds are noticeable.

BUD SCALES: Medium, rounded, closely appressed.

LEAVES: Bright medium, mid-green, straight or very slightly curved forwards, sides parallel, very thick and flat, keeled below, top quarter tapering to a medium to blunt point slightly drawn out at the tip, sharp to the touch. Two to three (often softened) rows of stomatic lines above and below, not extending to tip. *Size*: 10–15 mm long (shortest around the terminal cluster) by seldom over 1 mm wide, very glossy, arranged radially to semi-radially, held at 40/45°, horizontally, 20° above and 10–30° below. Aberrant leaf at 60°. Leaves on top of shoot point forward partly hiding shoot. Leaves form parallel outline, ending in a cluster of very short incurved leaves, not hiding the bud. Leaves are set close together, and are very stiff to the touch.

SHOOTS: Medium orange above, light orange below, with slight sheen, glabrous. Pulvini are prominent and orange-brown. Shoots are rather thick but flexible. Annual growth 60–80 mm, much less where the side terminal buds develop, giving the "clustered" effect. Side shoots at 45° to branch, variable.

– – 'Clanbrassiliana'. This was the earliest dwarf form of the Norway Spruce to be discovered, having been first described in 1836, and since the original tree is still alive in Tollymore Park, near Newcastle, Co. Down, Northern Ireland, in a spot open to the public for all to see the confusion over its identity is surprising and quite unnecessary. It may be partly due to a tendency years ago to regard 'Clanbrassiliana' as a collective name covering any dwarf form of *P. abies* and partly to the existence of varieties having points of similarity with 'Clanbrassiliana' (some of them in part also sharing its name) but the regrettable fact is that it is not at all easy to find true to name. Some eminent English and Continental nurseries send out 'Clanbrassiliana Elegans' in its place and on page 231 I am taking the liberty of using a photograph of the stock plant at one time maintained in a famous Irish nursery, as an illustration of 'Gregoryana', a variety which has little in common with 'Clanbrassiliana'.

'Clanbrassiliana' forms a broad and spreading, a globose or sometimes a squatly upright bush (doubtless influenced much in habit by pruning in early life), very slow-growing and with a crowded branch system with large, conical, red-brown buds and

▲ 180 *Picea abies* 'Clanbrassiliana'. Detail of foliage. Note the variation in leaf size and vigour.

◄ 181 *Picea abies* 'Clanbrassiliana'. The original tree in Tollymore Park, Newcastle, Co. Down, N.I.

rather wiry-looking foliage in which each leaf appears curved, is held edgeways, is widest about mid-way along its length and tapers thence gradually to a fine point with a drawn-out sharp tip. One feature always met with in the true plant is the noticeable difference in vigour (i.e. annual growth and leaf length) at different parts of the plant, and sometimes between adjacent shoots. The branching system is spreading with the main side branches ascending at 10–20°, more at the crown of the plant. The leaf-spray is flat, slightly up-cupped, so that the bush is more or less regular in growth but without any noticeable appearance of growth in layers.

BUDS: Medium red-brown, long-conical with sharp point, 4–5 mm (terminal), 2–3 mm (other) glossy, very resinous in winter so as to make the buds then appear light grey in colour. Number in terminal cluster 1–3, rarely 4; frequently there are two additional horizontal buds near terminal cluster and again at the base of the current year's growth and (rarely) one additional bud half-way. Buds are prominent because of their size and bright colour.

BUD SCALES: Large, pointed, fringed with resin, closely appressed.

LEAVES: Medium, bright to dull mid-green. Leaves emerge at a narrow angle to shoot; those on top of shoot are straight, elsewhere they curve away sharply near their base and are thence straight or (most frequently) curved outwards. *They are widest at the centre*, are thick and flat in cross section with a raised mid-rib and are *held edgeways to the shoot*. The upper half of the leaf tapers gradually to a long fine point ending in a fine long drawn-out tip pointing forwards, sharp to the touch.

224

182 *Picea abies* 'Clanbrassiliana Elegans'. Compare with *Ill. 180*

Two to three broken rows of stomatic lines above and below, not extending to tip. *Size*: 5–10 mm (or more) by 0·5–0·75 mm wide, with slight sheen, arranged radially to semi-radially, held at 60–80° horizontally and 30° above and 70–80° below (angles measured at the tips of the leaves). Aberrant leaf at 90–100°, not always present. Leaves on top of shoot point forward, nearly hiding shoot. Leaves form oval to tapered outline. There is no concentration of leaves around terminal bud, but normal leaves point forward at ±30° and end in line with each other, giving a "squared off" appearance. Leaves are set close together, and are flexible to the touch. SHOOTS: Light grey-brown above, creamy or greenish-white below, glossy, glabrous. Pulvini are not prominent. Shoots are thin and flexible; annual growth 20–50 mm, very noticeably variable between strong shoots carrying long leaves and weak shoots bearing short to very short leaves.

Any tendency to coarseness of growth should be checked by cutting away growth that is out of character before it gets too extensive.

– – **'Clanbrassiliana Elegans'** forms a broadly conical plant with a branching system of no clear pattern and with very dense, irregular growth. The main branches rise at 10–45°; the leaf-spray is basically flat but each shoot arches over downwards so that the whole spray droops, all growing tips being held at −10°. My description is taken from plants at Glasnevin: in other examples I have seen this drooping at the tips is not so evident. This form is often distributed by nurseries here and in Holland as 'Clanbrassiliana', from which form it is quite distinct.
BUDS: Medium red-brown, ovoid, with blunt (occasionally long) point. 2–3 mm (terminal), 1·5–2 mm (other), with slight sheen. Solitary terminal bud, with usually a pair of sub-terminal buds; other lateral buds few: buds noticeable.
BUD SCALES: Medium, rounded, not fringed, appressed.

225

LEAVES: Medium, bright mid-green, straight or curved backwards, widest at the centre, rhombic, held edgeways, narrowing gradually to a long, symmetrical point drawn out to a long, fine, translucent tip, sharp to the touch. One (occasionally two) rows of very small stomata above and below, extending to tip. *Size*: 6–8 mm long by 0·5–0·75 mm wide, glossy, arranged imperfectly radially, held at 50–60° horizontally, 20–30° above and 50° below. Aberrant leaf at 90°. Leaves on top of shoot point forward, partially hiding shoot. Leaves form an oval outline. Leaves are set close together and are stiff to the touch.

SHOOTS: Light yellow above, very pale yellow below, glossy, glabrous. Pulvini are prominent. Shoots are thin and very flexible. Annual growth 20–30 mm, side shoots at 60–70° to branch. Bud sheaths persistent three years, dark brown to black.

– – **'Clanbrassiliana Stricta'** is indistinguishable in old plants from 'Clanbrassiliana Elegans', and even if it is not actually the same clone (which it could well be) is not in my opinion sufficiently distinctive to justify retention of the name.

– – **'Decumbens'** forms a flat, spreading plant, never over 30 cm high by 1 m across. It is very similar to 'Nidiformis', but the branching system is more horizontal and so does not produce a "nest" effect, and the leaves lack the wiry look of 'Nidiformis' and are a lighter and yellower green. Growth is irregular and very dense; branching system with no clear pattern.

The description was taken from a plant twenty-five years old in Mr R. F. Watson's collection at Taunton, in August 1964. There is some confusion with 'Dumosa' here as the description given by Hornibrook (especially his reference to a rhubarb leaf) relates to the latter variety as here described. The plants he donated to Glasnevin may as young plants at the time have been decumbent but they are now large upright-globose and are I think identical with the Westonbirt plant from which my description of 'Dumosa' is taken.

BUDS: Medium red-brown, conical, with sharp point 2–3 mm, very uniform all over plant, dull, resinous in winter. Solitary terminal bud, with frequently two sub-terminals, usually three to four lateral buds irregularly spaced. Buds inconspicuous.

BUD SCALES: Rounded, fringed with resin, very closely appressed.

LEAVES: Medium, very bright yellow-green, straight especially near tips, elsewhere often curved forwards, with parallel sides tapering towards tip, thick but flat; mid-rib prominent, with a sharp, oblique point, drawn out to a fine tip, sharp to the touch. One to three rows glistening white stomatic lines above and below. *Size*: 12–20 mm long (shortest near the tips) by uniformly 1 mm wide, glossy, arranged semi-radially, held at 70–90° horizontally and at 40° above; no aberrant leaf. Leaves on top of shoot point forward, not hiding shoot. Leaves form parallel outline, several short leaves, pointing forward, surrounding the terminal bud. Leaves are set close together, and are flexible to the touch.

SHOOTS: Light brown above and below, dull, glabrous. Pulvini are prominent. Shoots (except for strong leaders) are thin and very flexible; annual growth 40–70 mm,

Picea abies 'Decumbens'.　　　　　　　　184 *Picea abies* 'Diffusa'.

fairly uniform all over plant, side shoots at 20–40° to branch, the angle being notice-ably variable. Forms a flat open spray, not very regular, with all young shoots curving slightly downwards. Branches 0–20° above the horizontal, arching over to 0°, save for a few weaker shoots at steeper angles.

– – **'Diffusa'.** From the bad record of survival of these dwarf spruces in the climate at Kew I expected to have to put this name on the "Lost to Cultivation" list, especially as it had never apparently strayed into commercial production, but several years ago I came across several old plants in a cottage garden in Gloucestershire which appear to be of this variety, and two of these are now in the Pygmy Pinetum at Devizes.

They answer very well to Hornibrook's description except that instead of making a wide-spreading bush like the plant at Kew mentioned by Hornibrook in his first edition (but apparently no longer there in 1938) my plants have formed very attractive bee-skip shape bushes about 75 cm tall and the same across and are maintaining this shape and a dense uniform outline by sending up several nearly vertical shoots carrying radial foliage at the crown of the plant in addition to the normal side shoots carrying the thin, flattish, semi-radial foliage described by Hornibrook.

Apart from the different habit and the yellower green of the foliage, 'Diffusa' differs from 'Pumila' only in minor respects, as follows: Terminal buds in cluster contains 1–5 buds making buds more noticeable; mid-rib of leaves is slightly raised; the (usually transparent) leaf tips always point forwards; leaves are narrower (0·75–1 mm) but closer together so as to hide upper side of shoot and finish with usually a broken circle of short, stiff (not drooping), needle-like leaves pointing forward at ±20° around the terminal cluster; the shoots are thinner and the annual growth is

227

185 *Picea abies* 'Dumosa'. A young plant.   186 *Picea abies* 'Ellwangeriana'.

greater (50–60 mm). The 1–2 year leaf-spray is flat but by the third year it is twisted out of the place of the spray, resulting in a very dense and solid-looking plant.

'Diffusa' is a reliable and attractive garden form of great decorative value and should be better known than it is.

– – **'Dumosa'** forms an upright to spreading or upright conical plant, the growth being regular and dense; the branching system is noticeably in layers, the main branches all standing out at +10°. The plant increases in height by throwing up central leader growths, and these are apt (unless kept in check with the knife) to take over and the plant loses its attraction and grows tall and coarse. This description was made during August, from a large plant at Westonbirt Arboretum, Gloucestershire. This cultivar is frequently found labelled 'Decumbens'.

BUDS: Light orange-brown, long ovoid, with blunt point, 5–6 mm (terminal), 3–4 mm other, glossy. No true terminal cluster, but 5–6 lateral buds close to terminal bud, no other lateral buds. Buds noticeable because of the way they are grouped together near the terminal bud.

BUD SCALES: Medium, pointed, not fringed with resin, closely appressed.

LEAVES: Dark, dull mid-green, straight, or occasionally very slightly curved forward, sides parallel, thick but flat, grooved, with a medium point somewhat oblique, ending in a minute tip, not sharp to the touch. One or two rows stomatic lines extending to tip. *Size*: 10–15 mm long by 1 mm wide, shortest on top of the shoot above and below, glossy, arranged radially, held at 50–60° horizontally (up to 90° near buds), 20° above and 40° below. Leaves on top of shoot point forward not hiding shoot. Leaves form a parallel outline with a semicircular end (due to full-length leaves radiating at all angles from between buds), these are so narrow as to appear to be spaced apart and are flexible to the touch.

SHOOTS: Light yellow above, very pale grey below, with slight sheen and slight pubescence. Pulvini are prominent. Shoots are thin and very flexible; annual growth

228

50–70 mm, side shoots at all angles from 20–90° to branch, because the sub-terminal buds develop shoots radiating at all angles, all more or less in the plane of the spray, as the spokes of a wheel. This characteristic development year after year gives a definite pattern even to quite large branches.

– – **'Echiniformis'** (The Hedgehog Spruce) forms a very slow-growing, neat, globose or cushion-shaped plant of dense, irregular and congested growth. It is often confused with 'Gregoryana' and occasionally with 'Veitchii'.

BUDS: Light brown with slight sheen and light yellow-green centres where not covered with scales; large buds cylindrical with rounded tips, 1–3 mm diameter, very irregular in size. Growth is very congested and irregular and may occur in either of two ways, viz. strong shoots 15–20 mm long with normal leaves and a small terminal cluster (3–5 buds of assorted sizes), or a congested type of growth in which a cluster of buds has developed into a mass of short shoots 3–5 mm long with tiny leaves, each carrying its own terminal cluster, the effect being a congested mass of buds and leaves up to 15 mm across. These two types of growth often alternate. There is an occasional lateral bud on the long shoots, near the base. These large bud clusters are a very prominent feature on some plants, but are not always present.

BUD SCALES: Usually small and very closely appressed, but occasionally they are pointed, loosely appressed and with tips free.

LEAVES: Medium, dull, yellow to grey-green, sharply turned out at base, thence straight or slightly curved forward, parallel, with the top half tapered to a sharp, more or less symmetrical point, sometimes drawn out to a short tip, *very sharp to the touch*, very narrow but thick and of rhombic cross section, but held *flat*; the mid-rib not being prominent. Three to four very broken rows of stomatic lines above and below, extending to tip. *Size*: 12–15 mm or occasionally longer by 1–1·25 mm wide with slight sheen, arranged radially and held at all angles to the shoot. Occasional shoots bear much wider and thicker leaves. No aberrant leaf. The uppermost leaves on the strong shoots stand off at 70–90° (or even more) in a roughly star-like ring, *below* the terminal cluster. The large bud clusters are a confused mass of buds and small to very small leaves pointing more or less forward. *Leaves on strong shoots are few and spaced well apart*, and are stiff and prickly to the touch—hence the popular name.

SHOOTS: Light brown with slight sheen, glabrous. Pulvini are flattened, giving shoot a "crocodile leather" appearance. Relative to their length the shoots are thick and very stiff. The erratic development of the buds gives a congested and completely patternless growth.

– – **'Ellwangeriana'** forms a dense, robust-looking and spreading plant with ascending branches but no central leader. Growth from lateral buds lies in a flat spray, but where terminal buds are numerous these develop clusters of almost radial shoots, giving a somewhat "tufty" look to the plant. Makes a good-sized bush in time, but is useful on the larger rockery, especially as the bush can be kept in character indefinitely by cutting out all very coarse growth as it appears.

BUDS: Medium orange-brown, conical, with sharp point, 3–5 mm, uniform all over the plant, resinous in winter. Number in terminal cluster up to ten, lateral buds very numerous, sometimes in clusters. Buds noticeable because of their number, but intermingled with leaves.

BUD SCALES: Medium, pointed, fringed with resin, very closely appressed.

LEAVES: Dark, bright, mid-green, mostly straight, occasionally curved upwards, parallel, thick and stout, mid-rib prominent above and below, with a symmetrical, medium point slightly drawn out at the tip, sharp to the touch. Two to three rows glistening white stomatic lines above and below. *Size*: 12–15 mm long by 1 mm wide (width very uniform all over the plant), with slight sheen, arranged almost radially on strong roots, elsewhere semi-radially, held at 60° horizontally (up to 90° on some shoots, less than 60° near the tips), 20° above and 40° below. There is an occasional aberrant leaf, at 90°. Leaves on top of shoot point forward, not hiding shoot. Leaves form parallel outline, with a few short leaves, pointing forward, amongst the terminal buds. Leaves are set close together, and are very stiff to the touch.

SHOOTS: Medium orange-brown above and below with slight sheen, hairy. Pulvini are very prominent. Shoots are very thick and stiff; annual growth 40–60 mm, side shoots at 45° to branch.

– – **'Globosa Nana'** forms a dense, globose to broadly conical plant with main branches spreading and ascending at all angles from 10° upwards (up to 80° in the case of very strong laterals). There is no trace of the usual flat spray because the terminal cluster develops into shoots at all angles, even an occasional shoot *pointing inwards*, and this gives a characteristic dense and "prickly" look to the plant.

This description was taken from a plant in the nursery garden at Glasnevin, a propagation from the original plant in the Murray Hornibrook collection. When young it is an attractive and quite distinctive form of globose habit, but it is apparently apt to throw up coarse leader growth and will soon lose character if these are allowed to remain, and this may be one reason why this form is now very rare in cultivation.

BUDS: Dull, dark brown with lighter centres; flat ovoid to globose with rounded tip; 3–5 mm (terminal), 2–3 mm (other). Number in terminal cluster 5–6, occasionally more, well distributed around the shoot, occasional lateral buds on strong shoots only. Buds are prominent.

BUD SCALES: Small, rounded, numerous, fringed with hairs, loosely appressed.

LEAVES: Light, bright, grey-green, straight, sometimes very slightly curved backwards, widest at the centre, upper half narrowing gradually to a symmetrical, blunt point with a fine tip, sometimes much drawn out and sharp to the touch. Three to four broken rows of stomatic lines above and below extending to tip. *Size*: 6–8 mm long by 1 mm wide with slight sheen, arranged radially, held at 30° horizontally, 20° above and 40–50° below. Aberrant leaf at 50° projects beyond the other leaves. Leaves on top of shoot point forward, partly hiding the shoot. Leaves form a parallel outline,

187 *Picea abies* 'Gregoryana'. *Picea abies* 'Echiniformis' is similar, but with fewer and longer needles.

finishing with a double circle of small, straight leaves pointing forward but not hiding the terminal bud. The sub-terminal buds carry the aberrant leaf. Leaves are set close together, and are stiff to the touch.

SHOOTS: Medium orange-brown above and below, with slight sheen, very slightly pubescent. Pulvini are prominent. Shoots vary between thin and very thick and are flexible. Annual growth 30–60 mm, side shoots held at all angles from 20° to 60° to the branch, noticeably irregular in direction.

– – **'Gregoryana'.** This is one of the slowest-growing and most attractive forms. When young it forms a dense, bun-shaped to globose plant which could be roughly described as a closer-growing form of 'Echiniformis', but the *leaves are shorter and closer set and held edgeways*, and 'Gregoryana' lacks the strong shoots often thrown out here and there by that variety, so forms a smaller, denser-looking plant. With age both 'Gregoryana' and 'Echiniformis' are apt to lose the simple globose form which is their main attraction, the plants opening up into a cluster of globose masses somewhat suggesting a small, inverted bunch of grapes, but this tendency can be checked indefinitely by careful "stitch-in-time" pruning.

BUDS: Very pale yellow-green, invariably globose, tips not covered with scales. 1–1·5 mm diameter (terminal buds) with slight sheen, not resinous in winter. Number and size of buds in terminal cluster very variable (up to ten or more), with one or two lateral buds at base of strongest shoots only. Buds very noticeable because of their number.

BUD SCALES: Small, pointed, not fringed with hairs, very closely appressed.

LEAVES: Medium, dull grey-green, apparently round like a needle but actually rhombic in section, held edgeways, straight, parallel, with the top quarter tapering gradually to a sharp, symmetrical point slightly drawn out to a fine tip, a little sharp to the touch (but much less so than in 'Echiniformis'). One to two (rarely three) rows of stomatic lines above and below extending to tip. *Size*: 8–12 mm long by 0·5–

231

0·75 mm wide, glossy, arranged radially, held irregularly at all angles, but mainly at 70–90°. The uppermost leaves on the shoot stand out in a star-like circle at the base of the terminal cluster, *exposing all its buds*. Because of its congested growth these interlock with leaves from adjoining shoots, forming an impenetrable mass. An occasional short leaf points forwards. Leaves are set close together, and are stiff to the touch.

SHOOTS: Light brown with slight sheen, slightly hairy. Pulvini are prominent, brown. Shoots are thick but flexible. Annual growth is very variable from 5 to 20 mm. The erratic development of the buds gives a congested, patternless growth which is so dense as to smother all foliage in the interior of the plant.

– – **"horizontalis"**. This and the varietal names *"pendula"*, *"prostrata"* and *"parviformis"* occur in old books with insufficient descriptions to permit of identification, so they should not now be used.

– – **'Humilis'** forms a small, dense, globose plant of very congested growth with no clear growth pattern. Parts of the plant may consist of a congested mass of close growth in which the buds and leaves are more or less normal and healthy in appearance and size, and other parts which are a still denser mass of tiny buds and leaves. It is possible that this form arose by selection of propagating material from the dense growth occasionally seen on plants of 'Pygmaea' ('Humilis' could well be described as a diminutive form of that cultivar) for plants that are intermediate in character are to be found.

As a pot plant or in a trough it can be quite interesting (the growth in a good specimen is almost unbelievably congested) but it is more curious than beautiful and has no value as a garden plant.

BUDS: Light bright orange (lighter in centre), 2–3 mm (terminal buds) down to less than 1 mm (other), with slight sheen, resinous in winter. Number in terminal cluster varies considerably from one to eight or more, so that congested parts of the plant are little more than a dense mass of buds. As a result, buds are very prominent.

BUD SCALES: On large buds are medium, pointed and very closely appressed.

LEAVES: Dark, bright, mid-green, straight or (occasionally) curved backwards, parallel-sided and very thick, with prominent mid-rib, narrowing abruptly to a sharp point slightly drawn out (on large leaves) to a fine tip. Two to three very broken rows of stomatic lines above and below, extending to tip. *Size*: 2–10 mm long by 1 mm or less wide, glossy, arranged radially. Irregularly held at all angles from 10° to 75° to shoot, and on some strong shoots arranged spirally at the tip, where a dense cluster of short leaves pointing forward surround the terminal cluster without hiding it. Where the growth consists of a confused mass of buds the leaves are very small indeed. All leaves are set close together, and are stiff to the touch.

SHOOTS: Light grey above, very light grey below, glossy, glabrous. Pulvini are prominent. Shoots are thick and stiff; annual growth anything from 5 to 30 mm, side shoots at all angles to branch.

▲ 188 *Picea abies* 'Humilis'. A very old plant in Pinetum Schovenhorst, Putten, Holland.

189 *Picea abies* 'Inversa'. Young plants being stem-trained in a Dutch nursery. ▶

– – **'Inversa'** is a truly pendulous form that needs to be stem-trained when young, otherwise it becomes merely a prostrate or trailing plant. The regular development of the three terminal buds give a flat two-year spray, in which the growing tips are held up at +10° (i.e. 10° above the plane of the spray), but on pendulous branches these, of course, hang down almost vertically. The name was at one time spelt "*inverta*", but I use the spelling in general use today.

'Inversa' is quite easily distinguishable from 'Reflexa' by its thin flexible branches and by the colour and type of its foliage.

BUDS: Medium dull red-brown, long ovoid with blunt point, 5–6 mm (terminal buds), 3–4 mm (other), dull, resinous in winter. Number in terminal cluster one, but always two sub-terminal buds and on strong shoots one pair of lateral buds midway along the shoot. Buds inconspicuous.

BUD SCALES: Large, pointed, fringed with resin, loosely appressed, with tips free and sometimes recurved.

LEAVES: Light, bright, mid-green, straight, or occasionally very slightly curved up or forwards, parallel-sided, thick, rhombic in section, held edgeways, mid-rib prominent, especially on lower side of leaf, the top quarter tapering to a medium, symmetrical point usually with a blunt tip, not at all sharp to the touch. Two or three (or more below) rows of rather small stomata extending to tip. *Size*: 8–12 mm long (longest at centre of shoot) by 0·75–1·25 mm wide, glossy, arranged semi-radially, held at 60–65° horizontally (noticeably uniform), 30° above and 40–50° below. The aberrant leaf at 90°, borne also by the sub-terminal buds, is long and very noticeable. Leaves on top of shoot point forward, not hiding shoot. Leaves form an oval outline finishing with an open circle of shorter leaves pointing forward around terminal bud (not obscuring it) often noticeably twisted. Leaves are set close together, and are·stiff to the touch.

SHOOTS: Medium brown above and below, glossy, pubescent. Pulvini are prominent, orange-red. Shoots are thinnish and flexible. Annual growth 30–50 mm, side shoots uniformly held at 50–60° to branch.

– – **'Knaptonensis'** forms a cushion-shaped to globose plant wider than high with no clear pattern in the branching system. Because of irregular development of the buds the leaf-spray is confused and congested, giving a rather untidy look to the plant.

This (now very rare) form is not unlike 'Pygmaea' in general appearance, but in the buds, colour of leaves and habit is quite distinct from that cultivar.

BUDS: Dull, medium orange-brown, ovoid, with sharp point, 3–4 mm (terminal), 2–3 mm (other), glossy. Number in terminal cluster usually three, lateral buds numerous. Buds noticeable.

BUD SCALES: Medium, rounded, fringed with hairs, very closely appressed.

LEAVES: Light bright yellow-green, straight, occasionally curved forwards, sides parallel, round, thick and fleshy, ending abruptly in a symmetrical point drawn out to a short nipple-like tip, not sharp to the touch. Two to three scattered rows of very small stomata above and below, not extending to tip. *Size*: 5–7 mm long by 1–1·5 mm wide, very glossy, arranged radially, held at 30–50° horizontally, 20–30° above and 30–40° below. Aberrant leaf at 70°. Leaves form a vaguely parallel outline ending in a circle of rather short leaves around but not hiding the terminal bud. Leaves are set very close together, and are very stiff to the touch.

SHOOTS: Light orange-grey above, medium orange-grey below, with slight sheen, glabrous. Pulvini are prominent, the leaves being so closely set on the stem that this has the appearance of tiny narcissus bulbs closely packed together, each bearing one huge leaf. Shoots are thick, but not noticeably stiff. Annual growth 10–12 mm, side shoots held at 45–50° to branch.

– – **'Maxwellii'.** There seems considerable uncertainty as to the identity of this form and of the related forms **'Merkii'** and **'Pseudomaxwellii'**. I have seen several forms, in this country and on the Continent, which differ sufficiently from each other to justify their being regarded as distinct cultivars, but none that I could identify beyond reasonable doubt with the descriptions given by Hornibrook in his Second Edition. So I must leave this group for further study, and readers can help in this by drawing my attention to authentic specimens of known origin and recorded history.

– – **'Microsperma'** forms a broadly conical plant with a spreading, symmetrical branch system, the branches standing up at all angles from horizontal (to +60° in the case of the strongest branches). The shoots which develop from the terminal and

190 *Picea abies* 'Microsperma'. The arching habit that is characteristic of this variety can be plainly seen.

"half-way" clusters referred to below are too crowded to lie in a flat spray. The upper ones commence at an angle of $+20°$ and arch gracefully over. This slight arching effect, repeated all over the plant, gives an attractive and characteristic appearance to this variety.

This is an attractive form which looks as though it would become large eventually. Its foliage, held "edgeways" is not unlike a form of *P. orientalis*. The arching twigs and the flattened terminal bud cluster, repeated about mid-way along the year's growth on strong shoots, is quite characteristic. It should be better known than it is.

BUDS: Bright, dark red-brown conical (leading buds ovoid) with sharp points, 4–6 mm (terminal), 2–4 mm (others), with slight sheen. Number in terminal cluster 5–8 (more on main leader growths), always (on lateral shoots) in two definite groups on each side of the terminal bud. A second and similar cluster is found half-way along strong shoots; otherwise there are few lateral buds. Buds are conspicuous.

BUD SCALES: Small, pointed and blunt, fringed with hairs, loosely appressed.

LEAVES: Dark bright mid-green, curved abruptly away from shoot at base and thence slightly forward forming an elongated "S" shape, with parallel sides, rhombic in section, held edgeways, mid-rib not prominent, with a sharp, oblique point and a sharp tip not drawn out but often ending in a slight suggestion of a hook, not sharp to the touch. One to three long straight rows of stomata above and below extending to tip.

Size: 6–8 mm long by 0·5–0·75 mm wide, longest at the centre of the shoot, glossy, arranged imperfectly radially, held at 70° horizontally, 20–30° above and 40–50° below. Aberrant leaf at 90°. Leaves on top of shoot point forward, not hiding shoot. Leaves form a parallel outline and finish in a double circle of very short, straight leaves held at 30° around the terminal bud but not hiding it from view. The buds in the terminal cluster carry the aberrant leaf. Leaves are set very close together, and are stiff to the touch.

SHOOTS: Medium brown above, medium grey-brown below, glossy with slight sheen, dull, very slightly pubescent. Pulvini are prominent, orange-brown. Leading shoots are very thick, but laterals are thin and flexible. Annual growth 30–50 mm, side shoots held at 40–90° to branch, the previous years' bud scales persistent and noticeable—very dark brown.

– – '**Mucronata**' forms a broadly conical plant with growth uniform and regular and very dense. The main branches sweep up to 60° (or occasionally to 90°) these branches bearing their leaves radially. It is a robust and strong-growing variety which gets large in time: easily recognizable by the curved main branches and the numerous large buds.

BUDS: Bright, medium orange-brown, ovoid, with blunt point, 7–8 mm (terminal), 4–6 mm (other), dull. Solitary terminal bud, but lateral buds numerous, especially so near terminal bud, and buds are a prominent feature of the plant because of this.

BUD SCALES: Large, pointed, fringed with resin and closely appressed, except the uppermost scales on the main terminal buds, which look rather like a tiny hyacinth bulb.

LEAVES: Dark, bright, blue-green, thick but flat; mid-rib not prominent; straight except that top third is curved upwards slightly; parallel, top quarter tapering very gradually, ending abruptly in a fine tip only slightly drawn out; sharp to the touch. One to three broken rows of stomatic lines above and below, not extending to tip. *Size*: 10–17 mm long by 1 mm wide, glossy, arranged almost radially, held somewhat irregularly at 40–50° horizontally and 30–40° above and (occasionally) below. Aberrant leaf at 90° or more. Leaves on top of shoot point forward, not hiding the shoot. Leaves form a more or less parallel outline, with a cluster of short, round leaves, pointing forward, around but not hiding the terminal bud. Leaves are spaced well apart and are stiff to the touch.

SHOOTS: Light orange-brown above and below, glossy, very slightly hairy. Pulvini are prominent. Shoots are very thick and very stiff, annual growth 20–50 mm, side shoots are held at 30–45°, usually in a flat spray.

I have only seen a small plant of '**Oldhamiana**'. It had buds similar to 'Mucronata' but the leaves were shorter, 10×0.75 mm and much more closely set, and it had pale greenish-yellow shoots. Otherwise, as a small plant, it appeared close to the latter variety.

– – '**Nana**' forms a broadly conical plant to 1·5 m high with most erratic growth. Main shoots at ±45° above horizontal, this angle varying considerably. Parts of the bush are of close and relatively uniform growth, but at the top and here and there at the sides strong, coarse vertical shoots will arise. These will often follow up with the normal growth the following year.

It is not, at a quick glance, unlike a very coarse edition of 'Pygmaea' but these occasional coarse, vertical shoots with their distinctively different, sparse, divergent, noticeably square and often curved leaves are quite unlike that variety.

191 *Picea abies* 'Nana'. 192 *Picea abies* 'Nana Compacta'.
Despite the similarity in name, these two varieties are quite distinct.

'Nana' is a very uncommon form. This description was taken in August from the best specimen of this cultivar I know, a plant over fifty years old at Iford Manor, Bradford-on-Avon, Wilts.

BUDS: Light orange-brown round-ovoid with rounded tip. Size very variable, from 2 to 6 mm (terminal) to 1·2 mm (other), dull. Sometimes one large terminal bud, sometimes many smaller buds of different sizes in an irregular cluster, lateral buds very uncommon. Buds inconspicuous.

BUD SCALES: Large, thick and pointed, fringed with hairs, loosely appressed.

LEAVES: Medium bright mid-green, usually straight, but noticeably curved outwards on a few coarse shoots. Small leaves rhombic, large leaves square, with blunt, noticeably oblique point, slightly drawn out to a very fine tip, very sharp to the touch. Two to four broken rows of stomatic lines above and below not extending to tip. *Size*: very variable, from 2 to 16 mm long (sometimes even less on congested shoots) by 0·5–1·5 mm wide; glossy, symmetrically radial, normal leaves held at 10–20° but this angle is increased up to 70° on the coarse shoots, and the outline of the shoot is similarly variable. A cluster of much shorter leaves, pointing forwards, completely covers the terminal bud, where solitary. Leaves are overlapping on weak and are spaced widely apart on coarse shoots and are very stiff to the touch.

SHOOTS: Light orange above and below, glossy, glabrous. Pulvini are very prominent. Shoots are very thick and very stiff; annual growth variable, from 5 to 50 mm (on the strong, coarse shoots to 100 mm), side shoots at 45° to branch, this angle varying considerably.

237

– – **'Nana Compacta'** is quite unlike 'Nana' in every way. As grown in this country it is a very dwarf and slow-growing form which makes a sturdy-looking, flattened-globose plant with very compact and dense foliage; short dark-green leaves and very many, prominent, large, crimson-brown buds in flattened clusters. At the sides of the plant the branches are ascending at 20–30°, the branchlets are thin and the foliage is in more or less flat sprays in which by the second year there is a good deal of overlapping, but towards its crown the plant throws up strong, thick shoots ascending at a steep angle (but never upright) carrying up to eight large flat buds. The foliage is everywhere radial or nearly so; on side growth this arrangement is much flattened, on the coarse, upright shoots it is nearly symmetrical, but the bud clusters are still somewhat flattened.

I have not seen old plants of this cultivar so do not know its ultimate growth capabilities but it could doubtless be maintained for many years as a low, spreading bushling by regular removal of the strong shoots mentioned above.

It is not unlike 'Ohlendorffii' in some respects but there need be no confusion. 'Nana Compacta' always forms a flattened-globose plant in which the branch system is compact and altogether lacking the stiff-erect habit of 'Ohlendorffii'; the buds are larger, more numerous and much more prominent, and the leaves are dark- (not yellow-) green (*Ill. 192*).

BUDS: Dark red-brown, ovoid with blunt point, 4–5 (terminal), 2–3 mm (other) (with some minute buds on weak shoots), glossy, sometimes resinous in winter and sometimes glossy as though varnished. Number in terminal cluster 1–5 in a flattened group (more numerous on the strong, ascending shoots), other lateral buds rare. Buds are very prominent.

BUD SCALES: Medium, pointed, often fringed with resin, closely appressed.

LEAVES: Dark, dull, mid-green, reflexed at base, thence straight or nearly so, rhombic to square in section, held edgeways, with mid-rib prominent, parallel sided, narrowing at the tip to a medium, symmetrical point sometimes slightly drawn out, not sharp to the touch. One to two rows of stomatic lines above and below almost extending to tip. *Size*: 4–7 mm long by 0·5 mm *or less* wide, with slight sheen, arranged radially even at sides of plant although there much flattened. Leaves are held at 60–70° horizontally, 20° above and, irregularly 40–60° below. Aberrant leaf at 90–100°, usually carried by sub-terminal buds. Leaves on top of shoot are few and scattered and do not hide the shoot. Shoot has a parallel outline. There are few, if any, leaves at the end of the shoot, the leaves continuing normally right to the base of the terminal bud. Leaves are set close together, and are stiff and the plant is a little prickly to the touch.

SHOOTS: Light yellow-grey or grey-green above, whitish-yellow or pale green below, glossy, glabrous. Pulvini are prominent, orange-brown. Side shoots are thin and flexible, coarse ascending shoots very thick. Annual growth 20–30 mm side shoots held at 30–50° to branch.

193 *Picea abies* 'Nidiformis'. One of the most popular and reliable of these dwarf forms.

– – **'Nidiformis'** is one of the commonest and most reliable dwarf forms of the Norway Spruce, and is usually found true to name. It forms a spreading to prostrate plant of dense and fairly regular growth. The main branches at first rise at $+50-70°$ and arch over to $±10°$ at the growing tips. This habit tends to leave a cone-shaped depression in the centre of young plants to which the variety owes its name, but this characteristic is usually lost as the plant ages.

It can be distinguished by the presence of a row of tiny, vicious, glassy hooks (too small to be seen by the naked eye) on the lower edge of every leaf. So far as I know this characteristic is shared only with 'Decumbens', in which variety the hooks are fewer and present only on a few of the leaves. In 'Decumbens', also, the leaves are wider and of a lighter green and they form a parallel (not tapered) outline and lack the "wiry" look that is a characteristic feature of 'Nidiformis'. As with all these low-growing forms 'Nidiformis' will cover a large area in time, building up height slowly at the centre.

BUDS: Dark brown, ovoid, with blunt point, 1–2 mm (terminal), 1–1·5 mm (other). Terminal bud solitary with usually two sub-terminals, and occasionally one other lateral. Buds are inconspicuous.

BUD SCALES: Medium, rounded, not fringed with hairs, very closely appressed.

LEAVES: Dark, dull, mid-green, curved out sharply at base, thence straight or slightly curved forward, with parallel sides, rhombic, with a series of sharp transparent hooks on the bottom edge of the leaf which ends in a sharp, very oblique point, rather drawn out to an up-turned tip, slightly sharp to the touch. One to two rows of stomatic lines

239

▲ 194 *Picea abies* 'Ohlendorffii'. Colour: yellow-green, becoming dark green later.

195 *Picea abies* 'Pachyphylla'. The plant at Glasnevin illustrated in Hornibrook's Second Edition. ▶

above and below extending to tip. *Size*: 5–7 mm long by 0·5–0·75 mm wide; with slight sheen, arranged imperfectly radially, held at 80–90° horizontally, 30° above and with an occasional leaf at 80° below. Aberrant leaf at 90°. Leaves on top of shoot point forward, not hiding shoot. Leaves form a tapered outline, with circular end, where a few shortish leaves point forwards, not hiding the bud. Leaves are set close together and are very "wiry" both in appearance and to the touch.
SHOOTS: Light yellow-grey above, almost white below, glossy, glabrous. Pulvini are prominent. Shoots are thin and very flexible; annual growth 30–40 mm; side shoots at 30–70° to branch (noticeably variable).

– – 'Ohlendorffii' forms a globose plant (later becoming broadly conical) with an ascending-spreading branch system and branchlets growing at all angles, not in flat sprays. Many of the growing shoots arch over slightly. In a young plant growth is dense and regular, but with age the outline becomes irregular because of strong branches which sweep up to form sub-leaders.

This is the plant commonly met with in the trade under this name. It corresponds only reasonably well with the description given by Hornibrook, as the leaves at their tips in the cultivar I am describing always curve away from the shoots and the branches are not in fan-like sprays as he suggests. It was at first thought to be a form of *P. orientalis*, the foliage being not unlike that of that species, but is now accepted as belonging to *P. abies*.
BUDS: Bright medium to dark orange-brown, long ovoid with pointed tip, 2–3 mm,

240

occasionally more (terminal), 1·5–2 mm (other), glossy. Number in terminal cluster irregular, usually 3–5, occasionally up to ten on very strong shoots, with usually one or two lateral buds on strong shoots. Buds very noticeable, especially in young plants.
BUD SCALES: Small, rounded, often fringed with white resin, very closely appressed.
LEAVES: Light, bright yellow-green. All leaves begin at a narrow angle to the stem and curve outwards and backwards, especially so in case of leaves on lower side of shoot, and are square or round like a needle, parallel for most of their length but tapering at each end and ending with an oblique, sharp point, much drawn out to a fine tip pointing forwards along the shoot, not sharp to the touch. One to four irregular rows of very small stomatic lines above and below, not extending to tip. *Size*: 4–8 mm long by 0·5–0·75 mm wide, glossy; arranged radially on leading shoots and on small plants, semi-radially on side growth of older plants, held (at their tips) at 40–50° horizontally, and 10–30° above and 60° below. Aberrant leaf at 90°. Leaves on top of shoot point forward, almost hiding shoot. Leaves form parallel or tapered outline ending in a double circle of short leaves pointing forwards (10–30°), covering but not hiding the terminal bud. Leaves are set very close together, and are stiff to the touch.
SHOOTS: Light brown above, very light brown below, glossy, glabrous. Pulvini are prominent. Shoots are thin and flexible. Annual growth 30–60 mm, side shoots held irregularly at 40–50° to branch.

– – 'Pachyphylla' is probably the most distinctive form of any. It forms a globose (later an upright) plant of extremely slow growth, and bears thick, fleshy leaves quite unlike those typical of the species. It seldom makes sufficient growth to provide material for propagation, so will always be rare. The "small plant at Glasnevin" of which Hornibrook wrote in 1938 is still less than 1 m high by half as much across, so that 'Pachyphylla' could claim to be reliably dwarf, but it is merely a curiosity. It is much sought after by collectors.
BUDS: Medium brown, globose, 2–3 mm (terminal), 1–2 mm (other), with slight sheen, solitary terminal bud, lateral buds rare, occasionally one or two at base of current year's growth. Occasionally no terminal bud develops and this leads to the ultimate death of the shoot. Buds inconspicuous.
BUD SCALES: Medium, rounded, so closely appressed as to be indistinguishable as separate scales.
LEAVES: Medium, dull mid-green, curved forwards, tapered to each end the upper side convexed, the lower side keeled, giving a boat-shaped cross-section; very thick and fleshy in appearance, ending in a very blunt, oblique point, not drawn out, but occasionally ending in a short nipple-like tip, not sharp to the touch. Five to six rows stomatic lines above and three to four below, sometimes extending to tip. *Size*: 10–15 mm long by 1·25–1·5 mm wide, glossy, arranged radially, held at all angles 20–90°, standing out more in the centre of the shoot than at either end and noticeably spirally arranged, ending at the tip with a circle of small leaves not covering the bud. Leaves are spaced widely apart, and are very stiff to the touch.

241

196 *Picea abies* 'Procumbens' in Mr H. G. Hillier's collection.

SHOOTS: Very light grey above, medium grey below, glossy, glabrous. Pulvini are prominent. Shoots are thick and stiff. Annual growth 5–20 mm.

– – **"pendula"**. This name has been used rather loosely by different writers to describe forms that are now impossible to identify. It is best to abandon the use of the name. The two truly pendulous forms coming within the scope of this book are 'Inversa' and 'Reflexa'.

– – **'Phylicoides'** can hardly claim to be a dwarf form as it grows into a large open bush or a gaunt small tree. The foliage is quite distinct—yellow-green its first year, becoming blue-green the second season. *Size*: 6–7 mm long, parallel sided, rhombic in cross-section, held edgeways, often curved away from shoot. The side branches are few and frequently quite pendulous. It is quite unlike any other cultivar of *P. abies*, but is more of a curiosity than a plant of beauty or garden value.

– – **'Procumbens'** forms a very strong-growing and healthy-looking, flat-topped, procumbent plant with foliage in stiff, widespread, flat (slightly up-cupped) sprays held at 20–30°. The leaves are longer than in any other low-growing variety I have seen and reduce regularly in length from the base of the year's growth to the terminal bud. The invariable development *downwards* of the supernumerary sub-terminal bud (where it occurs) is characteristic.

There is a good plant of this form at Red Lodge Nursery, Chandler's Ford, Hants, and a fine specimen at "Jermyns", Ampfield, near Romsey, Hants, the residence of Mr H. G. Hillier, on the bank near the front door.

It is probable that this is the stronger form referred to by Hornibrook (Second Edition, 1938, 168), in which case I have not yet located the true 'Procumbens', which according to Hornibrook's description has its branches spreading horizontally over the ground and its foliage forming an *oval* outline. He gives *P. excelsa* var. *prostrata* Schn. (1913), 230 as a synonym and I notice Dr Boom does the same in his book. If there are in fact the two forms and the one I do not know agrees with Hornibrook's description it may be we should regard the form I describe here as 'Prostrata'. I must leave the point unsettled at present.

BUDS: Light orange-brown, conical with sharp point, 4–5 mm (terminal), 3–4 mm (other), dull, not resinous in winter. Number in terminal cluster usually three. Where a fourth bud is present *it always points downwards*; lateral buds are numerous and occur all round the shoot. Buds are inconspicuous.

BUD SCALES: Small, rounded, fringed with hairs, very closely appressed.

LEAVES: Light, bright, mid-green, straight, parallel sided, thick but flat, mid-rib sunk, with top half of leaf tapering to a sharp symmetrical point, slightly drawn out to a transparent tip, sharp to the touch. Three rows of stomatic lines above and below extending to tip. *Size*: 10–17 mm long (shortest above and towards the tip of the shoot) by 1–1·5 mm wide, glossy, arranged semi-radially, held at 60–80° horizontally, 20–30° above and an occasional leaf at 40° below. Leaves on top of shoot point forward. Shoot has a *very noticeably* tapered outline ending in an irregular and variable cluster of small leaves pointing forward or nearly so around the terminal bud, but not hiding it. Leaves are set close together, and are very stiff to the touch.

SHOOTS: Medium orange-brown, glossy, glabrous. Pulvini are prominent. Shoots are very thick and stiff. Annual growth 50–100 mm, side shoots at 70° to branch.

– – **'Pumila'** and its associated colour forms present a difficult group, for the descriptions we have inherited would suggest that they are identical in all respects save colour of foliage. It would, however, be nearer the truth to say that all they have in common is a leaf which is widest at about one-third of its length from the base (tapering thence gradually to the tip), and the habit of carrying their leaves semi-radially and lying in distinct ranks or rows, the leaves in each rank being shorter and pointing more nearly forward than those in the rank below it. In a single twig this arrangement is quite neat but it gives a rather jumbled appearance to the plant viewed as a whole.

'Pumila' is very much less common than 'Pumila Nigra' (described below) which has quite a different habit of growth, but as Hornibrook merely describes the latter as "similar to the type, but with much darker green foliage" confusion has perhaps been inevitable, and as the leaf shape is shared also with 'Clanbrassiliana' a mix-up with that already sadly distracted plant is also apt to occur. There are several plants of 'Pumila' as I now describe it, in a bold and very effective group about midway along the entrance drive at 'Grayswood Hill', Haslemere, Surrey, the residence of that great gardener Mr G. L. Pilkington, through whose kindness young plants are now established in the Pygmy Pinetum, where they are close enough to an old plant of 'Pumila Nigra' for easy comparison (*Ill. 198*).

'Pumila' forms a low, spreading bush with a more or less irregular outline and with the lower branches wide-spreading and procumbent, but the upper ones more erect. The foliage is a rich, bright mid-green. The sprays are slightly up-cupped but because of the small angle of divergence of the side branches there is much overlapping of shoots, so the flat "plate-like layers" described by Hornibrook are often much obscured. The whole bush has a very soft and "cushiony" feel, and the foliage is everywhere uniform and regular, lacking the irregular leaf size between one shoot and another which is an invariable feature of 'Clanbrassiliana'.

BUDS: Light orange, conical-ovoid with blunt point, 2–2·5 mm (terminal), 1·5–2 mm (other), dull. One horizontal pair of lateral buds close to the solitary terminal bud, rarely one additional bud $\frac{2}{3}$ along shoot. Buds inconspicuous.

BUD SCALES: Medium, rounded, not fringed with hairs or resin, appressed.

LEAVES: Light, bright mid-green, turned out at base, thence straight, thin and flat, mid-rib prominent, widest at $\frac{1}{3}$, upper $\frac{2}{3}$ with a long taper to a sharp, oblique point drawn out to a very fine, transparent tip, not at all sharp to the touch. One or two rows of stomatic lines above and below, extending to tip. *Size*: 6–10 mm long by 0·5–0·75 mm wide, glossy, arranged semi-radially in ranks, the lowest held at 60° (upper ranks at a lesser angle) horizontally, 20° above and with leaves in the lowest rank hanging irregularly to 70° below. Aberrant leaf at 80–90°, borne by sub-terminal buds. Leaves on top of shoot point forward, not hiding shoot. Leaves form a parallel outline with leaves of normal length continuing to the very tip of the shoot and are held forwards and downwards so as to give a "drooping" appearance to the shoot. Leaves are spaced well part and are flexible and soft to the touch.

SHOOTS: Medium yellow-brown above, medium yellow below, glabrous. Pulvini are prominent. Shoots are thin and very flexible. Annual growth 20–30 mm, side shoots held at 40–50° to branch.

– – **'Pumila Argentea'.** Murray Hornibrook's original plant, presented to the National Botanic Garden, Glasnevin, Dublin, is now a large tree of no distinctive character or peculiarity in colour of foliage. It may have been, at the time he described it, a case of chlorosis due to some mineral deficiency in the soil in which it had been potted, but in any case the name can now be dropped.

– – **'Pumila Glauca'** is very similar to the following cultivar, 'Pumila Nigra'. In some plants the branches rise perhaps a little more steeply, but other than that the only difference I can detect is that the stomata are more numerous and show up a glistening white under a ×25 magnification, instead of the dull white of 'Pumila Nigra'. This is sufficient to give a barely discernibly glaucous look to the leaf examined closely with the naked eye, but the plants as a whole are indistinguishable.

197 *Picea abies* 'Pumila Nigra'. Colour: dark green.

I do not think the difference is worth maintaining, except in very comprehensive collections—if that.

– – **'Pumila Nigra'** is the commonest of the group which carries the name and is an excellent and reliable variety. It forms a wide-spreading plant, seldom reaching to 1 m high but covering a large area in time.

The regular development of the horizontal pair of lateral buds produces a spray which basically is flat, but as all the shoots twist upwards, and as the narrow angle of divergence results in considerable overlapping the effect of flatness is lost after the second year and the general effect is that of a dense, irregular plant with *all the main growing shoots rising stiffly at an angle of 30–45° all over the plant.* Of all the forms which form low, wide-spreading plants 'Pumila Nigra' carries its main branches at the steepest angle and can thus be readily distinguished from the truly procumbent forms even at a distance.

There are large specimens in the rockery at the Botanic Garden, Bath, and at Stourhead in Wiltshire, near the main entrance.

BUDS: Light orange-brown, conical with blunt point, 2·5–3 mm (terminal), 2–2·5 mm (other), dull, resinous in winter. Solitary terminal bud with a horizonta lpair of laterals very close and frequently also one or two midway (also horizontal), seldom any others. Buds are inconspicuous.

245

BUD SCALES: Small, rounded, fringed with resin, very closely appressed.

LEAVES: Dark, dull, blue-green, turned out at base, thence straight, thin and flat, tapered to each end, widest at one-third from base, tapering gradually but narrowing abruptly to a blunt, oblique point drawn out to a minute, transparent tip pointing forward, a little sharp to the touch. The mid-rib is raised, giving the leaf an appearance of being grooved. Two to four broken rows of small, creamy-white stomata above and below extending to tip. *Size*: 8–12 mm long (less on top of shoot and towards the tip) by 1·0 mm wide, glossy, arranged semi-radially in distinct ranks, each rank at a different angle, giving a dense and untidy look to the shoot; held at 40–60° horizontally, 20° above (and 30–70° below wherever the long leaves in the lowest rank hang forwards and downwards). Aberrant leaf at 80–100°. Leaves on top of shoot point more or less forward, almost hiding shoot. Leaves form a tapered outline squared off abruptly at the tip, where a circle of very small leaves pointing forward at 0–30° and often twisted cover but do not hide the terminal bud. Aberrant leaves borne by the sub-lateral buds project and so are very noticeable. Leaves are set very close together, and are stiff to the touch.

SHOOTS: Medium brown above, medium orange-brown below, glossy, glabrous. Pulvini are prominent. Shoots are thin and very flexible. Annual growth 30–50 mm; side shoots at 50° to branch, this angle being noticeably uniform all over the plant.

– – **'Pygmaea'** is, next to 'Clanbrassiliana', the oldest recorded dwarf form of *P. abies* and they both remain equally popular, but unlike the latter variety, 'Pygmaea' seems to have been able to maintain its identity and so is usually found truly named. There are some very old plants in existence, including those at Leonardslee, Horsham, Sussex. The history of these plants was recorded by Hornibrook and they have now added more than a quarter of a century to their age without much increase in size, so the variety can be regarded as reliably dwarf, provided that (as a former head gardener at Leonardslee once privately admitted to me to having always done) any strong, coarse growth be cut out of the bush as soon as it develops.

If, as I believe, 'Humilis' is a cultivariant resulting from selection of cutting wood from the particularly tight, congested growth that occasionally develops in a plant of 'Pygmaea', the distinction between these two cultivars (as I suggest also in the case of the 'Gregoryana' group) is somewhat arbitrary, and intermediate forms occur.

'Pygmaea' forms a very slow-growing, globose to broadly conical bush usually seen less than 1 m high, although capable of reaching twice that height after a century or so of steady growth. The growth is very dense and congested, and in its own irregular way uniform all over the bush, except that an abnormally strong shoot will sometimes appear here or there as a result of which the plant develops a rugged and picturesque outline, and occasionally (due perhaps to a local concentration of the virus—or whatever agent it is that caused the dwarfing in the first place) a branch will

198 *Picea abies* 'Pumila'.

199 *Picea abies* 'Pygmaea'.

develop an extremely dense habit with the shorter leaves, reduced shoot growth and abnormal bud-formation associated with 'Humilis'. There is an interesting example in the Pygmy Pinetum at Devizes in which the two types of growth are in such contrast that it is difficult to realize they are on the same plant.

BUDS: Medium orange-brown, globose (large buds cylindrical with rounded tip), 2 mm (terminal), 1 mm (other), glossy or with slight sheen, not resinous in winter. Up to three buds in terminal cluster, but most shoots carry a solitary terminal bud. Lateral buds are frequent at base of current year's growth, otherwise rare.

BUD SCALES: Variable: sometimes large and pointed; more often small, rounded and tightly appressed.

LEAVES: Dark, bright, mid-green, straight, rhombic to nearly square, parallel-sided, narrowing abruptly to a symmetrical point with a very fine drawn-out tip, sharp to the touch. Two to three broken rows of stomatic lines above and below, usually extending to tip. *Size*: 5–8 mm long by 1 mm wide, with slight sheen, arranged radially on strong shoots, discernibly set spirally on shoot and often twisted, occasionally noticeably so; held at 30–45°, the leaves on lower side of shoot longer and at a wider angle than those above and finishing with a circle (frequently of smaller) leaves pointing forward around but not hiding the terminal bud, often twisted. Leaves are set very close together, especially on the weaker shoots, on which they are also much smaller than on strong shoots.

SHOOTS: Light to very pale yellow or grey, glossy and glabrous. Pulvini are prominent. Shoots are thick but relatively flexible. Annual growth 10–30 mm, *very variable*, the different shoots, even adjoining ones, differing noticeably in vigour and size of leaf. Side shoots are at 30–45° to branch, the angle being very variable.

The habit is congested, the branching system irregular and following no particular pattern, and the foliage is usually sufficiently dense to smother all growth in the interior of the plant.

200 *Picea abies* 'Reflexa' in Mr A. H. Nisbet's collection at Brooker's Farm, Gosport.

– – **'Reflexa'** (sometimes met with under the incorrect name "*pendula*") is a truly pendulous form which requires to be stem-trained to the required height unless it is to be grown as a prostrate plant. In this form it can be very effective if planted at the top of a large rockery down over which its branches will cascade, the growth in the centre of the plant building up into a dense mat of lusty, stiff branches richly clothed with foliage. As with so many of the forms with dark foliage it is particularly attractive during early summer, when the soft green of the new foliage makes a vivid contrast with the old. It is the strongest-growing and most outstanding of any of the pendulous forms of *P. abies*.

BUDS: Bright, light orange-brown, long ovoid, with blunt point, 6–8 mm (terminal), 5–7 mm (other), dull, resinous in winter. Number in terminal cluster 3–6, lateral buds numerous, especially on strong leading shoots. Buds are very prominent, especially in winter.

BUD SCALES: Large, pointed, fringed with resin, loosely appressed with upper part recurved, sometimes curled right back.

LEAVES: Dark, dull, grey to blue-green, usually straight or nearly so, the mid-rib prominent, with parallel sides with the top quarter of its length tapering gradually to a symmetrical, medium point with a blunt, transparent tip, not sharp to the touch. One to four broken and irregular rows of stomata above and below, extending to tip.

201 *Picea abies* 'Remontii' in the H. A. Hesse nursery at Weener, Ems, W. Germany.

Size: 10–12 mm long by 1–1·25 mm wide, with slight sheen, arranged radially, the upper leaves short, lying along the shoot, the lower leaves long and hanging forwards and outwards, held uniformly at 30–35° horizontally, 10–15° above and 50–60° below. The aberrant leaf, being long and held at 90°, is very noticeable. Leaves on top of shoot point forward, partly hiding shoot. Leaves form a parallel outline, finishing with a thin circle of short, needle-like leaves pointing forwards and usually closely appressed to the terminal bud; often twisted. Leaves are set close together, and are stiff to the touch, appearing stiffer than they are.

SHOOTS: Light grey above and below, dull, pubescent. Pulvini are prominent, orange-red. Shoots are *very* thick and stiff, annual growth 50–120 mm; side shoots held at 60° to branch, each growing branch forming a saucer-shaped spray with slightly recurved shoots (hence the name) which only become pendulous the second year.

– – 'Remontii' is an attractive and popular form, but not one of the most dwarf. It is usually seen as a conical bush of about the shape of the well-known *P. glauca* 'Albertiana Conica' and it reaches to about 3 m high. The foliage is a bright mid-green and the growth is neat and regular, in flat sprays with a regular ramification (due to the development of the two sub-terminal buds) distinctly traceable back into the older growth. The growing tips are at ±5° but the growth is too dense to have any appearance of being in layers.

249

202 *Picea abies* 'Repens'. A fine specimen in the National Botanic Garden, Glasnevin, Dublin.

Where a larger specimen is required this is one to be recommended. There is a fine specimen in the National Pinetum at Bedgebury, Kent.

BUDS: Light, conical or ovoid with blunt point, 2–3 mm (terminal), 1–2 mm (other), glossy. Solitary terminal bud with one or two laterals very close to terminal bud, other lateral buds very rare. Buds noticeable.

BUD SCALES: Medium, pointed not fringed, closely appressed.

LEAVES: Light to medium, bright mid-green, curved out near base, thence straight; widest at centre, held edgeways, mid-rib prominent, with the top half tapering abruptly to a slightly drawn-out tip, not sharp to the touch. One to three broken rows of stomatic lines above and below extending to tip. *Size*: 5–7 mm long (always the longest leaves are below, hanging down) by 0·5–0·75 mm broad, with slight sheen, arranged imperfectly radially, held at 60–80° horizontally and 30° above and 70–90° below. No aberrant leaf. Leaves on top of shoot are short, and point forward, not hiding shoot. Leaves form a tapered outline (sometimes noticeably so) and finish at the tip with a close circle of very short leaves pointing forwards, with their tips reaching to the tip of the terminal bud. Leaves are set close together, and are flexible to the touch.

SHOOTS: Medium brown above, light brown below, with slight sheen, glabrous. Pulvini are prominent. Shoots are fairly thick, but flexible; annual growth 20–30 mm; side shoots at 50–60° to branch.

– – **'Repens'** forms a prostrate to spreading plant which gradually builds up in the centre by super-imposition of later growth. The growth is regular, dense and uniform.

250

203 *Picea abies* 'Tabuliformis'. Many plants of this variety are completely prostrate, and the specimen shown was probably trained up as a young plant.

The regular development of the two sub-terminal buds year by year results in a regular, flat leaf spray and as the angle to the horizontal at the growing tips is $\pm 5°$, the growth appears noticeably in layers.

The following description was made from the two old plants in the National Botanical Garden at Glasnevin, Dublin, part of the original Murray Hornibrook collection received in 1921–2.

BUDS: Bright medium orange-brown, conical to ovoid with sharp point, 3–4 mm (terminal), 2–3 mm (other), with sheen. Number in terminal cluster three, with usually one lateral bud additionally on each side. Buds inconspicuous.

BUD SCALES: Medium, pointed, fringed with hairs, very closely appressed.

LEAVES: Light, bright mid- to yellow-green (the colour being variable) twisted out at base, thence straight, widest at the centre, flat, wiry-looking and narrow but relatively thick, with the mid-rib prominent, tapering to a sharp, symmetrical point, slightly drawn out to a fine tip sharp to the touch. One or two broken rows of stomatic lines above and below extending to tip. *Size*: 8–10 mm long by never over 1 mm wide; glossy, arranged semi-radially but much flattened, the leaves twisted to bare the stem beneath, held at 70° horizontally, 30° above and 60° below. Aberrant leaf at 80–90° or more. Leaves on top of shoot point forward, not hiding shoot. Leaves form tapered outline, ending in a cluster of shorter leaves radiating at all angles, not hiding the bud. Leaves are set closer together than their narrowness suggests and are flexible to the touch.

SHOOTS: Medium orange-brown above, light brown below, with slight sheen, glabrous. Pulvini are not prominent. Shoots are thin and very flexible. Annual growth 30–50 mm, side shoots held at 45–50° to branch, uniform all over the plant.

– – **'Tabuliformis'** forms a spreading plant, usually seen as a low, prostrate mat with horizontal branching system and foliage in flat regularly tri-pinnate sprays with the growing tips tending to droop, held at 0 to −5°. The foliage itself is not particularly

251

dense but as there is much overlapping of shoots, the plant builds up a dense thatch at the surface of the plant and gains height with age by the smothering of the growth beneath. Growth in older plants is consequently in distinct layers, but always the top of the plant is flat, hence the name. There is a very old plant in the National Botanic Garden at Glasnevin, Dublin, from which this description is given, and another in which the layer effect is very evident at Jermyn's House, Ampfield, Hants, the residence of Mr H. G. Hillier, which I think is the same cultivar.

BUDS: Medium orange-brown, ovoid (occasionally almost globose), with sharp point, 2–3 mm (terminal), 1–2 mm (other), dull, not resinous in winter. Solitary terminal bud with one or two sub-terminals (alternate), occasionally one or two lateral buds, on strong shoots only. Buds almost invisible.

BUD SCALES: Large, rounded, not fringed, loosely appressed.

LEAVES: Medium bright yellow-green, straight but twisted at base, sides parallel, rhombic in cross-section, held edgeways, the mid-rib prominent, with top quarter tapering to a long, sharp point sometimes a little drawn out to a sharp tip, not sharp to the touch. One to four rows of stomatic lines above and below extending to tip. *Size*: 7–10 mm long (longest in the centre of the shoot) by 0·5–0·75 mm wide; with slight sheen, arranged semi-radially, held at 60–70° horizontally, 20° above and occasional leaves to 40° below. Aberrant leaf at 90°. Leaves on top of shoot point forward, not hiding shoot. Leaves form an oval outline ending in a thin circle of leaves around the bud. Leaves are set rather wide apart and are flexible to the touch.

SHOOTS: Light brown above, medium grey below, glossy, glabrous. Pulvini are prominent. Shoots are very thin and flexible. Annual growth 20–30 mm, side shoots held at 50–60° to branch, the angle noticeably uniform all over the plant.

Picea glauca. The White Spruce is usually a tree up to 25 m, the species being widely distributed in Canada and the Eastern United States. It has given us several good dwarf forms. *P. glauca* now includes, in var. *albertiana*, a geographical variety from Alberta, Canada, at one time treated as a separate species and the change gives rise to a nomenclatural conundrum in regard of the cultivar long known in cultivation as *P. albertiana conica*. This should now by a strict application of the Rules become *P. glauca* var. *albertiana* 'Conica', or perhaps (as I see Dr Boom gives it in his book) *P. glauca* 'Conica', but the former is pompous and the latter has the disadvantage of looking like a different plant. It has so long been known in the trade as 'Albertiana Conica' that I prefer to keep this as the cultivar name. Perhaps the International Registration Authority will settle the point for us by legalizing the name.

– – 'Albertiana Conica'. It is of interest to know how plants have reached our gardens and Dr Donald Wyman of the Arnold Arboretum, writing in *The American Nurseryman* for 1st November 1961 gives the following account of the origin of *P. glauca* 'Albertiana Conica'.

"In 1904, when Professor J. G. Jack and Alfred Rehder of the Arnold Arboretum

204 *Picea glauca* 'Albertiana Conica'. Deservedly a popular favourite, but very prone to disfiguring attacks by mites and aphis.

were doing a little botanizing work together in southwest Canada, they found themselves at Lake Laggan, Alberta, in the Canadian Rockies, waiting for a train. When they found the train was several hours late, they wandered off into the woods nearby and found four dwarf evergreen seedlings, all of uniform size, which were different from anything they had seen before. These they dug and shipped back to the Arnold Arboretum at once. They later turned out to be dwarf varieties of the white spruce, *Picea glauca*, and were named by Rehder *P. glauca conica*. It was found that these trees could be propagated by cuttings and in due course they were distributed throughout the botanic gardens and nurseries of the northern temperate regions of the world."

Dr Wyman goes on to relate of his having many years later found reversion on a large plant of this cultivar and of having saved seeds from that plant from which all the seedlings came as normal *P. glauca*.

'Albertiana Conica' is now one of our most prized dwarf conifers. It naturally forms a dense, conical bush (with a little trouble taken in cutting out any unwanted growth, such as a duplicate leader, it can be retained to a height of 2 m or more, looking as though it had been turned out on a lathe) with attractive fine, dense, soft, grass-green foliage. It is unfortunately a little intolerant of wind and liable to damage by red-spider and mites.

BUDS: Medium red-brown, cylindrical with rounded tip, 2 mm (terminal), 1·5 mm (other), not resinous in winter. Number in terminal cluster usually three, lateral buds numerous (on strong shoots only). Buds inconspicuous.

BUD SCALES: Small, rounded, very closely appressed, persisting for several years.

205 *Picea glauca* 'Echiniformis'. Colour: grey-green.

LEAVES: Light, bright grass-green, aromatic when crushed, reflexed at base thence straight or curved forward or downwards; very thin, fine and round in section like a needle, grooved, parallel, tapering gradually to a sharp point with a long, fine tip, not sharp to the touch. One row of stomata above and below, not extending to tip. *Size:* 8–12 mm long by not more than 0·5 mm wide, dull, arranged radially, held at widely varying angles, the longest leaves below the shoot hanging forwards and downwards. No aberrant leaf. Leaves form an irregularly parallel outline and finish with a dense clump of short leaves pointing forward, covering but not hiding the bud; along the rest of the shoot the leaves are set spaced well apart. Leaves are flexible and are soft to the touch.

SHOOTS: Light yellow, glossy, slightly hairy. Pulvini are prominent, orange in colour. Shoots are thin and flexible; annual growth 30–60 mm, side shoots at 30–70° to branch.

– – **'Echiniformis'** (frequently for some inscrutinable reason mislabelled "*P. echiniformis glauca*") forms a low, dense, cushion-shaped plant with closely set branches and thick, greyish-green foliage curved forward along the shoot, which is completely covered from view by the leaves, as are also the terminal buds.

The whole plant has a curious "limp" appearance quite unsuggestive of a hedgehog and it bears no resemblance whatever to *P. abies* 'Echiniformis', with its shining globose buds and long straight, stiff needle-like leaves.

254

BUDS: Medium brown, variably cylindrical to globose, yellow-green at centres with rounded tip. 2–3 mm (terminal), 1–2 mm (other), dull or with slight sheen. Number in terminal cluster (ill-defined) three, buds noticeable.

BUD SCALES: Medium, rounded or sometimes pointed, closely appressed or with pointed tips free.

LEAVES: Light, dull, yellow-green with a heavy bloom which gives a grey or blue-green effect, curved, parallel sided and round like a needle, with an obtuse, oblique point with short tip. *Size:* 5–7 mm long, very narrow, very glaucous, arranged radially, held at 40–45° horizontally and 20° above. Leaves are set close together, and are flexible.

SHOOTS: Medium brown above and below, very flexible. Annual growth 15–30 mm, occasionally more, side shoots at 45° to branch.

– – '**Nana**' forms a globose plant with upright-spreading main branches which carry large and prominent buds, and with more or less flat sprays with straight and (to all appearances) stiff branchlets which are held at all angles from horizontal towards the sides of the bush but ascending steeply at its centre. It is quite rare in cultivation and is at once distinguishable from the commoner 'Echiniformis' by its habit of growth, and large, brown buds.

BUDS: Bright medium brown. Strong terminal buds, globose, 4–5 mm; other buds, conical with sharp points, 1–4 mm, dull. Number in terminal cluster one, with 4–5 side buds, arranged spirally, very close to terminal bud on leading shoots, more distant on laterals, with the horizontal pair dominant. Seldom more than one other lateral bud. Buds are very prominent and noticeable, especially at the top of the plant.

BUD SCALES: Thin, papery, pointed, not fringed with resin, loosely appressed.

LEAVES: Very light, bright grey-green, straight, with parallel sides, thick and needle-like, ending in a blunt, oblique point sometimes slightly drawn out to a transparent tip, not sharp to the touch. Three to four rows stomatic lines above and 2–3 below, not extending to tip. *Size:* 5–7 mm long (according to the vigour of each shoot, but uniform in length on each shoot) by less than 1 mm wide, dull, arranged radially on upright shoots, imperfectly radially on side branches, held at 40° horizontally, 20° above and 40° below. No aberrant leaf. Leaves on top of shoot point forward, partially hiding shoot. Leaves form a parallel outline ending with double circle of short leaves around the terminal bud like the petals of a half-closed daisy. Leaves are set close together and are stiff to the touch.

SHOOTS: Medium grey above and below, dull, glabrous. Pulvini are prominent. Shoots are of medium thickness and very flexible although (because of their straightness) they appear to be stiff. Annual growth 25–45 mm; side shoots held at 50° to the branch.

– – '**Nana Glauca**' is presumably a more glaucous grey form than the preceding. It is mentioned by Dr Boom but I have not seen it.

▲ 206 *Picea mariana* 'Beissneri Compacta'.

▲ 207 *Picea mariana* 'Beissneri Compacta'. A tree over 2 m high in H. A. Hesse nursery, Weener, Ems, W. Germany.

◀ 208 *Picea omorika* 'Nana'. A young plant.

▼ 209 *Picea mariana* 'Nana'. Colour: grey-blue.

Picea mariana. The Black Spruce is another American species of large-tree dimensions in nature that has given us one or two delightful dwarf forms. At the northernmost limit of its range it is dwarfed by the climate to a shrub a few feet high, so it should be possible to introduce quite low-growing clones, as has been done in the case of *Abies balsamea* var. *hudsonia*. The species was at one time named *P. nigra* and this name can still be met with in collections and catalogues.

– – **'Beissneri'** although slow-growing, is hardly a dwarf form as it is a conical tree that will reach 5 m or more, but the German nursery firm H. A. Hesse, Weener-on-Ems, Germany, list a dwarf form **'Beissneri Compacta'** which they describe as a globose to pyramidal dwarf form to 2 m high by as much broad, with leaf shape and colour as in the species.

– – **'Doumetii'** is another pyramidal form densely furnished with fine, thin silvery-green leaves, but as it reaches 5 m or more, it too is too large for much consideration here.

– – **'Nana',** on the other hand, is quite one of the best dwarf conifers we have, reliably dwarf (seldom seen over 50 cm) forming a neat, round little bush with fine, short, bluish-grey foliage held radially on shoots which all more or less radiate from the centre of the plant, giving it a very well-mannered and "petite" appearance. A delightful little plant!

BUDS: Medium brown, globose, 2 mm (terminal), 1 mm (other); dull, not resinous in winter. Terminal bud usually solitary or with one very small bud adjoining, but with several lateral buds not far distant. Buds are noticeable.

BUD SCALES: Small, pointed, not fringed with hairs or resin; tips free-standing.

LEAVES: Actually a dark, dull blue-green, but the numerous large white stomata give the plant an almost blue-grey appearance; straight, round in section, parallel, tapering gradually to a long, sharp point (frequently noticeably oblique, giving a curved appearance to the leaf) sometimes much drawn out to a long, fine tip, not sharp to the touch. Two to four rows of very prominent stomatic lines above and below, extending to tip. *Size*: 5–7 mm long (shortest on upper side of shoot) by less than 0·5 mm wide, with slight sheen, arranged radially, held at 40–70° horizontally and 20–30° above and with the lower leaves curved to 80° below. Aberrant leaf at 70–80°, not very noticeable. Leaves form a parallel outline rather squared off at the tip, where leaves shorter than usual form a single circle around the terminal bud. Leaves are set fairly close together, and are very flexible.

SHOOTS: Medium brown above and below, dull, very hairy. Pulvini are not prominent. Shoots are thin and very flexible. Annual growth 20–30 mm. The growth of shoots from three or four lateral buds (often more vigorous than from the terminal bud itself) gives a dense and congested pattern of growth with no trace of the usual flat leaf-spray. The branches are at all angles, mostly pointing outwards.

The plant sometimes met with as **'Pygmaea'** (or occasionally under the incorrect name *P.* "*nigra pygmaea*") seems to be indistinguishable from 'Nana', being (if it differs at all) merely another clone from the northernmost limit of the range of *P. mariana*.

Picea omorika. The Serbian Spruce, although a pyramidal tree to 30 m, has given us two dwarf forms.

– – **'Expansa'** is a wide-spreading, almost prostrate shrub, not more than 1 m high but covering a large area, with ascending branches and typical foliage.

– – **'Nana'** forms a globose to conical plant of a pleasant informal outline and attractive foliage. The leaves are slightly convex above, a medium yellow-green without stomata; below they have up to seven rows of closely packed white stomata in each of two noticeable, broad, glaucous bands. As the leaves are twisted to show both sides the foliage has a bi-coloured appearance which gives an attractive look to the plant, especially if it is planted on raised ground where it is seen from below. The effect of a few strong-growing side branches is to give an uneven outline to the plant.
BUDS: Light medium brown, long ovoid, with blunt point. 3–4 mm (terminal), 2–3 mm (other), dull, not resinous in winter. Number in terminal cluster 3–5, lateral buds unusual. Buds inconspicuous.
BUD SCALES: Large, narrowly pointed, not fringed with hairs or resin, very loosely appressed.
LEAVES: Dark, bright, dull, yellow-green above; convex, with a prominent mid-rib below; straight, parallel and with rounded or very obtuse point with a tiny pointed tip, not sharp to the touch. No stomata on upper side, two broad bands of up to seven rows of white stomata below, not extending to tip. *Size*: 7–8 mm long by 1·5 mm wide, dull, arranged semi-radially on lateral shoots, held at 80–90° horizontally and 20° above (often curving to 0°) and irregularly below. No aberrant leaf. Leaves on top of shoot point forward, almost hiding shoot. Leaves form a parallel or slightly tapered outline with a semi-circular end where leaves a little shorter than normal project beyond the terminal bud, partly hiding it from view. Leaves appear (because of their width) to be very close together, and are stiff to the touch.
SHOOTS: Light brown above and below, dull and very hairy. Pulvini are prominent. Shoots are thick but not very stiff. Annual growth 20–40 mm, side shoots held at 60° to branch. The growth is irregular and informal and very dense; the branching system is ascending, strong branches rising at 30–50°, others at 0° to +20°, never below. Foliage is in flat sprays, with each shoot slightly arched.

Picea orientalis is normally a tall, densely branched pyramidal tree, but it has given us several dwarf forms. The leaves are arranged semi-radially and are much shorter than in *P. abies*; a dark, shining green; rhomboidal to square in cross section with a blunt, oblique or rounded point. The leaf cushions are usually much swollen.

– – **'Aureo-spicata'** is hardly a dwarf form, but it is very effective for many years grown in a container. The young growth is a rich creamy-white, darkening to a rich gold by late summer. The contrast with the old foliage is most effective.

– – **'Gracilis'.** Although ultimately a small tree, this form is very slow-growing and is interesting when young or as a pot plant. It forms a round-topped (eventually pyramidal) bush, very densely set with branches carrying short, radially set leaves of

210 *Picea orientalis* 'Gracilis'.

a very bright grass-green. The development of all the buds in the terminal cluster and the lateral buds results in little trace of a flat spray, especially as several main branches are apt to rise at a steep angle and become sub-leaders, so there is much interlacing of branchlets, some of which grow inwards towards the centre of the plant.

BUDS: Medium red-brown, with sharp point. 2–3 mm (terminal buds no larger than the others and quite hidden) with slight sheen. Number in terminal cluster 1–6, lateral buds numerous on strong shoots. Buds are inconspicuous.

BUD SCALES: Medium, rounded, not fringed with hairs or resin and closely appressed.

LEAVES: Medium, very bright mid-green, straight or slightly curved forward, with sides parallel, round like a needle with upper quarter of their length tapering to an oblique, medium point not drawn out at the tip or sharp to the touch. One to four very broken rows of stomata above and below, not extending to tip (especially on lower side, where they are sometimes only near the base of the leaf. *Size*: 5–7 mm long by 0·5–0·75 mm wide, noticeably glossy, arranged radially everywhere, held at 50° horizontally, and 40° above and 50° below. Aberrant leaf at 60–70°. Leaves form a tapered outline ending at the tip in a bunch of leaves pointing forward in a close cluster, completely hiding the terminal bud, especially on the leading shoots. Leaves are set close together on weak shoots but on leaders are wider apart and are stiff to the touch.

SHOOTS: Medium brown above, light brown below, glossy, hairy. Pulvini are prominent, shoots are thin and very flexible (except for the strong leader growths). Annual growth 30–70 mm. Main side shoots held at 40–60° to the branch.

211 *Picea pungens* 'Glauca Prostrate'.

– – **'Nana'** can at first sight be mistaken for a form of *P. abies* with very small leaves, such as 'Ohlendorffii'. It forms a globose to ovoid plant seldom over 1 m high, and the tiny leaves and dense uniform growth make it a most distinct and desirable form. Each year's growth is in the form of a small, slightly drooping spray with the main branches radiating outwards in all directions, but the wide angle of divergence of the branchlets produces much inter-crossing and keeps the growth very dense and lacking any appearance of being in layers.

BUDS: Bright, light brown; conical with blunt tip, 1·5 mm (terminal), 1–1·5 mm (other), with slight sheen. Number in terminal cluster 1–3 (in line horizontally), very inconspicuous and with lateral buds uncommon.

BUD SCALES: Medium, rounded, not fringed with hairs or resin, tightly appressed.

LEAVES: Light, bright mid-green; with stems appressed but leaves turn sharply outwards and are thence slightly incurved along their length. Leaves parallel-sided and round like a needle, thick, ending abruptly in a blunt asymmetrical point, not drawn out or sharp to the touch. *Size*: 3–5 mm long (shortest near the tip and on top of the shoot) by much less than 1·0 mm wide, with a slight sheen, arranged radially, held at 50° horizontally, 30° above and 40° below. No aberrant leaf. Leaves on top of shoot point forward, not hiding shoot. Leaves form a parallel outline. A cluster of nearly full length leaves point forward not hiding the terminal bud. Leaves are fairly wide apart and are very flexible.

SHOOTS: Light yellow-brown above, light yellow below, dull, glabrous. Pulvini are prominent, shoots are thin relatively to their length and flexible. Annual growth 15–25 mm and shoots stand off at an angle of 70° (very uniform all over the plant).

260

212 A reverting plant of *Picea pungens* 'Glauca Prostrate'.   213 *Picea pungens* 'Globosa'.

Picea pungens, the Colorado Spruce, is one of the most beautiful of trees, especially in its glaucous blue forms, several of which have received cultivar names.

These are all tall-growing, pyramidal trees but the species has also given us several slow-growing seedling forms which are all most attractive garden plants. They differ from the type in vigour, length of leaf and habit.

– – **'Compacta'** is the oldest form to have been recorded, and I reproduce below part of an article by the late Alfred Rehder which is understood to have been the last article written by him before his death at the age of eighty-five.

It appeared in *Plants and Gardens, Autumn 1949* (the Brooklyn Botanic Garden Record), a copy of which was kindly sent me by Henry Teuscher, of the Botanic Garden at Montreal, who was the Guest Editor for that issue.

"*Picea pungens* f. *compacta*. From typical *Picea pungens* Engelm (*P. parryana* Sarg.) this form is chiefly distinguished by its habit, forming a dense, compact flat-topped bush broader than high, with horizontally spreading branches closely set with short shiny yellow branchlets; leaves crowded, rigid, spiny-pointed, slightly incurved, $\frac{1}{4}-\frac{3}{4}$ inch long, dark green, with 4 or sometimes 3 stomatic lines on each side.

"The original plant was, according to Sargent, 3 feet high in 1897. According to Hornibrook, the plant at the Arnold Arboretum was 7 feet high and twelve feet in diameter in 1923 and now it is about 8 feet tall and 14 feet in diameter.

"*Picea pungens* f. *compacta* was raised from seed sent by Dr. C. C. Parry from Pike's Peak, Colorado, in 1863, to the Harvard Botanic Garden, as stated by C. S. Sargent in Gard. and For. **10**: 481 (1897), where under *Picea parryana* the following note appears: 'Among the seedlings raised from Dr. Parry's first seeds is a dwarf form

261

which is still less than 3 feet in height and a handsome, broad, round-topped bush.' Grafts of this plant were received at the Arnold Arboretum in February 1890. This clearly shows that the statement made by several authors, that this form originated at the Arnold Arboretum, is not correct."

– – **'Glauca Prostrate'.** Any of the forms of this spruce can give rise to the procumbent cultivariant form described on page 26 by the selection of graft scions from side growth and these should all receive a cultivar name in this form to indicate their cultivariant status.

'Glauca' is a collective name covering all glaucous blue forms, so cultivariants of this type should come under the name 'Glauca Prostrate' unless they are propagated from named clones, in which case they would be **'Koster Prostrate', 'Moerheimi Prostrate',** or as the case may be. As explained in the chapter on *Abies* they are stable unless and until some damage induces them to make true leader growth, after which it is difficult to retain them in the required prostrate habit. Where such cultivariants are derived from a form (such as 'Koster') which itself has a pendulous branch-habit, they form most attractive plants. Such are sometimes found under the name "*glauca pendula*".

– – **'Globosa'** is a dwarf, globose form to about 1 m tall; branchlets thin, 5–8 cm long, light yellowish-brown; winter buds ovoid, apex pointed, light brown; scales broad, apex rounded; reflexed; leaves crowded, imperfectly radial, 8–12 mm long, about 1 mm thick, slightly sickle-shaped, glaucous, with 3–4 stomatic lines on each side. It is sometimes listed as 'Glauca Nana'.

– – **'Hunnewelliana'** has figured in all the textbooks since Hornibrook first wrote of it in 1923 as a dwarf form, but Mr Walter Hunnewell informs me that it is now about 8 m high and 5 m across, and as to his knowledge it has never been propagated we can afford to lose sight of this name.

– – **'Montgomery'.** This is a beautiful dwarf blue form of the Colorado Spruce—of compact habit and very symmetrical shape. The original plant forms part of a large collection of conifers given by the late Col. R. H. Montgomery to the New York Botanical Garden in 1947 and was named in his honour. It originated as a chance seedling in the Eastern Nurseries. This is a very desirable form, hardy and resistant. It is very slow-growing—the annual growth being about 7 cm. The needles are long, stiff, pungent and grey-blue.

PINUS

The pines seem, for some reason not apparent to me, to be the most glamorous of all the conifers, with a particular appeal to poets, and the dwarf forms apparently share in this attraction to some people.

There are several pine species so slow-growing that they can be made use of for several years, but the truly dwarf forms of the arborescent species are not many, and the forms obtainable in the nursery trade are very few. So far as I am aware, the truly dwarf forms of the arboreal species have all originated from Witch's Brooms.

I have been unable to study this group as thoroughly as I should have wished in the time available and to do so now would delay the appearance of this book unduly. I hope to rectify this in any subsequent edition and would welcome information from readers especially as to the whereabouts of old specimens of any of the dwarf pines, or of Witch's Brooms on any of the species of pine in which no dwarf form has yet been recorded.

Pinus cembra. The Arolla or Stone Pine grows to tree size in its natural state. It has five needles persisting for three to five years, crowded on the shoot, erect, rather rigid, 6–9 cm long, the margins finely toothed except at the leaf tip. It can be recognized from the other five-leafed pines by the orange-coloured down on the young shoots. In the wild it is found from the Central European Alps to the Carpathians at high altitudes, and in a second area from North-eastern Russia through Siberia. It becomes more dwarf as the eastern edge of the distribution is approached so that in Japan this plant becomes *P. pumila*. There is therefore reasonable ground for regarding that species as a variety of *P. cembra* and it is therefore not surprising that uncertainty exists as to the correct classification of some dwarf forms. The Kew Handlist (1961) for instance, lists var. *chlorocarpa* under *P. cembra*, but for vars. *pumila* and *pygmaea* refers us to *P. pumila*.

– ⸝ var. **chlorocarpa** Beissn. 1899, is an arboreal form presumably distinctive on account of the colour of its fruit, but Messrs Hillier and Son of Winchester, Hampshire, have for many years been distributing a dwarf cultivar as **'Chlorocarpa'**. In his recent book Mr H. G. Hillier describes this as "a very beautiful bush forming many rival leaders of equal size. It makes a compact bush with its primary branches erect. The leaves are less crowded than in *P. pumila*, being distributed in tighter, but wider-spaced bundles; they are, too, a little longer and with more conspicuous stomatic bands." He adds that in about thirty years the stock plant in his nursery has reached about 1·5 m by 1·5 m. Dr Boom suggests that this may be a form of *P. pumila*.

– – **'Globe'**, a new variety which I have not seen, is described by Dr Boom as "dwarf, globose, very compact, to 2 m across; leaves only 5–7 cm long, thin, glaucous. A very conspicuous form found in the Gimborn Pinetum at Doorn, in Holland and introduced to the trade by L. Konijn and Son, Tempelhof Nurseries, Reeuwijk near Boskoop."

– – **'Nana'.** Although Mr Hillier gives this as a synonym of 'Chlorocarpa', Dr F. G. Meyer in *Plant Explorations 1963* speaks of having acquired under this name a "dwarf, slow-growing plant 90 cm to a little over 1 m, leaves green with white lines, which originated in Germany before 1910". As plants were obtained from the same firm (Konijn) as the previous cultivar it is possible that they are the same, Dr Boom having regarded the latin-form name used by Dr Meyer as illegitimate and requiring replacement under the Cultivar Code with a "fancy" name. But in this case, if the plant has been known on the Continent since 1910 it is unbelievable that the name 'Nana' did not find its way into print somewhere between then and 1st January 1959 (the date of the embargo on new latin names).

– – **'Pygmaea'** Carr. Dr Meyer also records having obtained under this name as "a dense form making a small bush 45–60 cm tall, dense, with spreading and pendulous branches". This he states originated in Europe before 1855. Dr Boom adds: "leaves short, very irregular in length, curved, not falling off".

And there for the moment we must leave them. What a case for a national (or preferably a world-wide) reference collection!

Pinus densiflora. The Japanese Red Pine is a two-leaved pine allied to our native *P. sylvestris*, but distinct therefrom in its larger and more slender, dull-green leaves, glaucous branchlets and larger cones. Of the following dwarf forms only 'Umbraculifera' is to my knowledge available in this country.

– – **'Oculus-draconis'** ("Dragon's Eye" to you, my reader) is a slow-growing form with leaves carrying two yellow bands so that the shoot when looked at from the tip shows alternate yellow and green rings, hence the name. But never having seen a dragon (or this cultivar either, for that matter) I cannot vouch for this.

– – **'Pendula'** is not a dwarf form and makes a straggly, untidy plant unless stem-trained when young. Hornibrook describes it as "a pendulous, sometimes prostrate form which looks best when allowed to fall over a bold rock". I have not seen this form, nor **'Globosa'** ("Bandaisho" of Japanese Gardens), which is described, as one would expect from the name, as being a dwarf form of globose habit and as having shorter leaves.

– – **'Pumila'.** This is listed by one German nurseryman and is described by Dr F. G. Meyer in *Plant Exploration 1963* as "a dense, slow-growing plant, conical in shape with bright green foliage, which originated in Europe".

– – **'Umbraculifera'.** This is the "Tanyosho" of Japanese gardens and is the only variety readily obtainable in England. It forms a dense, rounded or flat-topped bush, eventually a tree to 4 m high, with rich green, typical foliage but cones very much smaller than in the type, often borne on quite young plants. It is a very attractive plant which could be well made more use of on larger rockeries.

214 *Pinus densiflora* 'Umbraculifera' in the Pygmy Pinetum. It will become a large plant in time.

Pinus griffithii is a species that has been much pushed around, having at one time been called *P. excelsa* and appearing now in the current Kew Handlist as *P. wallichiana*. It has given us one dwarf form in **'Nana'**, a dwarf bush with leaves much shorter and much more silvery than in the type. I have not seen it.

Pinus heldreichii. In its geographical form, var. **leucodermis,** the Bosnian Pine, this species is sufficiently slow-growing to form a useful garden tree, and several seedling selections have been made.

– – **'Compact Gem'.** This is the name given by Dr Boom to a selected and very slow, dense form that is occasionally met with in this country as "*Dwarf form*" and is referred to by Mr Hillier as "*compacta*", both of these names now being inadmissable under the Code of Nomenclature.

– – **'Pygmy'** is a low, dense compact form found as a seedling in the Pruhonitz Arboretum, Czechoslovakia. I have not seen it.

P. koraiensis, the Korean Pine, is normally a tall tree related to *P. cembra*, from which it differs in its longer leaves with whiter inner surface and by the margins having

265

215 A group of *Pinus mugo* on the rockery at the Royal Botanic Garden, Kew.

more numerous teeth which continue to the apex of the leaf. The resin canals are three in number against two in *P. cembra*, and the cones are longer and the scales less formal in outline.

– – **'Winton'** is described by Mr H. G. Hillier as "an extremely beautiful bush, wider than high. It differs from forms of *P. cembra* in its usually longer winter buds, and longer and less straight leaves with more conspicuous stomatic lines, which give the bush a blue-green colour." Mr Hillier's largest specimen in thirty years has reached 2 m high by nearly 5 m across, so it is slow-growing but hardly, perhaps, a dwarf form to most people.

Pinus mugo. The Mountain Pine (Mugo is a local name) is a very variable species with a distribution in nature throughout Europe from the Pyrenees to the Balkans. As well as the type (sometimes referred to as var. *mughus* or var. *mugo*) botanists recognize three geographical forms vars. *pumilio* (Haenke) Zenari, *rostrata* (Entoine) Hoopes and *rotundata* (Link) Hoopes. The only constant distinction lies in the shape and size of the cones but the latter two varieties are more usually of arboreal size and so outside the scope of this book.

All the varieties vary considerably from seed and even of var. *pumilio* the expectation from seedlings would be plants too large for most rockeries, but excellent for use on

216 *Pinus mugo* 'Gnom'.

217 *Pinus mugo* 'Mops'. Named clones must be propagated by grafting.

a rough embankment or where space permits. But selected, close-growing forms have been named and are propagated by grafting and these are excellent garden plants. As it is difficult to say under which botanical "varietas" these cultivars should be listed I give them as cultivars of the type.

– – **'Compacta'** is a selected form in cultivation with dense, almost globose shape and slender bright green leaves. There is a good illustration of this form in *The Cultivated Conifers in North America* by L. H. Bailey, 1933. Several dense and slow-growing selections have been made in the nurseries of Europe. Of these the only one I know to be available in this country is **'Gnom'**, which becomes a globular, dense bush to 2 m high and as broad; branchlets very numerous (3–5 from each branchlet of the previous year); winter-buds oblong-conical, resinous; leaves crowded, radially set, 3·5–4·5 cm long, dark green. Others are **'Hesse'**, described as having its young needles twisted, a rich dark green 7–9 cm long, a dense, close growing, cushion-shaped form with short branches; **'Kobold'**, globular, dense, compact; branches stout; winter-buds 3–5, widely set, varying in length, 5–12 mm long, thick, apex blunt, conspicuously brown; leaves crowded, straight, 2–3·5 cm long, 1 mm broad, green; leaf-sheaths on young branchlets rather long, membranous, resinous; and **'Mops'**, perhaps the densest form of all, winter-buds crowded, varying in length, 1–2 cm long, narrow, brown, resinous; leaves on young branchlets tapering, nearly straight, 2–4·5 cm long, 1·8 mm broad; leaf sheaths short, dark brown.

– – **'Slavinii'** is a low, spreading form raised from seed by B. H. Slavin, Superintendent of Parks at Rochester, New York, U.S.A. I do not know whether it is still in cultivation.

267

Pinus nigra. The Corsican Pine (formerly *P. laricio*) is a variable species from Central Europe with leaves in pairs, persisting for four years, very dense on the branches, stiff, stout and straight or nearly so, 10–15 cm long. It has given us several dwarf forms.

– – **'Hornibrookiana'** is an interesting form raised from a "Witch's Broom" found on an Austrian pine in Seneca Park, Rochester, New York, by Bernard Slavin. He described it in 1932 as "a low, somewhat shrubby plant with many stout, ramified, ascending branches covered with stiff, straight, sharp-pointed, lustrous, dark green leaves 5 cm long. It has a very compact stubby appearance." Specimens growing at Durand, Eastmans Park, are now 50–80 cm high. It is available in America but not, as far as I know, in this country.

– – **'Pygmaea'.** A very slow-growing, dense, globular or procumbent bush; the leaves stiff and twisted and irregularly set, 5–6 cm long and forming a dense mat or mop-head. It is a mountain form from Mount Ansaro, Italy. There is a very old plant in the University Botanic Garden at Cambridge on which the foliage turns brownish-green in winter, but there may be other classes in cultivation. It should not be confused with *P. sylvestris* 'Globosa Viridis'. The forms **'Balcanica'**, **'Moseri'**, **'Nana'** (this turned out to be not a dwarf form at all), **'Montrosa'** and **'Prostrata'** seem to be no longer with us (*Ill. 225*).

Pinus parviflora (the Japanese White Pine, beloved of the "Bonzai" addicts) is a tall tree in the wild but does not grow to its normal height in this country. It can be readily distinguished from the other five-leafed pines by its short, blunt leaves, conspicuously white on the inner surfaces, and by its cones. The leaves are 2–4 cm long, ±1 mm broad, apex usually blunt, margins finely toothed, bluish- to grass-green, inner side with a very conspicuous band of stomata in three to four rows. As it retains its leaves until the third or fourth year it is always "well furnished" and makes an attractive tree. No doubt the shortness of the leaves is the reason for its being occasionally quite incorrectly referred to as "*P. parvifolia*".

For a species so beloved of that keen-eyed nation of gardeners the Japanese it has given very few seedling dwarf forms. Such as are known have been raised in Europe, and even these are probably more accurately described as slow growing.

– – **'Brevifolia'** is an ascending form; narrow; branches few; branchlets few, short; leaves stiff, slightly curved, 2–3 cm long, almost 1 mm broad, with five to six inconspicuous stomatic lines on both inner sides, outside bluish-green. Mr Hillier states that the original plant on his nursery has reached 3 m high by nearly 2 m across in thirty years.

– – **'Gimborn's Pyramid'** is a compact, broad and slow-growing form; branches densely borne; branchlets erect, leaves very glaucous especially in spring. Raised from seed on the estate of van Gimborn, Doorn, Holland and introduced into cultivation by L. Konijn & Son, Reeuwijk, near Boskoop.

218 *Pinus pumila* in the Royal Botanic Garden at Edinburgh.

– – **'Nana'.** This name has been more than once used for slow-growing seedling forms, the first time having been by Carriere in 1867, but they all seem with time to have grown out of any tendency to dwarfness, so the name should no longer be used.

– – **'Oculus-draconis'** is an interesting collector's piece, similar in description to the form of *P. densiflora* with the same cultivar name.

Pinus pumila, the Dwarf Siberian Pine or Japanese Stone Pine (not to be confused with *P. mugo* var. *pumilio*) is very close to the European *P. cembra*, as a geographical form of which it is sometimes regarded, so that it is sometimes met with under the name *P. cembra* var. *pumila*. It differs mainly in habit, being a more or less prostrate shrub. The leaves are in fives as in *P. cembra* but usually shorter and more slender and often curved forwards. The margins are widely toothed along their whole length and the shoots lack the bright orange down of *P. cembra*.

– – **'Dwarf Blue'** is a dwarf form, wider than tall. There is a very good specimen in Arboretum Trompenberg, Rotterdam, Holland.

– – **'Jermyns'** is a slow-growing but pyramidal form, the mother plant of which is at "Jermyns", Ampfield, near Romsey in Hampshire, the residence of Mr H. G. Hillier.

– – **'Prostrata'.** Mr Hillier gives *P. cembra* 'Pygmaea' as a synonym of this form which, without further information, I am unable to separate from 'Dwarf Blue', above.

269

▲ 219 *Pinus strobus* 'Nana' in the collection of Mr R. F. Watson, at Taunton.

◄ 220 *Pinus aristata*. A very slow-growing species.

221 *Pinus strobus* 'Umbraculifera'. A fine specimen in Arboretum Trompenburg, Rotterdam.

Pinus strobus (bearing a wide assortment of vernacular names, the commonest being Weymouth Pine) is the tallest growing of the five-leafed pines which has given us dwarf forms. It is distinguishable from other species by the slender young shoots carrying tufts of short hairs on the otherwise glabrous shoots, below the insertion of the leaf bundles. The leaves are long, 5–12 cm, bluish-green, two to three stomatic lines on both inner faces, with apex blunt pointed, slender, straight, often held horizontally in summer but drooping in winter, remaining two years, leaf-sheaths 12 mm long, soon falling.

It has given us several forms which are relatively dwarf, but these are mostly plants requiring plenty of room, on a large rockery.

– – **'Minima'** is a minute form, described by M. Hornibrook in his first edition, which I have not been able to trace. It may be lost to cultivation or have subsequently shown a capacity to grow into a much larger plant than Hornibrook supposed, and so be lost to cultivation as a separable form.

– – **'Prostrata'** is a procumbent plant with normal leaves but with branches trailing on the ground, of which there is a good example at Kew. Hornibrook gives the history of the Kew form, but as plants of this type are found wild in Newfoundland and have turned up in seed-beds elsewhere it should perhaps more properly be viewed as a botanical form. Plants trained up to form a stem when young would form attractive pendulous trees, so **'Pendula'**, first mentioned by Nelson in 1866, was probably not a separate cultivar.

– – **'Pumila'** forms a dwarf, globose plant with long (8 cm) leaves of uniform length; fine, twisted, slightly incurved; silvery green. Branchlets slender, about 5 cm; winter buds oval, pointed, light brown, about 3 mm long with scales rather free. This, or a similar form, is often found as **'Nana'** and it may be that, as in the case of *Cedrus libani* 'Nana' the latter is a collective name covering several clones developed from different dwarf seedlings.

– – **'Radiata'** makes a rather open, tufted shrub, rather wider than high, which originated with a plant in the Arnold Arboretum, of which a good illustration, with description, is given by Hornibrook in his second edition.

– – **'Umbraculifera'** forms a broad dome-topped (hence the name) shrub; branchlets crowded, glabrous, reddish-brown; winter buds about 5 mm long; scales appressed; leaves in dense tufts, drooping and occasionally at the summit of a tuft some leaves appear barely half the length of the others, about 10 cm long, sharp pointed, very narrow, light green. It is readily distinguishable from 'Radiata' by its shape, the colour of the leaves and especially by their drooping habit.

There is need for further research on the dwarf forms of this species, working upon mature specimens. Witch's Brooms on large trees will occasionally bear

271

222 *Pinus sylvestris* 'Argentea' in Mr G. L. Pilkington's collection at "Grayswood Hill", Haslemere,
Surrey.

223 *Pinus sylvestris* 'Pygmaea' in the alpine collection
at Wisley.

abnormally small cones carrying viable seeds and a large number of seedlings
shewing genetic dwarfism are under test in the Arnold Arboretum, Jamaica
Plain, Mass.

Pinus sylvestris, our native Scots Pine, has given us several dwarf forms. These have
all originated as Witch's Brooms, to which this species seems rather prone, and as is
usual in such cases the growth is apt to be uneven and irregular and so the different
forms are hard to separate. They all make attractive pot-plants.

– – **'Argentea'** is one of the 'Beuvronensis' group (see below) with foliage an attractive
silvery-grey. It is a good garden form.

– – **'Aurea'** is not a dwarf form, but it grows very slowly and is worth a place in the
garden because of its habit of turning a clear golden-yellow in the winter, when colour
of any kind is at such a premium. As an older tree seen against a background of dark
evergreens it is most attractive.

– – **'Beuvronensis'** is stated to have originated in a Witch's Broom on a tree in a
nursery at Beuvronne, near Orleans, and as this is a place name this spelling should
be used.

It forms a very thickly growing, densely branched little bush with its branchlets
held almost at 90°. Hornibrook gives the following description.
BUDS: Pointed; oval; under 6·5 mm, some tips free; very resinous; brown-red.

272

224 *Pinus sylvestris* 'Beuvronensis'. A fine specimen in Mr H. G. Hillier's collection. The later growth is distinctly looser than that at the base of the plant, which has probably been growing more strongly since settling down in its present home.

BRANCHLETS: Annual growth about 35 mm; green; shiny; smooth.

LEAVES: In twos; about 12·5 mm; barely perceptibly serrulate; some slightly twisted, but most pressed tightly face to face by a disproportionately long (about 6·5 mm) leaf-sheath, which is white to pale brown.

'Beuvronensis' is, strictly speaking, a clonal name, as stated above. But it seems clear that more than one form has strayed into cultivation under this name and that it is now being used as a collective name to cover all these undescribed dwarf forms (and sometimes perhaps also 'Compressa', 'Genevensis', 'Nana' and 'Pygmaea' below). Further study of this group is needed, and I shall be glad to have my notice drawn to plants of such age and recorded origin as to give them indisputable claim to truly represent each of the published cultivar names or to be the mother plants of other forms worth separating and naming.

– – **'Compressa'** is a dwarf and extremely fastigiate form described in 1867 and not apparently now in cultivation.

– – **'Genevensis'**, described as "a distinct pygmy form of slow-spreading growth with foliage differing from 'Beuvronensis' by its very thin leaves, borne in dense tufts at the ends of the otherwise bare branchlets, which are held at a lesser angle to the branches" also appears lost to us as I have been unable to trace it.

– – **'Globosa Viridis'** is described as a dwarf, globose slow-growing form 1–1·3 m high, with crowded branches and short branchlets; leaves 10 cm long by 1·5 mm broad, rather stiff, much curved and twisted along their length. Dr Boom states that this form develops new leaves in late summer, which cover the terminal buds during the winter.
   This may be synonymous with 'Viridis Compacta' (below). It is sometimes confused with *P. nigra* 'Pygmaea', but its much longer and more noticeably twisted leaves (which give a somewhat tousled appearance to the bush) and the fact that the foliage remains green in winter distinguish it from that variety.

– – **'Nana'** is described as a small, spreading, stunted bush rarely above 50 cm tall, with thin, very short and erect branchlets; leaves widely spaced, short, straight and glaucous. Dr Boom states that this is the form often found in the trade as 'Pygmaea' and that the form distributed as 'Nana' is 'Watereri' (below). Mr Hillier states that it differs from 'Beuvronensis' by reason of its non-resinous buds in winter.

– – **'Pumila'.** A synonym of 'Watereri' (below).

– – **'Pygmaea'** forms a dense, round bush, very slow-growing to about 1 m, annual growth 25–30 cm, branchlets glabrous and shiny red; leaves 12–25 mm long, thick, stiff and very twisted; margins toothed, leaves less glaucous than in 'Watereri'. Leaf sheaths under 6 cm, dark brown; winter buds oval, printed, 4–5 mm, red, with tips of bud scales free and resinous in winter (*Ill. 223*).

– – **'Pyramidalis Compacta'** is (or was), a narrow, pyramidal form with steeply ascending branches and dense, incurved foliage described in detail by Hornibrook in 1923 but apparently no longer in cultivation. **'Saxatilis'** (a prostrate form) and **'Umbraculifera'** (a broad, rounded shrub of very open growth) also seem lost to us.

– – **'Viridis Compacta'.** I do not know and I think it is probably a synonym of 'Globosa Viridis'—a mistake on the part of Hornibrook who does not mention the latter name although it was published by Beissner in 1900. I retain the name in general use.

– – **'Watereri'** is a rather strong-growing, upright form which becomes too large for classification with the truly dwarf forms; it is probably a seedling form. The name 'Pumila' could claim priority, but because of the confusion arising with *P. pumila* and *P. mugo* var. *pumilio* I fully agree with Dr Boom and the Kew Handlist in preferring to use the name 'Watereri'. In his recent book Dr Boom records the origin of this

▲ 225 *Pinus nigra* 'Pygmaea'.

▲ 226 *Pinus sylvestris* 'Watereri' (syn. *P. s.* "*pumila*").

◀ 227 *Pinus sylvestris* 'Globosa Viridis' at Wisley.

▼ 228 *Pinus sylvestris* 'Beuvronensis'. A small plant in the Pygmy Pinetum that has been heavily thinned, exposing the trunk and main branches.

confusion, which apparently arose out of the old, sad, familiar story of a lost label. A Dutch nurseryman raised some young trees from scions taken from a nice plant which he had admired in a German garden. The owner had forgotten the name (it would of course have been 'Pumila') but he could remember that the plant had come from

229 *Podocarpus acutifolius.*　　　　230 *Podocarpus alpinus.*

the nursery firm of Waterers (of Bagshot, Surrey) so the young plants were distributed under the name *P. watereriana*. The name was reduced to its present form by Beissner in 1902, he not at the time recognizing it as the same cultivar he had written of as 'Pumila' in 1891.

'Watereri' forms an upright, pyramidal (later globose) bush with the main branches curving outwards and upwards so that all the growing tips are ascending. Annual growth about 5 cm, leaves 25–40 mm long, narrow, stiff, twisted, conspicuously glaucous grey-green. Winter buds ovoid, pointed, 6 mm, red, resinous; leaf sheaths persistent, white to brown, 8 cm. It was found on Horsell Common in about 1865 by the late Anthony Waterer, Senior, and the original tree, now about 7·5 m high and in excellent health, is still growing in the nursery at Knap Hill.

There are several other dwarf forms of *P. sylvestris* in cultivation in this country which are unidentifiable with any published names. These have doubtless originated from different Witch's Brooms (these are not uncommon on trees of this species) and more study in this group is needed in order to sort out which, if any, of these forms are sufficiently distinct to be worth naming.

231 *Podocarpus nivalis.*   232 *Podocarpus totara.*

PODOCARPUS

Although a large genus of evergreen trees or shrubs, mostly from Australia or New Zealand, only a few species are hardy enough for use outside in Great Britain. As a broad generalization, the Podocarps are of the same ornamental value as the Yews, for which at first sight they can be mistaken. Many species are important trees in their native countries, but when raised from cuttings in Britain they remain shrub-like, and so qualify for inclusion here.

Podocarpus acutifolius, although a tree up to 10 m high in New Zealand, is usually seen in Britain as a small bush with stiff and long main branches and short branchlets usually in whorls of three. The foliage is radial on all shoots and standing out at 80–90°, the leaves narrow and flat (15–25 mm long by 1–3 mm broad) on a short, flattened stem, tapering very gradually to a fine, prickly point, grooved above and with two narrow stomatic bands below. The colour is a brown- to orange-green according to the season.

Podocarpus alpinus forms a low straggly bush with small leaves 12 mm by 2 mm, crowded, indistinctly two-ranked, blunt or sharp pointed; the upper sides dull dark green; bands of stomata with prominent mid-rib beneath. It is very slow growing and of no particular attraction as a small plant. In its early years long, straggly growths should be shortened to encourage a dense habit.

Podocarpus andinus, the Plum-fruited Yew, is not reliably hardy in this country, especially when young, and it grows to tree size, so is outside the scope of this book.

Podocarpus hallii, at one time treated as a variety of *P. totara* is now regarded as a separate species. It differs in having a looser and more open habit and distinctly larger leaves.

Podocarpus macrophyllus merits inclusion here because it usually remains a small shrub and is remarkable for the size of its leaves, which on strongly growing plants may be 15 cm long by 6 mm wide.

– – **'Hilliers Compact'** is a slow-growing form with leaves 6–8 cm long, the mother plant of which in Mr H. G. Hillier's collection has only made a plant 1·25 m by 75 cm in twenty-five years.

Podocarpus nivalis forms a dense shrub up to 1 m high, usually wider than high, with leaves closely and irregularly arranged all round the shoot, 7–20 mm long by 1·5 mm wide, shortly and stoutly stalked, thick and leathery, pointed or blunt at the apex; dull green above, keeled and with two ill-defined white stomatic buds below. The fruit is a bright red.

It is hardy and suitable for a fairly bold spot on a rockery. In the Pygmy Pinetum there are at least two forms, varying in size and shape of leaf, and also a colour variant for which I suggest the descriptive cultivar name **'Bronze'.** This makes an attractive plant of quite unusual colouring and it should become popular when better known. I am informed by Mr Trevor Davies of New Zealand that the species is variable, on a regional basis.

Podocarpus nubigenus is another species of doubtful hardiness, with large leaves, 2·5–4 cm long by 3–4 mm wide.

Podocarpus totara at home is an evergreen tree 15–25 m or more high but in cultivation in Great Britain is usually seen as an upright to spreading bush, densely clothed with long, flat and fairly broad (15–25 mm by 3–4 mm) leaves, ending in a sharp and slightly prickly point; leaves borne more or less radially, light yellow-green with a sunk midrib above and two broad white bands of stomata below.

233 *Pseudotsuga menziesii* 'Fletcheri'. One of the finest of dwarf conifers.

PSEUDOTSUGA

Only two of the five species in this genus (which is neither spruce, fir nor hemlock) have given us recorded dwarf forms, but these have suffered several changes of name. *Ps. menziesii* was for a long time regarded as *Ps. douglasii* (its vernacular name is Douglas Fir, or, sometimes—to help on with the confusion a little—Oregon Pine), then for a time it was *Ps. taxifolia*. This was before it received its present name, which let us hope it will be allowed to retain. *Ps. glauca* was at one time regarded as a geographical variety of *Ps. menziesii* and there seems even now some residual doubt as to its right to specific status, and as is usual when such changes are made the old names linger on in labels and catalogues and cause much confusion.

The Pseudotsugas are most closely allied to *Abies* but they vary in that their cone scales are persistent, and they are distinguishable by their narrower leaves, soft to the touch, with coloured bases, and by the beech-like buds.

Pseudotsuga menziesii. The differences between this species and *Ps. glauca* are so small that, in the absence of fruiting parts the botanical position of some of the dwarf forms is indeterminate. I therefore list them all as cultivars of *Ps. menziesii*.

A large number of dwarf forms has been named from time to time. Of those listed by Hornibrook **'Astley'**, **'Cheesemanii'**, **'Compacta'**, **'Compacta Glauca'**, **'Compacta**

279

234 *Pseudotsuga menziesii* 'Fretzii'.   235 *Pseudotsuga menziesii* 'Brevifolia'.

Viridis', 'Dumosa', 'Globosa', 'Leptophylla', 'Nana', 'Nidiformis', 'Pumila' and **'Pygmaea'** are apparently not now in circulation in England, although several of them are listed in some American collections.

– – **'Brevifolia'** is a very slow-growing, picturesque, tree-like form with short pale-green leaves, straight or but slightly curved, arranged radially and standing out stiffly in all directions, with a pleasant fragrance when crushed. The buds are broadly ovoid with rounded tips. It differs from 'Fretzii' (below) in its narrower, apple-green leaves, and Mr Hillier states that it is less tolerant of lime than is that variety.

– – **'Densa'** is a dwarf, spreading, flat-topped tree with irregular horizontal branches, much ramified to matted branchlets clothed with leaves shorter than those of the species (12–20 cm). Whilst this form can be pruned into a symmetrical, formal shape, its normal habit develops individuality and character, and as a point of interest in small-scale plantings it is worthy of consideration.

– – **'Fletcheri'** is by far the commonest form in England and it is one of the most attractive of all dwarf conifers. Hornibrook gives a full account of its origin in his Second Edition. It forms a rounded- or flat-topped, picturesque, spreading bush with leaves radially set, or nearly so, 1·5–2 cm long (occasionally, on weak growth, much less) by 1·5–2 mm wide, twisted at the stem, thence usually straight but often

280

gracefully curved and twisted; green above with a sunk mid-rib, keeled below with two glaucous bands; winter buds long (to 1 cm), conical, finely pointed, red-brown, with bud-scales tightly appressed except at the base of the bud. The plant is soft to the touch (*Ill. 233*).

'Fletcheri', 'Cheesemanii' and 'Nana' were all found in the same batch of seedlings, but apparently 'Fletcheri' is the only form now obtainable in the nursery trade.

– – **'Fretzii'** is a slow-growing, curious form which makes a broad, conical bush (eventually becoming a small tree) with twisted ascending branches, very short branchlets and conical red buds coated with resin during the winter. The leaves are broader and shorter than in the typical form, 8–12 mm long by 2 mm wide, a dark, dull green above, arranged radially and usually much recurved. It is a form of interest to collectors but of no great beauty. As it is usually seen as a rather straggly, open bush it would probably pay for a little pruning in its early years.

– – **'Oudemansii'** is another collectors' item which also grows very slowly but eventually reaches tree stature. Its habit is pyramidal with ascending branches, the leaves are 10–16 mm long by 2–3 mm wide, parallel-sided and rounded at the tip, dark, shining green above with two light-green stomatic bands below.

– – **'Slavinii'** is semi-dwarf and of conical habit, broad at the base, narrowing towards the top, leaves crowded. It is obtainable in America, but not to my knowledge in this country.

SCIADOPYTYS

Sciadopytys verticillata, the Japanese Umbrella Pine, and the sole occupant of this genus is neither a pine nor a dwarf, but it is extremely slow-growing for many years, so is worthy of mention here, although eventually reaching tree size in a congenial spot in this country.

Its chief claim to interest lies in its unusual foliage and this always attracts attention. The true leaves are small and scale-like: these are scattered along the shoot but at its end there is a whorl of twenty or more pseudo-leaves 10–15 cm long by 2–3 mm wide, thick and flat, furrowed above and deeply so below, gradually tapering to a blunt tip divided in the middle where the two furrows join.

236 *Sequoia sempervirens* 'Adpressa'. One of the most beautiful of all dwarf conifers.

Sequoia

Sequoia sempervirens, the Giant Redwood, now stands alone in this genus, the Wellingtonia or Mammoth Tree of California (formerly *S. gigantea*) having had the generic name *Sequoiadendron* specially invented for it, although many people treat this as a joke and continue to use the old name.

Although one of the tallest trees in the world *S. sempervirens* has given us three excellent dwarf forms.

– – **'Adpressa'.** This dwarf form is probably a cultivariant of a tall variety of the species known as 'Albo-spica', as it will occasionally throw up strong, vertical growth with small, appressed leaves radially set. These must be cut right out at once if the dwarf characteristic is to be preserved, but if this be done 'Adpressa' will remain indefinitely a low, densely branched bush. In the summer when all the crowded, upright shoots are tipped with creamy-white it is probably the most beautiful dwarf conifer in existence. It breaks into bud freely from old wood and is improved by an occasional hard cutting back.

– – **'Nana Pendula'.** It is quite possible that this too is a cultivariant, but this time of the weeping form known as 'Pendula', which is described as having branches arched over and (in old trees) spreading over the ground. Cuttings of weak shoots taken from such a tree could be expected to produce plants of 'Nana Pendula' if stem-trained when young.

It is quite distinct from 'Adpressa' by its sprawling, open habit of growth and from 'Prostrata' (below) by its narrow leaves (*Ill. 238*).

282

237 *Sequoia sempervirens* 'Prostrata'. A plant in the Pygmy Pinetum that has been stem-trained to form a central trunk, giving the tiered effect necessary for this plant to look its best.

– – **'Prostrata'** is one of the most remarkable of dwarf conifers. It originated in a bud mutation on a tree in the Cambridge University Botanic Garden (hence the name 'Cantab' sometimes met with) which gave rise to a branch with flat leaves almost twice the usual width. Plants raised from cuttings taken from this branch had a completely prostrate habit.

Allowed to grow in this way the plant merely forms a widespread, dense, sprawling mat of no particular beauty, but if in its formative years one main shoot is trained up into a vertical leader the branches will spread out stiffly in horizontal layers and eventually it will become a large spreading plant, which with its wide leaves of an attractive and unusual shade of grey-green will seldom fail to attract attention.

I consider that it is most effective when planted against a wall or in front of a large rock so that it can only develop in a half-circle. It will never increase in height without further training up of a leader (the process is basically the same as the production of an espalier fruit tree) but it will spread out horizontally to cover a large area in time. Any strong branches carrying radially set foliage that sweep up from the horizontal must be cut out at once or the character of the plant will be soon lost. The leaves are sometimes killed in a hard winter. The plant is unharmed, but because the leaves persist for several years the dead, brown remains spoil its beauty for a long time, so it should be given a sheltered position if possible.

283

238 *Sequoia sempervirens* 'Nana Pendula'.   239 *Sequoiadendron giganteum* 'Pygmaeum'.

Sequoiadendron

Sequoiadendron giganteum the Mammoth Tree, itself growing to 100 m or more has given us one dwarf form in **'Pygmaeum',** but as would perhaps be expected of a pygmy giant it makes quite a large bush, to 3 m high. The growth is relatively crowded and dense, but strong leader growth appears and must be cut out betimes if the plant is not to become arboreal.

Taxus

Taxus is a genus of six or seven species which because their differences are solely in foliage and habit characteristics (the flowering and fruiting parts being identical) could be very well regarded as geographical varieties of a single species.

They are all very hardy and most accommodating as to soil and situation, thriving equally in acid or alkaline soil, standing pruning and clipping well and succeeding even in dense shade. This makes them a useful group even in the island climate of Britain, and in the more extreme climate of North America they are grown by the million and there, owing to the recognized fact that very similar clones when planted in the nursery in large quantities in adjoining rows or drifts appear surprisingly distinct, innumerable named forms are on the market which as individual plants are virtually impossible to distinguish.

The truly dwarf forms are few, but a number of the named forms are sufficiently slow-growing to be mentioned here. These, like the varieties of *J. communis*, seem to run either to a narrow fastigiate form or to a low and spreading habit. There are several striking golden and variegated forms, but generally the foliage is a dark, rich green, often almost a black-green, which in a mass can become sombre, so the yews should be planted with restraint. I have been unable to locate several of the forms described by Hornibrook.

Taxus baccata is the Common or (in America) English Yew. The leaves are spirally arranged, but on side branches are twisted into a pseudo-pectinate arrangement; linear, 12–13 mm long by 1·5–2 mm wide, gradually tapering to a fine point; dark (sometimes almost black-) green above and pale green, grey or yellowish with faint stomatic lines below.

– – **'Adpressa'** is strictly speaking a botanical form as it has appeared in the wild from time to time. It forms a large spreading shrub (eventually a small tree), with densely crowded branches and leaves that are much shorter and relatively broader than the common form, only 6–12 mm long by 2–4 mm broad, with a round apex ending in a sharp point. It is a fruiting form, the disc being shorter than the nutlet and it comes mainly true from seed.

– – **'Adpressa Aurea'** is a much more attractive form with growth similar to 'Adpressa' but forming a very much less vigorous plant, not exceeding 1·5 m high. The leaves on young growth are golden-yellow, elsewhere yellowish: female flowers only. There are also two fastigiate forms which I have not seen. Of these: **'Adpressa Pyramidalis'** is described as a pyramidal form with spreading branches and leaves only 1 mm wide, and **'Adpressa Stricta'** is a still more columnar form with vertical leader and short horizontal branches, with leaves up to 15 mm long by 3 mm wide. There is also a very attractive and deservedly popular form **'Adpressa Variegata'** with leaves persistently golden-yellow with a central green stripe. It forms a dense bush and grows much

▲ 240 *Taxus baccata* 'Adpressa Variegata'. A rich golden-yellow with green centre to each leaf.

◀ 241 *Taxus baccata* 'Amersfoort'.

larger than 'Adpressa Aurea'. There is a fine specimen at the Westonbirt Arboretum on the north side of Mitchell Drive near the Down Gate.

– – **'Amersfoort'** is a curious, slow-growing form with a stiff, open habit resulting from ascending main branches and few short branchlets. The leaves are numerous, oval, set radially, 5–8 mm long by 3–4 mm wide, rounded at the apex and abruptly pointed, dark glossy green above, lighter beneath. The leaves are slightly convex and this, with the raised mid-rib above, gives a curious thick appearance to the leaves and the whole plant is not at a glance unlike *Olearia nummularifolia*. It is more of a curiosity than a thing of beauty.

It can be readily distinguished from 'Adpressa' by its stiff habit, and by its "thick" leaves being twice as long as wide and radially set on the branches, whereas 'Adpressa' has a lax habit, the leaves are pectinate and are three times as long as they are wide.

– – **'Argentea'** is a very slow-growing, low bush with its young leaves variegated with narrow silver margins. It is not particularly effective seen from a distance, but is interesting as a pot plant or on a small rockery.

– – **'Cavendishii'** is a strong-growing and somewhat "untidy", spreading variety less than 1 m high but reaching to several metres across, with the main branches at the centre of the plant ascending at 45° and arching over to 0° but with all the growing

286

tips—especially at the outside of the plant—often decurved, sometimes even pendulous. The leaves are long, 20–30 mm long by 2–2·5 mm broad, the top third gradually tapering to a fine tip, very dark bluish-green above, with raised mid-rib; light green below, with two wide and usually deeply sunk bands of stomata giving a rim-like effect to the edge of the leaf. The leaves are arranged semi-radially, but almost every leaf is strongly curved outwards and upwards, often to 90° (*Ill. 245*).

This form is very similar to 'Repandens', differing in its arching, untidy habit and in its longer, darker green and more strongly curved leaves.

– – **'Compacta'** is one of the three dwarf forms produced by Messrs Den Ouden's nurseries, freer-growing than the other two and making a compact, oval, or conical bush of ascending branches, 1·3 m across; branches regularly spreading, compact, branchlets crowded, 4–6 cm long, brown; leaves radial, 5–10 mm long, 1 mm broad, slightly sickle-shaped, shining dark green above, paler and with a dark mid-rib beneath. Not unlike 'Paulina' in appearance, but much smaller in every way.

Mr H. G. Hillier writes as follows: "As received from the raiser this variety appears to be freer-growing than 'Pygmaea', with longer leaves and forms a more densely flat-topped bush".

– – **'Decora'.** The plant grown in England under this name is a very distinct form; a very slow-growing and most attractive garden variety, forming an upright, flat-topped bush with arching branches and lustrous foliage. The leaves are unusually large, up to 30 mm long by 3–4 mm broad, and are all curved upwards.

This agrees closely with Mr Hillier's description but not with Hornibrook's, who says of 'Decora' that it is "one of the tiniest of all yews and the only real pygmy among the flat-growing forms". Which variety he was actually writing of cannot now be ascertained, but it was certainly not our present plant (*Ill. 242*).

– – **'Ericoides'** is rather a mystery plant which used to be quite common but which is not now to be found. The probable explanation is that both it and **'Epacroides'** (to which the same remarks apply) were tender forms and perished during a particularly hard winter from collections once listing them. Both were slow-growing little bushes with small leaves, very narrow and heathlike. Hornibrook sets out the distinction between these forms, should either of them be still in cultivation.

– – **'Expansa'** (syn. 'Procumbens' Kent, 1900). A wide-spreading, procumbent form, frequently making an asymmetrical plant; branches slightly ascending but with tips decurved; leaves 25–30 mm long, dark green, often falcate, arranged pectinately.

I have not been able to identify this description with any plant I have seen. There is considerable uncertainty about several of these procumbent forms and it seems to me we have more names than plants. In some of the following I repeat previous descriptions pending further study of this group. Those with pendulous branches are very effective when planted at the top of a wall or steep bank.

287

242 *Taxus baccata* 'Decora'. The stock plant in Messrs Hillier and Son's nursery.

243 *Taxus baccata* 'Fastigiata'. The well-known Irish Yew. Colour: very dark green.

– – **'Fastigiata'** is the well-known Irish Yew. This and its colour variants **'Fastigiata Aurea'**, **'Fastigiata Aureomarginata'** and **'Fastigiata Aureovariegata'** become too large in time to be regarded as dwarf forms but in their early years they are very slow-growing and strictly columnar and are very useful for their architectural qualities.

– – **'Horizontalis'** is, properly speaking, a tree-form with branches strikingly horizontal but, as Mr Hillier states, it can be grown as a spreading bush characterized by the stiffness of all the growing tips.

– – **'Nana'** is a very dwarf form described by Hornibrook which I have not been able to identify. It is, if still in cultivation, a very dwarf, slow-growing form of rather spreading and straggly habit to 60 cm high, with short, thick and variable leaves sometimes falcate, *glossy dark green*, sometimes red-brown at the tips.

– – **'Nutans'** forms a very slow-growing low, rounded to spreading bush with a frame-work of irregularly spreading and crowded branches often nodding at the growing tips. The leaves are very irregular in shape, size, arrangement and distribution, a *shining dark green, light green beneath*. It is frequently confused with 'Pygmaea' (below).

288

244 *Taxus baccata* 'Nutans'. The foliage is very irregular in shape, size and arrangement.

– – **'Paulina'** forms a dense, compact, conical bush with long, dark green, glossy leaves, sometimes bronzing in winter. The branch system is ascending; the leaves are radially held, 5–15 mm long by 1·5 mm wide, flat and dark blue green above and keeled, a light mid-green below, each leaf close to the shoot at its base but strongly decurved to 70–90° at its tip.

– – **'Procumbens'** Lodd. (Cat 1836) ex Loud. (1838), 2067, is described as "having its branches spreading at right angles to the stem and bright green leaves. Very low and spreading habit." There are several plants in the *Taxus* collection at the National Pinetum at Bedgebury, Kent which I believe to be this form. They are all low-growing (to 50 cm high), very dense, prostrate shrubs irregularly branched, and densely clothed with foliage on the young shoots but having many of the main branches bare. The leaves are very variable in size, up to 15 mm long by 2 mm broad, parallel-sided with a fairly abrupt taper ending in a fine and very sharp drawn-out point. The young twigs and buds are green, the leaves are held up stiffly, often nearly vertically, and are green above, bronzing slightly in winter and light green below. The foliage has a somewhat "wiry" feel if brushed with the hand. Annual growth 50 mm.

– – **'Prostrata'** Bean (1916) 581, is described as "a low, trailing form, lower and flatter than 'Procumbens' and other prostrate forms". In the *Taxus* collection in the National Pinetum at Bedgebury is an old plant of a very low, spreading form which I have never seen elsewhere and which answers to the description. It is a very flat-topped plant 50 cm high by 1·5 m across with the habit of *Picea abies* 'Nidiformis' (including its "nest-like" formation). It has a very horizontal branching habit and it is densely and quite regularly clothed with semi-radial foliage. The leaves are 20 mm long by 2 mm wide, straight or nearly so, held up at a ±45°, a shiny dark green above with a prominent mid-rib, very light green below. Annual growth 6–8 cm, all growing tips are horizontal except at the edge of the plant where they tend to droop slightly.

Further research may decide whether or not this is, in fact, 'Prostrata', but it is an attractive form that should be in more general circulation.

– – **'Pseudo-procumbens'** Hornb. (1939) 241 is described as a low-growing, regular bush with rounded top and pendulous elongated branches in thick layers. Leaves light green 12–30 mm long. Hornibrook describes as a characteristic of this form the presence of two terminal buds, of which the stronger makes a shoot pointing downwards and the second a smaller shoot pointing upward. This should make this form quite distinctive, but if so I have never seen it.

– – **'Pumila Aurea'.** Although from the brief descriptions given by Hornibrook (who had only seen small plants) it is difficult to be sure, I think this must be the form represented by two very old plants at Bedgebury at the top of the bank. They are now flattish, irregularly globose plants 75 cm high by 1·5 m across, of dense growth and tapered leaves 20 mm long by 2 mm wide, densely set, arranged imperfectly radially and all pointing well forward and of a rich golden-yellow, almost orange in the general effect. The young shoots are yellow, the buds pinky-brown to yellow. It is an extremely attractive form, outstanding for colour, and one that should be more planted.

So far as colour is concerned, this plant agrees with old descriptions of **'Elvastonensis',** of which I have not been able to trace an authentic specimen. But these old descriptions are very brief and make no reference to habit of growth, so whether or not the names are synonyms I cannot say.

– – **'Pygmaea'** is probably the smallest form and I have not seen it true in this country. It is described as making a conical or ovoid little shrublet with crowded, ascending main branches and short branchlets with very short, radially held leaves, a *light grass green*. There is a good illustration of this form in *Die Nadelgehölze*, 1402.

The descriptions available for several of these small-leaved dwarf forms are far from adequate and in the absence of a representative collection they are quite impossible to disentangle satisfactorily. Because of its variability, I fancy that 'Nutans' often does duty under other names. The plants in the Pygmy Pinetum are too small as yet to be of much help so I shall be glad of any information which readers can supply as to the whereabouts of mature and authentic specimens of any of these forms.

– – **'Repandens'** is a strong-growing and spreading variety 30–40 cm high by 2–2·5 m across, often confused with the very similar 'Cavendishii'. It has a somewhat stiffer and more prostrate habit, the leaves are smaller—15–25 mm long by 2 mm broad, tapering gradually to a long, fine point, a shining dark green with the same raised mid-rib above and two bands of stomata, but the leaves are either straight or very

245 *Taxus baccata* 'Cavendishii'. *Taxus baccata* 'Repandens' differs mainly in the shape of its leaves.

246 *Taxus baccata* 'Repens Aurea' in John Scott and Co. nursery at Merriott, Somerset.

247 *Taxus baccata* 'Semperaurea'. A young plant. With age it will extend its main branches and become more irregular in outline.

much less curved and they point forwards and upwards (but never to 90°) in two distinct rows so as to form a V-groove. I give the differences between 'Repandens' and the very similar 'Cavendishii, under that form, but I have been unable to distinguish a form sometimes met with under the name **'Pendula'.**

I have seen a golden-variegated form being grown under the name **'Repens Aurea'** which should be popular when it becomes more available. The legitimacy of this name is questionable and it may have to be replaced with a "fancy" name to comply with the Cultivar Code (*Ill. 246*).

– – **'Semperaurea'** is by no means a dwarf form, but because of its colour and habit it is desirable as a young plant and being slow-growing can be made use of for some years. It makes a delightful specimen on a lawn, especially where it will be seen against a background of dark evergreens or a shadow mass. It forms a spreading shrub to 1·5– 2 m high by much more across with no trunk but with its (eventually numerous) main branches ascending at a steep angle and with numerous, short, side branches. The leaves are 10–20 mm long by 2·5–3 mm broad, a bright golden-yellow, paler below, keeping their colour well throughout the year.

– – **'Standishii'** is a very slow-growing fastigiate form with golden-yellow leaves 20–25 mm long by 3·5–4 mm across with a raised mid-rib. A most desirable little plant.

Taxus cuspidata, the Japanese Yew, is a hardy, slow-growing form that thrives in North America, where innumerable clones have been selected and named. From the English Yew it can be distinguished by the yellowish tinge of the under-surface of the leaves and by the longer, more oblong, winter buds with looser and more pointed

292

248 *Taxus cuspidata* 'Nana'. A young plant: it will become a large, spreading bush in time.

scales. It has given us several dwarf forms which, although not particularly outstanding, are useful because of their extreme hardiness and adaptability.

– – **'Densa'** forms a dense, cushion-shaped little bush with erect branches, leaves dark green.

– – **'Minima'** is an extremely slow-growing upright form of irregular habit with many short branchlets and relatively long leaves, a lustrous dark green. Hornibrook states that it is the smallest conifer hardy in North America, but today I should say that *Thuja occidentalis* 'Hetz Midget' had better claim to this distinction.

– – **'Nana'** is a wide-spreading bushy form seldom over 1·5 m high but often much more across. It grows somewhat irregularly, with a few strong and stout main branches and many short side branches; leaves radially set, 20–25 mm long by 4 mm broad, broad and blunt pointed, flat with a slightly raised mid-rib, dark green, sometimes lighter green above. The name "*brevifolia*" under which it is sometimes found is objectionable because of the confusion arising with the species of that name. It can make a fine pot specimen, especially if the foliage is greatly thinned out.

Taxus × media is a hybrid between *T. baccata* and *T. cuspidata* of which several clones have been selected and named in America. They are intermediate in characteristics between the two parent species and are all rather too vigorous for inclusion here.

THUJA

The *Thuja*, first cousins of the *Chamaecyparis*, differ from their relatives mainly in the cones, which are egg-shaped or rounded with flat, oblong and usually thin scales, quite unlike the top-like scales of that genus. The similarity in foliage, especially in the juvenile stage, can give us difficulty in identifying our treasures when (as is usual with our dwarf forms) we are restricted to the foliar characteristics.

Thuja koraiensis, like several other conifer species, forms either a pyramidal to fastigiate tree or a low-spreading, almost trailing bush. With the former we have nothing to do here, but the low-growing form is very useful and attractive where there is room for it to spread over a fairly large area of ground. The leaf spray is bright, dark green, flat and typically thujoid, the underside being very thickly coated with a white glaucous bloom which is not easily brushed off. The crushed foliage is less objectionable than is *Th. occidentalis*, it having a rather pleasant "medicated" smell.

Thuja occidentalis. The American Arbor-vitae is normally a tree of no particular attraction. The foliage is much flattened, the lateral pair folded and overlapping the facing pair which bear (usually prominently) a raised round to oval resin gland. The species can be usually recognized by the presence of this gland and even in abnormal foliage forms by the unpleasant acrid smell of the adult foliage when bruised. The species is found in nature mainly on marshy ground and does not thrive in dry soil, so presumably the dwarf forms will also do best in moist situations.

Th. occidentalis has given rise to numerous dwarf forms which are good garden plants, but mostly they share the habit of this species, and turn dull green or dirty brown in the winter.

The nomenclature of these dwarf forms is all at sixes and sevens because the original descriptions were very brief and inadequate and because dwarf seedlings can turn up at any time which are but little different or barely distinguishable from the existing clones. Several writers have attempted to get round this by describing such cultivars as they knew and picking on a likely variety to treat as a collective name to cover the remainder. This almost always leads you into trouble. Beissner, in 'Compacta', lighted on a name which had already been bagged (and as I now suggest restricting the use of this word—more appropriately so) for a compact rather than a dwarf form. Hornibrook with 'Froebelii' fared little better, for it seems now certain, so far as certainty is possible, that 'Froebelii' is synonymous with 'Hoveyii', which he described separately and outside his 'Froebelii' group.

Mr Hillier in his recent book suggests some very wholesale lumpings together, but sympathetic as I am with his feelings with regard to the present confusion I cannot but help feeling he has over-simplified matters, as within his synonymy he includes clones which are quite discernibly distinct and in some cases different enough to have quite separate garden uses. I therefore give full descriptions of all the clones I have in the Pygmy Pinetum or know "personally" and have quoted other published names as synonyms of these whenever I could be reasonably sure of being right. In the case of other clones which I could not honestly fit in anywhere, and do not myself know, I have repeated earlier descriptions for what they are worth.

There remains undoubtedly a number of unnamed clones arising from later seedlings that are more or less similar to those I have described. I suggest that the names I have treated as synonyms be allowed to drop out of use and that nurserymen take the trouble to ascertain that their propagating material comes from true stock and not from any of these unnamed clones. These should not be propagated from unless and until one of them, with time, proves itself to be sufficiently distinctive to justify its being named as a new cultivar.

The dwarf forms lend themselves to a simple grouping, as under.

Juvenile Foliage Forms

'Ellwangeriana Aurea'
'Ericoides'
'Ohlendorffii'
'Rheingold'
'Tetragona'
'Watereri'

Globose Habit

'Globosa'
'Globularis'
'Little Gem'
'Pumila'
'Recurva Nana'
'Reidii'
'Umbraculifera'
'Woodwardii'

Conical Habit

'Cristata'
'Cristata Aurea'
'Ellwangeriana Aurea'
'Holmstrupensis'
'Hoveyii'

Bun-shaped Forms

'Caespitosa'
'Dumosa'
'Pygmaea'
'Recurva Nana'

Colour Forms (Golden)

'Ellwangeriana Aurea'
'Lutea Nana'
'Rheingold'

Abnormal Foliage Forms

'Batemanii'
'Bodmeri'
'Filiformis'
'Ohlendorffii'
'Tetragona'

Miniature Forms

'Caespitosa'
'Hetz Pygmy'
'Minima'
'Ohlendorffii'

Colour Forms (Variegated)

'Beaufort'
'Wansdyke Silver'

249 *Thuja occidentalis* 'Caespitosa'. 250 *Thuja occidentalis* 'Dumosa'.

– – **'Bodmeri'** forms a dense, conical shrub; it is a monstrous form with thick main and side branches. The normal leaf-spray is entirely missing, the leaves are more or less closely appressed to the stem and, being often folded or keeled, give (sometimes exaggerated) a tetragonal appearance to the shoot. The foliage is a rich deep green, there being little or no differentiation between the facial and lateral pairs.

This is an abnormal foliage form of a type that has cropped up in several of the *Thuja* and *Chamaecyparis* species, where it has frequently been given the name of 'Lycopodioides', so it is not surprising that our present variety is sometimes, quite incorrectly, so labelled. In *Cultivated Conifers in North America*, L. H. Bailey gives the following description: "A monstrosity form with thick, clumpy growth due to shortened more or less curved branches and dense overlapping foliage green beneath." This description does not at all fit our plant as we know it in Europe but Bailey adds "the plant known as **'Batemanii'** is said to be this variety" and it may well be that his description was in fact of that otherwise unrecorded variety, which I have not seen.

– – **'Caespitosa'** is a very slow-growing plant which forms a low, hemispherical bun wider than high. The foliage is very congested and irregular. There is no flat leaf-spray formation in the ordinary sense, but the leaves are either closely appressed around an almost cord-like shoot with the points of the lateral leaves free-standing, or they occur on shoots which are very much flattened out (to 2·5 mm) and there are occasional shoots bearing juvenile foliage. It is an attractive form, which should be better known.

– – **'Compacta'**, as its name properly indicates, is a compact form of the species. It forms an ovoid to conical bush much larger and looser in growth than the dwarf forms, but I mention it as it has appeared in earlier works on the dwarf conifers. It has a large flat spray with the branchlets parallel and with the ultimate shoots short and uniform in length so that the space is more or less filled up, without the overlapping

296

251 *Thuja occidentalis* 'Recurva Nana'.   252 *Thuja occidentalis* 'Cristata Aurea'.

that is characteristic of 'Globosa', for a coarse, open specimen of which a young plant of 'Compacta' could be mistaken.

The colour is deep green, developing a deep, glaucous bloom the second year. This gives the plant as a whole a much darker appearance.

– – **'Cristata'.** The name, and the reference to the "cock's comb-like branches" in the descriptions are apt to give the impression that this uncommon variety is more exciting than is really the case. I have only seen it in Holland where (from memory, not from notes), it was an upright, rounded bush, rather open and with rather narrow foliage finer than in 'Globosa' but not so fine as in 'Sphaerica'; the sprays held at all angles and curved in a way which to me suggested inspiration for a designer of scroll ironwork rather than a cockscomb—certainly there was nothing cristate about it. The foliage developed mostly on only one side of the shoot.

– – **'Cristata Aurea'** is a variation in which the foliage is a dull yellowish-green, its stems orange. It is slower growing so forms a smaller plant.

Under this name one English nursery (no longer in existence) was for some years distributing plants of *Thuja plicata* 'Rogersi', so a number of collections will probably have that plant wrongly labelled.

– – **'Dumosa'** (Syn. "*nana*" Carl., "*Antarctica*" Hort., *Thuja minor* Paul, "*plicata dumosa*" Hornb., "*plicata llaveana*" Hort., "*wareana globosa*" Beissn. 1881. I am not entirely satisfied that I have identified this form. It was described by Carriere as "A spreading little bush, densely clothed with numerous short, tufted, flat, fan-shaped branches growing in all directions, thickly set with short, forked, two-edged (much flattened?) branchlets. Of a glossy light green above, much paler below." To this description Gordon in his "Supplement" of 1862 adds, "This kind forms a dense, confused little bush, seldom growing more than 60–90 cm high, somewhat resembling in its branchlets the Nootka Sound Arborvitae (*Thuja plicata*) but of a much lighter

297

253 *Thuja occidentalis* "Ellwangeriana Aurea".   254 *Thuja occidentalis* 'Ericoides'.

colour." It is doubtless this last sentence that has given rise to the inclusion some-times of the word "*plicata*" in the cultivar names, but as it serves no useful purpose and is, indeed, misleading it is best omitted. Under 'Recurva Nana' (below) I put forward a case for identifying 'Dumosa' with a form often met with in the trade under that name but distinct therefrom.

– – **'Ellwangeriana Aurea'.** There is a lot of confusion between this plant and **'Rheingold'** (*Ill. 263*), for which Murray Hornibrook is partly responsible.

The former is a slow-growing golden form which is ovoid when young but which eventually builds itself up into a pyramidal tree several metres high. Except as a very young plant it bears predominantly adult foliage with pinkish-brown shoots and golden-yellow foliage in flat sprays held at random angles, but even when large there can always be found a stray shoot or two near the ground bearing juvenile foliage.

Reading Hornibrook's description of 'Rheingold' in his Second Edition one is apt to jump to the conclusion that he is quoting Beissner's own words. But not a bit of it! What Beissner wrote of 'Rheingold' was, "differs from 'Ellwangeriana Aurea' because the plant is dwarf, globular, dense, to 1 m high, foliage juvenile, golden-yellow to brownish-yellow. I have seen the two plants and the differences are evident and confusion is not necessary."

Although the differences are, as Beissner says, evident when you have mature

▲ 256 *Thuja occidentalis* 'Pumila'. Detail of foliage.

◄ 255 *Thuja occidentalis* 'Pumila'. A very old plant at Glasnevin.

plants before you, differentiation by description is very difficult indeed and recognition in young plants almost impossible. 'Rheingold' tends to have smaller sprays which curl away from and develop branchlets out of the plane of the spray (unlike 'Ellwangeriana Aurea' where the sprays lie flat), holds its leaves slightly less appressed round the terminal buds, and always carries much more juvenile foliage, in which it will be found that the leaf is a little wider in proportion to its length and stands at a wider angle to the stem. But these differences are very small and the only constant feature is that 'Rheingold' is the dwarf form always retaining a good proportion of juvenile foliage. One result of the confusion between these two forms is that 'Rheingold' has frequently been labelled "*rheingold compacta*" to distinguish it from the stronger-growing form to which the name 'Rheingold' was erroneously thought to apply.

Both are excellent garden plants, and as Mr Hillier aptly remarks, "Perhaps the richest piece of radiant old gold in the garden at the dead of winter". They revel in the hardest weather and are indispensable for planting amongst winter-flowering heathers.

– – 'Ericoides' is the largest and strongest-growing of the fixed juvenile forms amongst the different conifer species that have been saddled with this cultivar name. It forms a large, blousy, ovoid to globose bush with erect, dense, twiggy growth densely clothed with very soft and flexible juvenile leaves of varying size (up to 8 by 1·5 mm) appressed near the growing tips, elsewhere held at an angle of up to 50°, each leaf

299

▲ 257 *Thuja occidentalis* 'Globosa' in the Pygmy Pinetum at Devizes.

258 *Thuja occidentalis* 'Filiformis'. ▶

almost invariably being incurved towards its tip. The colour is a soft, dull green in summer and changes to a medium brown—the colouring of walnut furniture—in winter.

Whilst not an outstanding variety it is not unattractive even in its winter colouring, which avoids the half-dead appearance of some cultivars of this species. Being easily damaged by snow it should not be planted in a situation where damage of this kind, by destroying its regular outline, would spoil the effect and it is probably most effective planted in an informal group.

In the nursery garden at the Royal Botanic Gardens, at Kew, I was recently shown a small plant, the origin of which had not been recorded, which would appear to be the cultivar **'Ericoides Glauca'** referred to by Hornibrook as having reached him from "Rostrevor", Co. Down, N. Ireland. I have searched in vain at "Rostrevor" for the mother plant and it is good to know that this variety has not, as I had feared, been lost to cultivation as it appears to be an attractive form.

– – **'Filiformis'** (syn. "douglasii") is a loose and rather open shrub, eventually a small tree, with long thread-like branches and few branchlets, these often pendulous at their tips.

300

This cultivar can be distinguished from the (much less common) thread-like forms of *Thuja orientalis* by the prominence of the resin gland on the back of the leaves and by the fact that although the entire growth is thread-like, always a few of the terminal growths of this cultivar are flattened as though they had been neatly gone over with a flat iron. Also the leaves have the characteristic odour of the species when bruised.

– – **'Globosa'.** This is a popular form the identification of which has not been made any easier by Hornibrook looking unknowingly at a plant of 'Woodwardii' (or so it would appear) when he wrote up his description of 'Globosa'.

'Globosa', as he rightly remarks, forms a compact, globose bush up to about 1·25 m high, and like many of the gardeners who plant it, it suffers from middle-age spread. But the foliage is a light—almost a grey-green, turning darker in winter. The sprays are flat and crowded, with much overlapping of the shoots, which are similar on both sides; irregularly glandular; flattened (rarely beyond 1·5 mm wide). The habit frequently seen with this species of developing the axial buds in the lower part of the year's growth only on one side of the shoot is well marked in this form and it is not uncommon to find a shoot on which only the upper buds have developed shoots until almost at the end of the season's growth. The main branches are ascending but the leaf sprays are held at random angles giving a very dense look to the plant.

– – **'Globularis'** I have not been able to identify with certainty. Beissner (1891) described it as "A very beautiful, globose form like 'Globosa' with lighter and looser twigs and a bright green, so that it offers an alternative for the beautiful *Thuja orientalis* 'Aurea Nana' for planting in rough situations".

On the bank at Glasnevin there is a plant in the original Hornibrook collection labelled 'Globosa' which is not that variety as above described. It is a more or less globose plant with ascending main branches and branchlets. These latter are pinky brown, with a much flattened (to 2 mm) leafy spray, rather open, symmetrically and attractively developed with alternate branchlets curving gracefully outwards but symmetrically furnished except at the base; a rich glossy green above, paler at the growing tips and a pale yellow-green beneath.

The attractiveness of this form is much enhanced by the leaf sprays being daintily curved out of the plane of the spray so that although the latter are vertical or nearly so the leaf tips are more or less horizontal.

This form answers very well to Beissner's descriptions of 'Globularis' (so far as it goes) and is I think probably that cultivar.

– – **'Hetz Midget'** is a tiny American form described as a true, tight, dwarf globe. **'Minima'** (Hort. Amer., non Hornb.) another American form, must be very similar, as it is described as an extremely dwarf and very slow-growing, tiny ball-shape, light green in colour turning bronzy in the autumn.

I only have small plants of these two cultivars; they both have neat and diminutive foliage in crowded sprays of the 'Globose' type, but very much smaller.

259 *Thuja occidentalis* 'Holmstrupensis'. Dark green. 260 *Thuja occidentalis* 'Hoveyi'. Yellowish-green.

– – **'Holmstrupensis'** is one of the few dwarf forms to give us a conical plant. It makes a slow-growing, dense cone of healthy-looking foliage and the colour is a very rich, deep green, well maintained except in hard winters. The foliage is in dense, flat sprays very much overlapping, flattened (uniformly to 2 mm), carried in vertical planes which more or less radiate from the trunk.

Because of its colour and shape this will be much more planted when better known. With very little attention it could be kept to quite a symmetrical outline and so should be useful in small formal gardens.

– – **'Hoveyii'** (syn. "*froebelii*" and "*spihlmannii*") is a slow-growing variety which reaches 3 m in time and which forms a globose to a squat-ovoid bush. The colour of the foliage is a light yellowish-green which is well maintained during winter. The older twigs are a yellowish to medium brown. The sprays are flat, regular and open, noticeably glandular front and back, the young shoots much flattened (to 2 mm wide). The sprays are identical on both sides and are carried vertically in parallel planes giving the bush a distinctly laminated appearance.

– – **'Little Gem'** shares with 'Pumila' the flattened globular shape of that variety when young, but there the similarity ceases. 'Little Gem' has glossy foliage of a deep, rich mid-green, darkening in winter, the foliage is conspicuously glandular on both sides

302

261 *Thuja occidentalis* 'Little Gem'. Deep green.   262 *Thuja occidentalis* 'Ohlendorffii'.

(which are similar) and much flattened (to 3 mm) as though each little spray had been passed through a mangle, and the ultimate branchlets twist and curve out of the plane of the spray. This last is further obscured by the eruption of tiny shoots at all angles from second year and older wood. The sprays are held at all angles, mostly perhaps horizontal or nearly so, but the effect of all these divergent shoots all over the plant give it a very dense appearance which can be accentuated to any required extent by a little pruning. It is one of the best garden forms.

– – **'Lutea Nana'** is one of the most desirable forms. It could well be described as a dwarf form of cultivar 'Lutea' (better known in America as the George Peabody Arborvitae). It forms an upright pyramid to about 2 m with dense, yellow-green foliage which develops in winter into a rich, glowing golden-yellow which bears comparison with 'Ellwangeriana Aurea'. It can be distinguished from that cultivar because the foliage is denser, wider (2 mm compared with the 1–1·5 mm of 'Ellwangeriana Aurea') and lacking its graceful lace-like quality: also it never carries juvenile foliage.

It is a variety that should be made much more use of in gardens because of its winter glory and its upright, formal habit of growth.

– – **'Ohlendorffii'** (occasionally met with under its alternative name 'Spaethii') is a horticultural curiosity. Left to itself it will form a clump of vertical shoots with closely set, decussate, juvenile foliage with strongly decurved leaves (up to 10 by 1·5 mm), and arising therefrom a smaller number of strong, thick, sparingly branched, vertical shoots bearing tiny adult leaves, which being noticeably folded or keeled and appressed to the stem give it a more or less square cross-section. In summer the plant

303

263 *Thuja occidentalis* 'Rheingold'. See page 298.

264 *Thuja occidentalis* 'Pygmaea'. Blue-green.

carries a pleasant two-tone effect, parts of the shoots being a dark green and parts a pinky-brown, but it lets itself down badly in winter.

There is another, and less common, form which could reasonably be described as a much coarser edition of 'Ohlendorffii'. It carries the same two types of foliage, but the few juvenile leaves are smaller and much less decurved, and the vertical shoots (which predominate) are much longer, thicker and more pronouncedly tetragonal (to 3 mm "across the flats"). This form is grown in some nurseries in France as 'Filiformis', a form to which it bears no resemblance at all. I am not sure how the Cultivar Code would apply in such a case, but for this form I suggest reviving the very descriptive name **'Tetragona'** quoted by Beissner in 1891 (without description) as a gardeners' synonym for 'Ohlendorffii', he evidently not being aware of the difference between these two very distinct forms.

– – **'Pumila'.** The early descriptions of this cultivar all refer to it as a dense, dwarf form growing broader than high, but the pictures of my type plant (*Ill. 256*) on the Rock Garden at Glasnevin show that in time it can build itself up to a height of 2 m or more. But no doubt it would maintain its globose shape indefinitely if any strong, upright growths were cut out as they appeared. The foliage is a deep, rich green above, lighter green beneath, in flat, regular, crowded sprays in which the angle of divergence of the branches and branchlets is noticeably less (40–50°) than in most forms,

304

with each branchlet slightly twisted so that the leaflets do not touch each other, even when they overlap. The growth is flattened (1·5–2 mm). The sprays, in a mature plant, are very gracefully held in nearly horizontal planes, the habit being very clearly seen in *Ills. 255* and *256*.

In colour it is not unlike 'Little Gem', but the foliage is narrower and very neat and regular, with no trace of the aberrant shoots of that variety.

– – **'Pygmaea'** (syn. "*plicata pygmaea*" Hornb.) forms a low, stunted bush with a very irregular branching system. The growth is in flat sprays, held at random, with a greatly reduced entre-nœud, so that the leaves are very densely crowded and over-lapping, and as they are much flattened (to 3 mm) the spray is very dense, and there is much overlapping of branchlets. The glands are prominent above and below, especially so as they are noticeable glossy. The flattening extends to the very tip of the shoot, giving it a distinctly "round-ended" look and, as Hornibrook noticed, these tips are liable to some form of die-back, but I have not had this variety long enough to trace its cause.

It is an attractive little plant with deep, blue-green foliage which contrasts nicely with the lighter green of the young growth in the summer.

– – **'Recurva Nana'** is an attractive form which is not by any means always found true. It forms a low, squat mound with very much flattened (uniformly from 2 to 3 mm) foliage in crowded sprays that are usually held nearly horizontally but with each growing tip recurved, and twisted as though one held one's hand spread out at eye level, palm downward, bent all the fingers slightly and twisted the wrist a little.

In its place there is often supplied a somewhat similar but much stronger-growing form which makes a flattened to globose bush with foliage that in places is similar to 'Recurva Nana', but less regularly recurved—some of the shoots indeed lying quite flat. This form gains height by throwing up strong, cupressoid, vertical shoots with an entre-nœud of anything up to 8 mm, having keeled and folded leaves with free, pointed tips. These shoots will make up to 12 cm growth in the year with few laterals, these having the normal thujoid foliage. The true identity of this form, which is quite common in cultivation, has long been obscure. Making allowance for the difficulties inherent in the translation of botanical terms the description given above follows the early descriptions quoted under 'Dumosa' reasonably well. So on the one hand we have a plant without a name, on the other a name without a plant and I feel we are on fairly safe and eminently logical ground to identify the form we are here dealing with as 'Dumosa', unless and until further information comes to light on the subject.

There should be no need for confusion between these two forms. In 'Recurva Nana' the growth is very regular all over the plant. The main branches rise at an angle, curve over and carry their sprays roughly horizontally and the regularly recurved foliage is of uniform width. In 'Dumosa', apart from the vertical shoots described above, the growth is much more irregular. Some shoots are vigorous, these being much flattened and usually recurved, but other growth is very tangled and congested,

265 *Thuja occidentalis* 'Umbraculifera'.

266 *Thuja occidentalis* 'Wansdyke Silver'. ▶

this growth being always narrower and thicker than in 'Recurva Nana' and not recurved.

– – **'Rheingold'**. See page 298 under 'Ellwangeriana Aurea'.

– – **'Sphaerica'** is a dainty little plant represented in several collections in this country which should be popular when it becomes more available. It has tiny, lance-like foliage quite the narrowest (1 mm or less) foliage of any *Thuja occidentalis* form I know and the sprays are all crimpled and curled in a most attractive manner. It makes at first a globose little plant but in time becomes upright, to about 1·5 m.

– – **'Spiralis'** is not a dwarf form but a narrowly columnar tree. Where a plant of formal and "architectural" character is required it takes a lot of beating. It is a densely branched, narrowly pyramidal form, with the ultimate branchlets short and regularly pinnately arranged, very much after the fashion of *Chamaecyparis obtusa* 'Filicoides', from which it can at once be distinguished by the smell of the crushed foliage. With a little systematic pruning back of the lateral shoots it can be induced to form a very narrow and dense plant indeed.

– – **'Umbraculifera'** is one of the best dwarf forms and easy to identify as it has the bluest-green mature foliage of any variety we have. It usually has several upright

306

267 *Thuja occidentalis* 'Woodwardii'. Forms a large, globose bush. Note the "parallel planes" in which the foliage lies.

main stems which later spread out to support the dense, dome-shaped crown which gives the plant the umbrella shape to which it owes its name. The twigs are conspicuously pinky-brown and the foliage is in flat sprays with the shoots irregularly flattened (to 2mm, usually less) and daintily laid out and curved *in the plane of the spray*. It turns a dark bronzy green in the winter. 'Umbraculifera' forms quite a large bush in time, but it is a bad transplanter so should be planted in a small size if possible.

There is another variety **'Reidii'** which sometimes passed as 'Umbraculifera' but it has a denser spray, wider (usually 2 mm or more) with the branchlets and shoots pointing forward at a narrow angle, and with one of the dainty grace of 'Umbraculifera'. 'Reidii' also forms a large plant in time and holds its colour well in the winter. It tends to get looser with age and is not one of the most attractive forms.

– – **'Wansdyke Silver'** is the name I suggest for a very slow-growing and congested form in the Pygmy Pinetum which has light green foliage in short sprays liberally splashed with creamy white, the colour being held all the year. The mother plant (the origin of which unfortunately is not on record) is a columnar little plant about 1m high which has not grown appreciably in five years, so that I do not think it can be any of the variegated forms of *Thuja occidentalis* that have been hitherto named. **'Beaufort'** has similar colouring but is a tall-growing variety.

It is a very attractive form for those who like variegated plants and it keeps its colouring well throughout the year. It should become popular when better known.

– – **'Woodwardii'** is a strong-growing, globose form with rich-green foliage in flat sprays which are held stiffly in vertical planes rather in the manner of some of the *Thuja orientalis* forms. The foliage is quite coarse and open, is very much flattened (to 3 mm) and is approximately the same colour on both sides of the spray. Although this form will reach to several metres high in time, Kumlien, in *The Friendly Evergreens*, 1933, 215, states that it continues to maintain a well-rounded shape even when large.

Thuja orientalis. This is normally a small tree to 10 m, or a large globose bush. The species is easily distinguishable from all other thujas and cypresses by the fact that its branches are held erect or curving upwards and carry the leaf-sprays in a vertical plane, these being of the same colour and appearance on both sides of the spray. The ultimate divisions are distinctly thujoid, the leaves are small and closely set, over-lapping, triangular and bluntly pointed. They are dotted with stomata, and the facing pair has a central groove. *Th. orientalis* was at one time regarded as a distinct genus, *Biota*, and the name survives in the popular names of some of its forms, for instance "Berckman's Golden Biota", so well known in the United States.

The species can be clearly distinguished (in all adult forms) by the foliage and habit as given above, and by the strongly hooked cone scales. The dwarf forms can be grouped as follows:

Juvenile and semi-juvenile foliage	*Golden foliage (Dwarf)*	*Golden foliage (Tall, conical)*
'Decussata' (see 'Juniperoides')	'Aurea Nana'	'Aurea'
'Juniperoides'	'Sieboldii'	'Beverleyensis'
'Meldensis'	'Bonita'	'Conspicua'
'Minima'		'Elegantissima'
'Rosedalis'		'Hillieri'
		'Semperaurea'

Foliage variants

'Athrotaxoides'
'Flagelliformis'
'Filiformis Erecta'
'Filiformis Elegans'

– – **'Athrotaxoides'** is an interesting, very rare and extremely slow-growing form with very thick branches and branchlets, these all being completely cupressoid, lacking any trace of the flat spray characteristic of the species and suggesting a very coarse edition of the foliage of *Chamaecyparis obtusa* 'Lycopodioides'. The only large plant I know is in the National Botanic Garden at Glasnevin, Dublin. This is probably the plant of which Hornibrook wrote in 1938 but it is now a flat-topped tree 2·5m high by 3 m across. There is a small plant in the Pygmy Pinetum.

– – **'Aurea'.** There have been several golden seedlings turn up from time to time, and those that have been brought into cultivation are difficult to tell apart. I cannot claim to have identified the particular clone that originally gave rise to this name, but the dwarf form **'Aurea Nana'** is in easy supply and is deservedly popular. It should be in every collection, however small. 'Aurea Nana' forms a round-topped, oval little bush, seldom over 60 cm high. The foliage is very dense and all the leaf sprays seem to be trying to lie in parallel planes, giving the plant a distinctly laminated appearance.

▲ 268 *Thuja orientalis* 'Athrotaxoides'. One of the rarest forms known.

◀ 269 *Thuja orientalis* 'Aurea Nana'.

This characteristic it shares with the much stronger-growing and upright form **'Semperaurea'** (often found as "*semperaurescens*") from which it is indistinguishable when small as both have the same rich golden-yellow colour in early summer and become pale green later. So far as I can at present say, plants supplied under such varietal names as "*aurea densa*", "*aurea compacta*", "*aurea globosa*", "*Millard's Gold*" and "*minima aurea*", are identical with 'Aurea Nana'.

– – **'Beverleyensis'** is a tall-growing form which grows into a narrow column, not unlike 'Conspicua' (below). The foliage is golden-yellow in the early summer, turning to green later. The leaf-tips on this form are sharply pointed and less closely appressed than is usual in this species, giving the foliage a somewhat false appearance of prickliness.

– – **'Bonita',** much planted in America, is described as a broadly conical slow-growing form of regular, formal outline with young foliage at first golden-yellow, soon turning to a bright green. I have not seen it.

– – **'Conspicua'.** Although this is by no means a dwarf, it is in my opinion the best of the upright to conical golden forms—the usual bright gold in early summer, but retaining its colour better throughout the year than any. It is a strong grower, always finishing at the top of the plant with a few pale yellow, rather scrawny, twigs—I beg their pardon—I mean with a few leading growths with extended entre-nœud and lighter colour.

309

270 *Thuja orientalis* 'Filiformis Erecta'.

271 *Thuja orientalis* 'Elegantissima'.

According to Dallimore and Jackson it was named by Berckmann, so it is presumably the plant entitled to the name "Berckmann's Golden Biota", but in American literature that much planted variety is often quoted as a synonym of 'Aurea Nana'. The illustration in *The Friendly Evergreens*, Kumlien, on page 220, is much more like "a young tree" of 'Conspicua' than even an old plant of 'Aurea Nana' as grown in Europe, but it might equally well be neither of these forms. Whichever clone it is, "Berckmann's Golden Biota" it is and "Berckmann's Golden Biota" it doubtless will remain, but it would be interesting to have its true identity established.

Other golden and/or green forms that make upright plants that are slow-growing but too large for most situations (save, perhaps, to fill a prominent spot temporarily until a sufficiently large plant of a slower-growing and dwarfer form is available) are **'Elegantissima'** (turns brown in the winter), **'Hillieri'** (foliage at first yellow, soon turning green) and 'Semperaurea' (see under 'Aurea' above).

– – **'Decussata'.** See 'Juniperoides', below.

– – **'Filiformis Erecta'** is a very distinct form in which the usual foliage in sprays is entirely absent, the whole plant consisting of tightly bunched shoots clothed with leaves (the facing and lateral pairs being of equal size) with only their pointed tips (1–3 mm long) free-standing. The branching system is strongly vertical, save for a few straggling shoots at the sides and the plant forms an upright-ovoid bush seldom seen

310

272 *Thuja orientalis* 'Juniperoides' (syn. "*decussata*").

more than 1 m but capable of reaching twice that height. Leaves yellowish-green in summer, greenish-brown in winter, an interesting plant.

– – **'Flagelliformis''**. There are several recorded forms with thread-like foliage. The early descriptions are very brief and it has been difficult to determine which names properly belong to the forms in cultivation.

A very good illustration of 'Flagelliformis' in *The Book of Evergreens* Hoopes 1868, 335 clearly relates to a strong, upright-growing form with foliage similar to 'Filiformis Erecta' but with much larger leaves standing off at a wider angle (except near the growing tips, where they are folded so as to give a square cross section to the shoot). The growth is not so densely upright and is a light, yellowish-green in summer. This form is doubtfully hardy. There is a good specimen on the upper bank at the National Botanic Garden at Glasnevin, Dublin.

At Cliveden in Buckinghamshire, one of the beautiful gardens made available to the public through the National Trust, there is a large specimen of a strong-growing thread-leaf form with dark-green foliage very similar to *Chamaecyparis pisifera* 'Filifera', and with pendulous branchlets. This is certainly not the 'Flagelliformis' of Hoopes' illustration and I think it may be **'Filiformis Elegans'** (described as having "glaucous foliage"). Other forms in the literature—**'Filiformis Nana', 'Intermedia'** and **'Tetragona'** I have not seen: they will probably turn out to be synonyms of the cultivars I describe.

– – **'Juniperoides'** (syn. "*decussata*") is one of several fixed-juvenile forms of *Th. orientalis* which all form rounded bushes growing to less than 1 m, all with very dense decussate foliage with acicular leaves free-standing for most of their length

311

273 *Thuja orientalis* 'Meldensis'. Dull green. Stiff to the touch.

274 *Thuja orientalis* 'Minima' (syn. "*minima glauca*").

with the tips tending to recurve. They are all most desirable garden plants. 'Juniperoides' has large leaves (the free-standing part up to 8 mm long, held at 60° to stem), light greyish-green in summer, turning a rich purplish-grey in the winter, the colour of the bloom on a ripe grape. Always the greyish look is due to a heavy glaucous coating which is easily rubbed off. This plant is the least hardy of the group and should be sheltered from keen winds.

– – **'Meldensis'** has smaller leaves (5 mm long, noticeably decurved, to 70°), stiff, dull green in summer and dull purplish-brown in winter. The foliage has a *stiff and rough feel* when the bush is patted on the top with the hand. This form occasionally throws out a spray of adult foliage. This determines for us the specific allegiance of this form and may be retained for its botanical interest, if the plant does not carry the process too far and begin to lose character.

– – **'Minima'** is a very slow-growing form with very small and closely set semi-juvenile leaves which are very harsh to the touch. Unlike the wholly juvenile forms, the difference between the lateral and facing pairs of leaves is quite noticeable, the young shoots are distinctly thujoid and the adult growth pattern in flat sprays is discernible. The foliage changes from light yellow-green in early summer to dark green later and becomes a rather dirty brown in winter. This is a defect, for in cold weather the plant looks almost dead. Although it is generally referred to as "*minima glauca*", I have never noticed any glaucousness about the plant and as there seems to be no other claimant to the simpler name, I suggest that the adjective "*glauca*" be dropped.

312

275 *Thuja orientalis* 'Rosedalis'. Cream in spring; green in summer; purple-brown in winter. Soft to the touch.

The plant is very popular for trough gardens, where its tree-like branching system can be made use of by pruning, even as a tiny plant.

– – **'Rosedalis'** is perhaps the most popular of the fixed-juvenile foliage forms, with its soft, narrow leaves (up to 7 mm long held at 45°) and its change of colour three times in the year. In summer it is a light green, in winter brown to plum-purple and in the spring it changes to a beautiful butter-yellow. It can be distinguished readily from 'Meldensis' by these colour changes, and at all seasons by the feel of the foliage, which is *very soft and yielding* to the touch. **'Rosedale'** appears to be lost to cultivation, so there would appear to be no case for retaining the more clumsy name "*rosedalis compacta*" suggested by Hornibrook.

– – **'Sieboldii'** is a very old variety, often met with under the names "*compacta*" and "*nana*", which forms a round-headed bush up to 2 m high, with the usual vertical branching system and a dense habit of growth. The foliage (which at first is golden-yellow) soon turns to and remains a bright mid-green, is very fine, open and lace-like in flat sprays in which each side shoot branches off at precisely 45°, and so evenly spaced out that there is little or no overlapping of shoots in the spray. The final shoots are about 1 mm wide and even three-year-old twigs are barely twice as thick. None of the plants I have seen has had the extreme tips of the branchlet spray bent over and outwards, as described by Hornibrook. It may be this is a seasonal phase of short duration.

313

277 *Thuja plicata* 'Hillieri'.

276 *Thuja plicata* 'Rogersii'. In time becomes an upright plant of looser growth.

Thuja plicata, the Western Red Cedar is normally a tree to 50 m or more but it has given us several excellent dwarf forms. The foliage is more nearly like *Th. occidentalis* than any other species but it differs in that the leaves are less conspicuously glandular and are streaked with white on the underside; also the foliage has a less objectionable smell when bruised.

– – **'Cuprea'** forms a low, spreading shrub with golden-bronze foliage. Both this and 'Rogersii' were raised by Mr Gardiner at the Red Lodge Nurseries, at that time at Southampton, from seeds from a tree of *Th. plicata* 'Aurea'.

– – **'Gracilis'** is a form in which the foliage is much lighter and finer than in the type, with the leaves much smaller. It is described as forming a slow-growing and broadly conical plant, but the largest plants of the golden form **'Gracilis Aurea'** which I have seen have been rather low, bun-shaped specimens in which the foliage at first glance could have been easily taken for *Chamaecyparis pisifera* 'Golden Mop'.

– – **'Hillieri'** is a dwarf form with foliage of reduced size and a very congested habit, the colour a nice rich green. It is probable that the dwarfness is due to the presence of some virus, and the growth is erratic as though its action was irregular through the plant. Some shoots are very dense and congested and others are long and vigorous.

314

and there are plants of 'Hillieri' about in which the congested character has been almost wholly lost. Care should be taken to use only the tight form of growth as propagating material.

– – **'Pumila'** is very similar to 'Hillieri' in foliage, but it forms a low, bun-shaped little plant, not more than 30 cm high by perhaps twice as much across.

– – **'Rogersii'** shares the golden-bronze colour of 'Cuprea' but it forms a much denser and more upright plant with very congested foliage which is dark green in the interior of the bush but a rich copper-bronze on all the exposed tips. It is slow to get going, but when well established it throws up strong vertical shoots by means of which the plant gains its upright shape. But if these are cut away it can be kept as an extremely dense, ovoid or globose little bush which is a glowing spot of colour at all seasons.

278 *Thuja plicata* 'Stoneham Gold'.

I have noticed that the colour varies considerably, some plants in the nursery rows appearing a creamy white, but I do not think this variation is sufficiently stable to "fix" as a distinct cultivar. No doubt someone will try to do this sooner or later.

– – **'Stoneham Gold'.** Although it will reach to 2 m or more high in time this form is very slow-growing for several years, so it should be planted more widely than at present because of its wonderful colour.

It forms an upright plant with dense growth of more or less typical foliage which is dark green—often almost black—in the interior of the plant but a rich orange-yellow on all the young shoots at its surface. This two-tone effect is very attractive and the golden colour is well maintained throughout the year on plants that are growing vigorously. Older plants would probably pay for hard pruning to induce strong new growth.

279 *Thujopsis dolobrata* 'Nana'.

THUJOPSIS

Thujopsis dolobrata is the sole occupant of this genus, which at one time was included in *Thuja*. A practical if not very scholarly way to describe its foliage is to liken it to foliage of *Thuja* that has been put through a mangle, becoming thereby squashed out very thin and much wider. It has given us one useful, if not particularly exciting, dwarf form.

– – **'Nana'** forms a wide-spreading bush, never more than 1 m high but often much more across, with smaller leaves and length of shoot than in the type. It seems indestructibly hardy and is very useful for a rough corner. I have noticed that the colour varies a good deal; at its best it is a nice, rich, grass green, but sometimes one sees it a dull yellowish-green, and all the forms are a poor colour in winter.

280 *Torreya nucifera* 'Prostrata'. A very large specimen at Glasnevin.

TORREYA

This is a small genus allied to *Cephalotaxus*, of which only one species *T. nucifera* has given us any recorded forms suitable for inclusion in this book.

Torreya nucifera is a Japanese species with foliage very similar to *Cephalotaxus harringtonia* var. *drupacea* but differing therefrom by the long, gradually tapered leaves ending in a very fine, sharp tip, with no noticeable mid-rib above and with two well-defined, narrow sunk bands of (sometimes pinkish) stomata beneath.

– – **'Prostrata'.** The plant mentioned by Hornibrook at Glasnevin has now become of large size, as will be seen from the picture above. Although he states that it was planted as a seedling I am of the opinion that its status is merely that of a culti-variant. It could very well have been a seedling that had accidentally lost its leader which has never been able to recover its normal habit. 'Prostrata' is a useful and attractive plant for ground cover in open woodland or wherever a large specimen not above 1 m high is required.

317

281 *Tsuga canadensis* 'Bennett' (syn. "Bennett's Minima").

282 *Tsuga canadensis* 'Cole's Prostrate'.

TSUGA

The hemlocks form a genus of ten species of tree of which several, when raised from cuttings, are slow growing; but only *Tsuga canadensis*, the Eastern or Canadian Hemlock has given us true dwarf forms.

The foliage is not unlike that of the yews, but the terminal shoots are thinner and usually pendulous, giving these trees a more graceful appearance. The leaves are actually borne radially on short stems which are pressed to the shoots, but they are twisted so as to lie in a more or less clearly defined double tier with the leaves in the lower tier longer than those above. The leaf stems spring from a cushion-like projection which at once distinguishes this genus from the leaf scar of *Abies* and the peg-like leaf base of *Picea*.

Tsuga canadensis. Although normally a tree to 30 m, this species is very variable from seed and has produced many dwarf forms, including some of the smallest conifers known. A native of Canada and the eastern United States, a large number of dwarf forms have been collected and named in North America, especially of recent years, only a few of which are available in Britain. They are not strikingly beautiful plants but many are interesting and useful, either in the garden or as pot plants. I am indebted to Mr Wm. T. Gotelli of East Orange, N.J., and Mr Joel. W. Spingarn of Baldwin, N.Y., for much of the following information.

– – **'Abbott Weeping'** (syn. "*Abbott's dwarf*") is a semi-prostrate shrublet with very dark leaves. In four years it reaches 20 by 10 cm.

318

– – **'Albo-spicata'** is a compact, slow-growing, pyramidal form with the growing tips white, the two-tone effect thereby produced being very effective during the spring. The colouring is somewhat variable, probably responding to soil or climatic conditions. A good specimen is most striking.

– – **'Armistice'** is a very slow-growing form which forms a flat-topped bush with a noticeably horizontal branching system, so that the deep, glossy, green foliage is in tiers.

– – **'Aurea'** (syn. "*Everitt's Golden*"). A compact and slow-growing pyramidal form which gets large in time. The leaves are rather broad and crowded and (in full sunlight) are golden-yellow when young, deepening to a glowing old-gold by the autumn.

– – **'Bennett'** (syn. "*Bennett's Minima*") is an attractive low-growing, spreading form. Leaves to 10 mm long, usually much less, light green and closely set; annual growth 15 mm. It forms a plant not unlike *Picea abies* 'Nidiformis' but seems to lose character as it ages, the variety 'Minima' being preferable in this respect. **'Fantana'** is a similar form but, according to Mr Gotelli, even less reliably dwarf.

– – **'Boulevard'** is an upright pyramidal form with dark green leaves and a crowded branch system.

– – **'Brandleyii'** I have not seen. Mr Gotelli writes, "A dwarf, slow-growing globose form which will in time develop into a bush 1 m or a little more in height". Leaves broad and long, dark green; tips not pendulous. Other cultivars of similar habit and growth are **'Compacta', 'Nana'** and **'Broughtonii'.**

– – **'Cinnamomea'** I only know as a small plant, but it apparently forms a symmetrical, globose bush; leaves slender and very small. It owes its name to the presence of cinnamon-brown hairs on the young twigs. Mr Gotelli writes, "This variety is easily distinguishable from the other Canadian hemlocks by the weeping habit of every branch-tip. It develops into quite a large bush, my largest specimen being about 1·25 m wide and high."

– – **'Cole'** (syn. "*Cole's Prostrate*") is an extremely dwarf form which, unless trained up or grafted on to a stem grows as a completely prostrate plant. The flattened main branches are mostly bare of leaves at the centre of the plant and appear to press themselves against the ground as though held there by suction. Mr Gotelli says of this variety, "It loves to cling to a rock or stone so is ideal for rock-garden use. The original plant found some years ago by Mr Cole had a spread of more than 1 m but was only 15 cm high. My oldest specimen was about the same size and it was about twenty to twenty-five years old. It is, in my opinion, one of the very best conifers for a rock garden".

– – **'Curtis'** (syn. "*Curtis Ideal*") forms an upright to globose bush of rather open habit with gracefully arching branches and all growing tips pendulous. Leaves to

15 by 2 mm but much less on growing shoots, loosely appressed to the stems, giving a "wiry" look to the plant.

– – **'Dawsoniana'** is a spreading or pyramidal variety with broad leaves (up to 12 mm long by 2 mm wide) tapering from a rounded base to a rounded tip, which is toothed; 2 rows of stomata in glaucous bands. Trunk and main branches upright, branches and branchlets horizontal, arching over to −45° at tips. Shoots pinky-brown.

– – **'Fremdii'** is a stiff, dense, slow-growing bush which eventually becomes large in this country. It carries crowded, short, comparitively broad and obtuse dark green leaves.

– – **'Globosa'** is an upright, spreading form with stiff ascending main branches at 60° and branches at 40°. Leaves are wide and short, open, tapering abruptly to rather an obtuse point. The largest plant I have seen is a young specimen at Kew about 60 cm high and wide, and this plant was not yet noticeably globose in habit.

– – **'Gracilis'** is a slow-growing form which makes a globose to spreading bush with all branch tips slightly pendulous. Mr Gotelli tells me that its habit is similar to 'Hussii', both having very short, twiggy branches and crowded leaves. A plant seventy-five years old in his collection was less than 2 m high.

– – **'Greenwood Lake'** is a very slow-growing, congested form with a crowded, irregular branch system. Leaves are 6 mm long by 1·25 mm wide, round at ends, very irregularly held on the branches, giving a very stunted look to the plant. A plant sent by Mr Gotelli to Mr Nisbet in 1956 is now 15 cm high and wide, very dense and rigid, with recurved tips to the branches.

– – **'Horsford'** (syn. "*Horsford's dwarf*") makes a congested, globose little bush with very short, obtuse, crowded leaves and branchlets recurving. Mr Gotelli's oldest specimen was a plant measuring 45 cm wide and high. The name is occasionally spelt "*Horosford*".

– – **'Hussii'** is a very slow-growing, upright form with very thick, light-brown branches and short, twiggy branchlets. The short leaves (to 10 by 1·5 mm) are very dark green and closely set. The growth is dense but irregular, so the little tree has a picturesque outline that is characteristic of this popular variety.

– – **'Jervis'** is one of the smallest forms. It makes a tight little bushling only a few inches high by as much across, with stunted, irregular branching and short (7 by 1·5 mm), medium green leaves densely and irregularly clustered on the shoots.

– – **'Kelsey's Weeping'** forms a low, spreading plant, reaching to several metres across, with horizontal main branches and growing tips pendulous. Leaves 10 by 2 mm, branches very flexible.

283 *Tsuga canadensis* 'Gracilis'.

284 *Tsuga canadensis* 'Horsford'.

– – **'Microphylla'** is a slow-growing form of normal habit but with tiny leaves. It eventually grows too large for the average rock garden.

– – **'Minima'** is a dainty, slow-growing form with ascending branches and branchlets arching over with their tips drooping to −10°. Leaves (up to 15 by 2 mm) are closely set on the shoots. Mr Gotelli says of this form, "A truly fine form which is suitable for use as an individual specimen. It is also suitable for a large rock garden as it will ultimately develop into a fair-sized plant. My oldest specimen was 1·25 m high, with a spread of 3 m. It was a very old specimen and I doubt whether it would ever have increased in size appreciably. One of the real assets of this form is that it does not lose its shape as it ages."

– – **'Minuta'** (*T. c.* var. *minuta* Teuscher, in *New Flora and Silva*, 1935, 274) is the smallest of the dwarf hemlocks known to come true from seed, and (because of the extremely short annual growth) it is one virtually impossible to propagate vegetatively.

An account of its finding by Mr Frank L. Abbott in 1927 is given in the *Brooklyn Botanic Garden Record* for Autumn 1949, 141. Mr Gotelli writes, "This is another very fine dwarf hemlock ideal for a rock-garden. The needles are very short, as they are in most of the truly dwarf forms. I doubt if the plant will ever exceed 45 cm. Its habit of growth is very compact and the plant is globose."

The variety **'Pygmaea'** is very similar in habit and growth, except that it may be even smaller and have shorter leaves".

321

285 *Tsuga canadensis* 'Pendula'.

– – **'Pendula'.** A number of pendulous forms of tree-like dimensions have come into cultivation. Pendulous forms will turn up at any time in the seedbeds, and these forms come fairly true from seed, so their number is legion, but only a few forms have been selected and named.

In his Second Edition Hornibrook gives the history of four of such plants found near the summit of the Fishkill Mountains by General Joseph Howlett about 1870 and in an article entitled "The Four Fathers of the Sargent Hemlock" in the American trade journal *American Nurseryman* of the 15th December 1962, Mr Alfred J. Fordham brings the account up to date. He gives an excellent picture of the plant which went to Charles Sprague Sargent of Brookline, Boston, Mass. (Hornibrook's plant No. 4). This he states is now about 9 m in diameter, well and thriving, and well cared for by its present owner Mrs Roger Ernst. It has developed a horizontal system of branches which has built up into the form of a broad mound, new growths following the contour of the branches underneath in a dense patch of foliage.

Mr Fordham also gives a picture of a tree in the Arnold Arboretum, grafted in 1881, which can be traced to the tree planted by General Howlett in his own garden at Matteawan (Hornibrook's Tree No. 1) and he tells me that the old Parsons Nursery which existed at Flushing, sent a propagator up to Matteawan to procure material from the original tree which was the only one to be widely propagated. The Arnold Arboretum tree has developed into an open, multi-stemmed, umbrella-shaped tree 10 m in diameter and about 4·5 m tall on a framework of trunk and heavy branches arising at angles, giving more elevation and less density than this tree seen in the Brookline form.

In *Trees and Shrubs Hardy in the British Isles* the late W. J. Bean gives three forms, vars. *pendula*, *prostrata* and *sargentii*. All the plants that I have seen in this country answer to the description given by Bean to his var. *pendula*—"A very attractive bush or small tree forming a hemispherical mass of pendulous branches, completely hiding the interior" and as they answer to the description of neither the Brookline plant nor the Matteawan form they must be assumed to have originated in another seedling—whether one of Hornibrook's trees 2 and 3 already dead in 1937 or not will probably never be known. The English form needs training to form a leader to the required height and in the absence of such training would form a plant exactly answering to Bean's var. *prostrata*, which cannot therefore be viewed as a valid name.

I therefore propose to clear up the matter as follows:

– – **'Brookline'** (new name). The form of which the original tree No. 4 is available as the type.

– – **'Sargentii** (*canadensis sargentii* Parsons 1896, *canadensis sargentiana* 1900). The form represented by the Arnold Arboretum tree, above.

– – **'Pendula'** (*canadensis pendula* Beissn. (1884)). The hemispherical plant described by Bean, in general cultivation in Europe, probably of more than one clone.

I regret having no fuller description of the American forms but perhaps someone having access to the plants will remedy this omission for us. It would be very useful if the forms could be distinguished from their foliar characteristics only. At Kew, near the lake, there are several unlabelled forms of *Tsuga canadensis* which might very well include these two American forms but they are too young to identify with certainty from the branching characteristics seen in the matured trees as described above.

– – **'Rugg's Washington Dwarf'.** A dense globose to cushion-shaped plant with congested growth. Foliage bronzy-yellow, especially in spring. One of the best small garden forms.

– – **'Stranger'** (syn. "*Strangeri*") leaves small and closely set in one plane.

– – **'Taxifolia'** forms an open, spreading bush, very soft to the touch. Leaves 15 by 2·5 mm, tapering to a rounded tip; branches all gracefully arching at the growing tips.

Tsuga mertensiana, the Mountain Hemlock, has given rise to one recorded dwarf form, 'Nana', but it is not, to my knowledge, in circulation. Mr Gotelli informs me that it does not develop a leader but has many radiating branches and glaucous foliage.

6 : Pests and Diseases

This chapter will fortunately be a short one because the pests and diseases associated with dwarf conifers are few and they are very simply controlled.

I have dealt in other chapters with the adverse action of frost, wind and strong sunlight, but in this very specialized book I cannot attempt to cover all the hazards of modern garden life with which our poor plants have to deal. Readers must turn elsewhere for information on how to deal with such things·as slugs, ants, wood lice, human feet (of all sizes), careless reversing and so forth, but I ought perhaps to give a warning on the subject of cats and dogs. These, the latter especially, can soon do great damage to the foliage of conifers which quickly gets "browned off" by their attentions. Dogs, in particular, once they have decided that a certain plant is a suitable substitute for a lamp post, return to it each time they are passing.

The remedy depends upon whether the animals in question belong to yourself or to your neighbours. If they are your own, the remedy is simple; give them away or have them put to sleep. If the offending animals are trespassers, the best remedy is a supply of pea gravel and a good catapult. Two or three direct hits at the psychological moment will soon persuade your friend of there being some connection between sudden pain and that particular bush, and he will learn to transfer his attentions elsewhere, none the worse for his lesson.

Whenever there is an attack by pest or disease, conifers always advertise their distress to a watchful eye, and any tree looking at all "off colour" or dull in appearance should at once be closely examined for the cause. Scale shows itself by the characteristic patches on the stems and I have found Taxus to be the most prone to attack. An invasion by aphis, red spider and mites of any kind, too small to see with the naked eye, will cause the foliage to look dull and lacking in the colour and rich lustre which is characteristic of a healthy conifer. This if unchecked leads to discoloration of the foliage and possibly the death of the tree. These pests will increase on a plant very rapidly during the spring and summer and quickly spread to other plants so a watch should be kept and as soon as any tree looks off colour a spray of some kind is indicated. A number of suitable compounds are available. In the nursery here I use a spray containing Demeton-Methyl, better known under its trade name Metasystox, but this is not available in small quantities to the public who can however obtain a somewhat similar product called Dimethoate, more usually known under its trade name as Rogor. (Both of these are Organo-phosphorus compounds, to be used—and stored—with a due sense of responsibility for the harm they can do if wrongly used.) These are both what is known as systemic insecticides, which means that if any part of the plant is wetted by the spray the chemical is absorbed into the sap which kindly takes over the task of distributing it to all parts of the plant and aphis, red spider and any sucking insects are quickly killed. The effect is very rapid, insect life being destroyed within hours, but if the foliage has already become discolored it will never regain its healthy appearance: evidence of freedom from the pest must therefore be looked for in the new leaves at the growing tips. I have found the Junipers and the Spruces most liable to be affected, and as the latter hold their leaves for two seasons, two years must elapse before the results of an attack will have disappeared, even although the attack itself has been dealt with. It is a good plan to follow up with a second spraying a week or two later. This will deal with any pest that has survived the first treatment and dispose of any further infestation subsequently hatched out.

Other effective sprays are available containing one or other of the chemicals BHC, malathion or the well-tried natural compound Derris, with or without Pyrethrum. These are of course sold under trade or brand names, but the active ingredient is usually disclosed or will be known by your chemist or other supplier.

There are dozens of species of these very small insects known to entomologists but as each of the above sprays seems to be effective in dealing with the lot, most gardeners will not be concerned with the identification in detail of their particular pest and so this is all the space that I really need to give to the subject, but having got this far I felt that I had not covered the subject very thoroughly. In particular I considered that any of the many diseases and pests of coniferous woodlands might possibly at any time descend to the attack of dwarf forms especially in any gardens situated near pine woods. I therefore consulted a plant pathologist friend of mine for advice as to standard textbooks to which I could refer and I feel that I cannot do better than to pass on to my readers his recommendations.

The first was a book entitled *Pathology of Trees and Shrubs* by T. R. Peace. This book covers diseases of temperate forests and ornamental trees and shrubs including those caused by fungi, bacteria, viruses and non-living agencies such as frost and wind. It is not a book that I could recommend for a weekend, for it is 3 in thick, but if you are prepared to take it away for your annual holiday and really stick at it for a fortnight, it should set you up for the rest of your lifetime as an accredited authority on these subjects amongst all your gardening acquaintances. One thing in particular that struck me very much in reading it was the large number of fungal diseases or rusts that spend part of their life cycle on this or that conifer and the rest of it on an entirely different host plant. This may be another conifer, or (according to the preference of the particular fungus) a poplar, currant, prunus, rhododendron, or even (of all things) groundsel. This only shows how much more important thorough weeding has been than we have ever believed or acted upon!

After having tackled this book, you will find *Insects of the British Woodlands* by R. Neil Chrystal, M.A., D.SC. relatively easy going, as this is a bare inch thick. It, too, deals very thoroughly with its subject and from it you should be able to identify any insect invasion you may experience, but it does not deal in any detail with the methods of control. If the insecticides already recommended do not do the trick help can doubtless be obtained from your local County Council Agricultural Adviser, and about February of each year the Ministry of Agriculture, Fisheries and Food produce a *List of Approved Products for Farmers and Growers* under the *Agricultural Chemicals Approval Scheme* containing very full details of all the chemicals available under the Scheme, with their uses and limitations. This list, I understand, can always be consulted at any sub-office of the Ministry and a copy is in most Reference Libraries, and as the development of chemical insecticides is constantly on the change, readers of this book will by studying the current list be able to keep themselves up to date even should the recommendations in this chapter become outdated.

Index

NOTE. Page references in bold type refer to the main descriptions, those in italics to illustrations, and references in ordinary type are to other references in the text.